DIRECTORY OF GRADUATE PROGRAMS IN APPLIED SPORT PSYCHOLOGY

Michael L. Sachs, Ph.D.
Temple University
Kevin L. Burke, Ph. D.
Georgia Southern University
Shawn Gomer, M.A.
Temple University
Editors

FIFTH EDITION

FITNESS INFORMATION TECHNOLOGY, INC.
P.O. BOX 4425
UNIVERSITY AVENUE
MORGANTOWN, WV 26504-4425

Library of Congress Card Catalog Number: 97-74988

ISBN 1-885693-10-9

Cover Design: Pepper Press
Copyeditor: Sandra R. Woods
Production Editor: Craig Hines
Printed by: BookCrafters

Printed in the United States of America
10 9 8 7 6 5 4 3 2 1

Fitness Information Technology, Inc.
P.O. Box 4425, University Avenue
Morgantown, WV 26504 USA
(800) 477-4348
(304) 599-3482 (phone/fax)
E-mail: fit@fitinfotech.com
Website: www.fitinfotech.com

Michael L. Sachs is an associate professor in the Department of Physical Education, College of Health, Physical Education, Recreation and Dance, at Temple University, specializing in exercise and sport psychology. He has been at Temple University since fall 1989. He received his Ph.D. in sport psychology from Florida State University in 1980 and was an assistant professor at the University of Quebec at Trois-Rivières from 1980–1983. From 1983–1989 he served as a research project coordinator in the Applied Research and Evaluation Unit in the Department of Pediatrics, University of Maryland School of Medicine. He has an extensive list of publications and presentations, including authorship as associate editor of *Psychology of Running* (Michael Sacks & Michael Sachs, Human Kinetics Publishers, 1981) and coeditor of *Running as Therapy: An Integrated Approach* (Michael Sachs & Gary Buffone, University of Nebraska Press, 1984; recently republished—1997—by Jason Aronson Publishers as part of their Master Works Series). *The Total Sports Experience for Kids: A Parent's Guide to Success in Youth Sports*, authored by Aubrey Fine and Michael Sachs (1996, Diamond Communications, Inc.), is another recent publication. He serves as an editorial board member and reviewer for numerous professional journals, including a position as Bulletin Board Editor for *The Sport Psychologist*. He is a licensed psychologist in Maryland, as well as a certified consultant, Association for the Advancement of Applied Sport Psychology. Dr. Sachs served as president of the Association for the Advancement of Applied Sport Psychology in 1991–1992. He is married and has two daughters. He is interested in all sports and enjoys running as his primary means of exercise.

Dr. Kevin L. Burke is an assistant professor and director of the Sport Psychology Laboratory in the Department of Health and Kinesiology at Georgia Southern University. He received a bachelor of arts degree in psychology and recreational studies (double major), with a minor in sociology from Belmont Abbey College in 1982. He also was a member of the men's tennis team and a National Association of Intercollegiate Athletics Academic All-American Tennis Team nominee, making the N.A.I.A. All-District 26 Tennis Team in both singles and doubles play. Dr. Burke received a master of arts degree in social/organizational psychology from East Carolina University in 1984 and doctor of philosophy degree in sport psychology from Florida State University in 1988.

A charter member and past secretary-treasurer of the Association for the Advancement of Applied Sport Psychology (AAASP), Dr. Burke also served on AAASP's original executive board as the first student representative. He has presented and published through local, state, regional, national, and international channels. In 1996, he coauthored a book entitled Tennis. Dr. Burke is currently an associate editor for the *Journal of Sport Behavior* and the

Journal of Interdisciplinary Research in Physical Education. He also serves on the editorial board for *Strategies.* He has served as a guest reviewer for the *Journal of Applied Sport Psychology, The Sport Psychologist,* and the *Journal of Sport & Exercise Psychology.* He also has served as a Sport Psychologist Digest compiler for the *Journal of Sport & Exercise Psychology,* and as associate editor for the AAASP newsletter. Dr. Burke has served as a Research Dissemination Committee member of the Research Consortium of the American Alliance for Health, Physical Education, Recreation, and Dance, and as a research works contributing editor for the *Journal of Physical Education, Recreation, and Dance.*

Dr. Burke has assisted professional, college, high school, and recreational athletes from various sports as a sport psychology consultant and is a certified consultant, AAASP. His current research interests are in optimism/pessimism, momentum, humor, concentration,sport officials, and the effectiveness of intervention techniques in sport and exercise. Dr. Burke has been nominated for the prestigious Dorothy V. Harris Young Scholar/Practitioner award, been selected for leadership training, and won an award for teaching. Dr. Burke has been an intercollegiate basketball official, and in 1997–8 began his eighteenth season as an interscholastic basketball official, in which he is certified at the state's highest level. He has served as head coach of three National Collegiate Athletic Association Division I tennis teams. Dr. Burke is a ranked United States Tennis Association competitor and recreational basketball and softball player.

Shawn Gomer is currently completing her doctorate in exercise and sport psychology at Temple University. She received a bachelor of arts degree in social psychology from Tufts University in 1990 and a master of arts degree in sport psychology from the University of Connecticut in 1994. After one year as a graduate assistant in the Department of Physical Education, Ms. Gomer was hired as the full-time undergraduate academic adviser in the department. She is responsible for advising approximately 400 undergraduate students in terms of university, departmental, and core curriculum. Because the position often entails counseling on various life issues, study skill problems, and career decision making, Ms. Gomer is grateful for the experiences she has had in her graduate sport psychology and counseling classes as well as her summer 1996 internship at an eating-disorders clinic. Her research interests include the psychological factors surrounding the transition out of a sport as well as the impact and implications of family systems on young athletes. As a former competitive tennis player, Ms. Gomer continues her participation by teaching tennis at the university level.

TABLE OF CONTENTS

TABLE OF CONTENTS ....

TABLE OF CONTENTS ....

Appendixes

Directory of Graduate Programs in Applied Sport Psychology

This publication is a directory of graduate programs in applied sport psychology. It has been developed by the Association for the Advancement of Applied Sport Psychology (AAASP) to assist students, faculty, and other interested persons in finding basic information about graduate programs in applied sport psychology.

The information contained for each program in this directory encompasses the following: address, contact person, telephone and fax numbers, electronic mail address, faculty substantively involved in the graduate program and their research/applied areas of interest, degrees offered, program information (students in the program, acceptance rates, admissions requirements, financial assistance available), internship information, and special comments concerning the program. The directory is intended to provide a starting point for students searching for a graduate program, as well as serve as a reference work for others in the field.

A number of disclaimers/caveats must be offered. First, aspects of programs change over time. It is important to contact programs in which you ("you" will be used in the directory to refer to the prospective student and hopefully make the directory somewhat more personal) might have interest and confirm the current status of the program (i.e., faculty present, degrees offered, financial assistance available, etc.). Second, no attempt has been made to define what is meant by a "program." A program may be a separate area of specialization within a department, or may simply be a "track" within an existing program. Numbers, types, and quality of courses and internship offerings differ across programs. Varying levels of preparation for work in applied sport psychology are available. It is *critical* that you check with the contact person for programs in which you might be interested and find out for sure whether your goals can be adequately met within the context of the program.

Information contained in this directory represents self-reports by the colleges and universities included. AAASP does not endorse any of the programs per se and has not undertaken an evaluation of any of the programs. It is assumed that students interested in particular programs will check them out carefully. The section on "Taking the Next Step: What to Ask as You Review the Directory," written by Patricia Latham Bach (a doctoral student in the Department of Exercise and Sport Sciences at the University of North Carolina at Greensboro), provides a significant expansion of information provided in the third edition—this may be helpful in checking out programs in which you're interested.

New Features

This edition of the directory is the fifth edition—the first edition was published in November 1986; the second in September 1989; the third in September 1992; and the fourth in September 1995. This fifth edition has several new indexes, and all information has been updated as of July 1, 1997, to be as current as possible.

A listing of a number of doctoral programs in clinical/counseling psychology that have indicated they offer opportunities to do work in sport psychology by taking courses in the exercise/sport sciences and enroll in practica has been provided (see Appendix D). This listing considers that in recent years many students interested in applied sport psychology have expressed a desire to obtain a doctoral degree in psychology with an emphasis in applied sport psychology. The relatively small number of psychology programs that offer emphases in applied sport psychology necessitates consideration of programs which do not have concentrations in exercise/sport but do allow students the opportunity to do some study in this area.

This is the fourth time such a listing has appeared in the directory. There may be programs that have been missed in trying to identify ones appropriate for the listing. If you're interested in the exercise/sport area and are planning on pursuing a doctoral degree in clinical/counseling psychology, it would be best to check with the programs in which you're interested to see whether the program is amenable to providing opportunities in applied sport psychology. It should be noted that not all clinical/counseling programs consider applied sport psychology (or even exercise and sport) a "worthwhile" area of study/practice, and you should be careful how this subject is broached, to avoid diminishing your chances of getting accepted to the program (assuming you would still want to attend a program if the attitude is negative toward applied sport psychology).

A listing of programs found in the fourth (1995) edition of the Directory that have been deleted and new programs that have been added to this fifth edition can be found in Appendix A.

Psychologist, Psychology, and Psychological

The primary use of the term "applied sport psychology" in this directory focuses on training in educational sport psychology. Educational sport psychology emphasizes the teaching of psychological skills (i.e., PST—Psychological Skills Training) such as goal setting, arousal control, concentration, imagery, and positive self-talk.

Some programs offer training in clinical sport psychology as well, but programs in which expertise can be developed in this area are considerably fewer. Clinical sport psychology encompasses psychological problems wherein expertise in clinical/counseling psychology is needed. These problems, which affect both sport participants and nonsport participants, include depression, anxiety, eating disorders, substance abuse, etc.

We realize there is a continuing debate within the field about the nature of "applied" sport psychology, and that work with exercise and sport participants often encompasses both educational and "clinical" components. The use of the term "applied" herein has been left sufficiently flexible to encompass programs with a variety of emphases, to provide this flexibility of opportunities for potential students in the field.

A smaller number of programs included in this directory have primarily an academic/research focus within sport psychology. These programs may appeal to those interested in a minimum amount of exposure to applications in the field and a maximum amount of exposure to the academic/research side of sport psychology.

We have attempted to address questions about the emphases of various programs by including a scale that has been successfully used by Norcross, Sayette, and Mayne in their excellent book, *Insider's Guide to Graduate Programs in Clinical and Counseling Psychology* (1996/1997 edition, New York: The Guilford Press) (see fuller discussion of this book in Appendix D). We asked programs to select one of the seven numbers on the following Likert Scale. Norcross et al. used this scale (with established validity) to have programs self-rate themselves along a clinically oriented to research oriented continuum. We thought that this might be an effective way (as modified) to address this for our field as well. Programs were asked to circle the number that best reflected the emphasis/orientation of their program:

Program Rating:

1	2	3	4	5	6	7
Applied Orientation			Equal Emphasis			Research Orientation

_____ Please check here if your program offers opportunities to pursue an applied orientation OR a research orientation (as opposed to an equal emphasis on both)

The following note was provided: "At the risk of starting a controversy over definitions, please note that research can be basic and/or applied, but simply indicates a focus upon research during one's program. An applied orientation means that the focus is upon applied/consulting work (which could be focused upon education/performance enhancement AND/OR clinical/counseling), with a requirement/encouragement to do such work in one or more settings. Some programs will have an equal emphasis on both, and are encouraged to note this, but many programs are clearly oriented towards one side or the other, and it will be helpful for students to know this."

Most programs provided the information requested. Your feedback on whether this information is helpful (and accurate!) would be appreciated.

The programs contained herein offer graduate degrees primarily in physical education/kinesiology/exercise science or psychology. You should note that use of the terms *psychologist*, *psychology*, and *psychological* is restricted by laws in each state and province. For more information concerning this issue, contact your state's (or province's) psychology licensing board or talk with faculty members at the programs in which you are interested.

There is an extensive set of literature on professional and ethical issues in applied sport psychology. Appendix G provides a reference list of books and articles that you may find useful in beginning your investigation of this area.

Internships/Practica

Information is contained within the directory on internships available in the various programs listed. It should be emphasized that there are internships and there are "internships"! More clearly, the term "internship" has different connotations for different programs. The term internship, when used with an APA approved clinical/counseling program, refers to a program requirement, and is likely to mean a full year's work that may encompass 2,000 hours of supervised work in an applied clinical/counseling setting. This setting may or may not (usually not) involve any sport psychology work. It should be noted that internships are not "affiliated" with clinical/counseling programs per se. However, internships must be approved by the programs (and usually, but not always, by the APA). Internship sites are often separate from the university and are generally quite competitive.

The term internship, when used with many of the physical education/kinesiology programs listed, is likely to mean a supervised, applied experience ranging from 90 hours or so to several hundred hours of work. This type of experience is often called a practicum, rather than an internship. In any case, we are using the term internship quite liberally here, and it encompasses both traditional internships and practica, with a focus on applied experiences in exercise and sport, and you should investigate specifically what internship/practicum opportunities are available in the programs in which you are interested. A few thoughts on internships are offered in Appendix C.

Background Reading in Sport Psychology

Questions are often posed about general background reading in sport psychology, examining theory, research, and practice (application). Appendix F provides a listing of basic texts in sport psychology, exercise psychology, and several general references. The following listing provides journals specific to sport psychology and several related journals in the sport sciences with frequent articles in the area:

Specific: *International Journal of Sport Psychology*
             Journal of Applied Sport Psychology
             Journal of Performance Enhancement
             Journal of Sport and Exercise Psychology
             The Sport Psychologist

Related: *Journal of Applied Psychology*
             Journal of Interdisciplinary Research in Physical Education
             Journal of Sport Behavior
             Perceptual and Motor Skills
             Research Quarterly for Exercise and Sport

In considering applied sport psychology in particular, individuals interested in this area often search for useful books, in both professional and trade publications. To facilitate locating some of these volumes, an updated version of an article by Michael Sachs (with assistance from Alan Kornspan, a doctoral student in the School of Physical Education at West Virginia University) entitled "Reading List in Applied Sport Psychology: Psychological Skills Training," which appeared in 1991 in *The Sport Psychologist* (volume 5, pp. 88–91) is provided in Appendix H.

Fitness Information Technology, Inc. (FIT) is the publisher of this fifth edition of the directory. FIT's address is P.O. Box 4425, University Avenue, Morgantown, WV 26504-4425; telephone number: 1-800-477-4348 or 304-599-3482; e-mail: fit@fitinfotech.com; website: www.fitinfotech.com. They have numerous other publications in exercise and sport psychology and you want to be sure to get on their mailing list. Another publisher of note is Human Kinetics. Human Kinetics is a major sport sciences publisher, and you can obtain a catalogue of their publications by calling 1-800-747-4457, or writing them at Box 5076, Champaign, IL 61820. There are other publishers in this area, but these are two who are the most specialized in sport psychology (and other areas within the sport sciences).

Careers in Sport Psychology

One of the most frequently asked questions about sport psychology concerns what one can do with a degree in the field. Division 47 (Exercise and Sport Psychology) of the American Psychological Association (APA), in joint sponsorship with AAASP and NASPSPA (North American Society for the Psychology of Sport and Physical Activity) has published a helpful brochure, "Graduate Training & Career Possibilities in Exercise & Sport Psychology." We have reproduced the brochure in this directory (see Appendix E).

The Division 47 Education Committee is also the author of an excellent brochure entitled "How Can a Psychologist Become a Sport Psychologist?" This brochure can be found on Division 47's web site—http://www.psyc.unt.edu/apadiv47/or you can write to the Committee Chairperson, Dr. Karen Cogan, at the University of North Texas Counseling Center, P.O. Box 13487, Denton, TX 13487. Dr. Cogan's e-mail address is Cogan@dsa.unt.edu

Certification/Licensure

As noted earlier, licensure as a psychologist is governed by state/provincial law (for the United States and Canada). Use of the terms *psychologist*, *psychology*, and *psychological* is restricted by these laws. For more information concerning this issue, you should contact your state's (or province's) psychology licensing board or talk with faculty members at the programs in which you're interested.

Certification, however, differs from licensure in that requirements are not based upon laws per se but are generally established by academic/professional organizations. These organizations attempt to identify the academic/practical background and sets of competencies that an "experienced professional" in the field should have. Certification programs in various areas of specialization within psychology are available, including sport psychology. Specifically, AAASP has a program that provides for certification as a "Certified Consultant, Association for the Advancement of Applied Sport Psychology." The criteria for certification are the following:

AAASP Certification Criteria

Necessary levels of preparation in the substantive content areas generally require successful completion of at least three graduate semester hours or their equivalent (e.g., passing suitable exams offered by an accredited doctoral program). However, up to four upper-level undergraduate courses may be substituted for this requirement (unless specifically designated as requiring graduate credit only). It is not always necessary to take one course to satisfy each requirement. However, one course or experience cannot be used to satisfy more than one criterion, except for number 2.

1.   Completion of a doctoral degree.

2.   Knowledge of scientific and professional ethics and standards (can meet requirement by taking one course on these topics or by taking several courses in which these topics comprise parts of the courses or by completing other comparable experiences).

3.   Knowledge of the sport psychology subdisciplines of intervention/performance enhancement, health/exercise psychology, and social psychology as evidenced by three courses or two courses and one independent study in sport psychology (two of these courses must be taken at the graduate level).

4.   Knowledge of the biomechanical and/or physiological bases of sport (e.g., kinesiology, biomechanics, exercise physiology).

5.   Knowledge of the historical, philosophical, social, or motor behavior bases of sport (e.g., motor learning/control, motor development, issues in sport/physical education, sociology of sport, history and philosophy of sport/physical education).

6.   Knowledge of psychopathology and its assessment (e.g., abnormal psychology, psychopathology).

7.   Training designed to foster basic skills in counseling (e.g., coursework on basic intervention techniques in counseling, supervised practica in counseling, clinical, or industrial/organizational psychology) (graduate level only).

8.   Supervised experience, with a qualified person (i.e., one who has an appropriate background in applied sport psychology), during which the individual receives training in the use of sport psychology principles and techniques (e.g., supervised practica in applied sport psychology in which the focus of the assessments and interventions are participants in physical activity, exercise, or sport) (graduate level only).

9.   Knowledge of skills and techniques within sport or exercise (e.g., skills and techniques classes, clinics, formal coaching experiences, organized participation in sport or exercise).

10. Knowledge and skills in research design, statistics, and psychological assessment (graduate level only).

At least two of the following four criteria must be met through educational experiences that focus on general psychological principles (rather than sport-specific ones).

11. Knowledge of the biological bases of behavior (e.g., biomechanics/kinesiology, comparative psychology, exercise physiology, neuropsychology, physiological psychology, psychopharmacology, sensation).

12. Knowledge of the cognitive-affective bases of behavior (e.g., cognition, emotion, learning, memory, motivation, motor development, motor learning/control, perception, thinking).

13. Knowledge of the social bases of behavior (e.g., cultural, ethnic, and group processes; gender roles in sport; organizational and systems theory; social psychology; sociology of sport).

14. Knowledge of individual behavior (e.g., developmental psychology, exercise behavior, health psychology, individual differences, personality theory).

●●●●●●●●●●●●●●●●●●●●●●

Further information concerning the certification process may be obtained from either Michael Sachs or Kevin Burke (see addresses and telephone numbers on the next page). AAASP is currently the only association providing certification in applied sport psychology.

You may also wish to consult an excellent brochure developed by the AAASP Organization Outreach and Education Committee entitled "Certified Consultant, Association for the Advancement of Applied Sport Psychology: Questions and Answers." The current Certification Committee chairperson is Dr. Bonnie Berger, School of Physical Education and Health Education, University of Wyoming, Laramie, WY 82070.

While students entering graduate programs would not be eligible for certification unless or until they hold the doctoral degree and meet the other criteria listed, this information may be of interest in planning a program of study and/or selecting a program in the first place. It should be noted that programs are not certified—*individuals* are certified as consultants. Certainly, your course of study should be determined by you and your adviser, and you can prepare for work in applied sport psychology in many ways. However, designing your course of study to meet (at a minimum) AAASP certification criteria, as well as state licensing criteria for training in psychology (at least the coursework/areas of study component), may provide additional options for someone interested in working in this area. The degree to which a program can prepare you for these goals may be an important consideration in your selection of a graduate program in applied sport psychology.

Comments, Questions, Feedback

We welcome your comments, questions, feedback, etc., on this directory, particularly concerning ways in which its usefulness can be enhanced in the future. Your editors are Michael Sachs, in the Department of Physical Education at Temple University (and a past president of AAASP); Kevin Burke, in the Department of Health and Kinesiology at Georgia Southern University (and a former secretary-treasurer of AAASP), and Shawn Gomer, a doctoral student in exercise and sport psychology at Temple University. Please feel free to contact us:

Michael L. Sachs, Ph.D.
Department of Physical Education—048-00,
Temple University
Philadelphia, PA 19122
(215) 204-8718 (office)
(215) 204-8705 (fax)
e-mail: MSACHS@VM.TEMPLE.EDU

Kevin L. Burke, Ph.D.
Department of Health and Kinesiology
Georgia Southern University
P.O. Box 8076
Statesboro, GA 30460-8076
(912) 681-5267 (office)
(912) 681-0381 (fax)
e-mail: KevBurke@gsaix2.cc.GASOU.edu

Shawn Gomer, M.A.
Department of Physical Education—048-00,
Temple University
Philadelphia, PA 19122
(215) 204-1953 (office)
(215) 204-8705 (fax)
e-mail: gome13@vm.temple.edu

Taking the Next Step: What to Ask as You Review the Directory

by Patricia Latham Bach, RN, MS
University of North Carolina, Greensboro

The process of becoming a sport psychologist is, in many ways, quite similar to that undertaken by an athlete who desires high-level achievement and excellence in a given sport. The attainment of this vision requires commitment, goal setting, attentional focus, positive-self talk, resiliency, and motivation, as well as the support of significant others, friends, and faculty. As you review this directory, realize that you have embarked upon one of the first of many steps which, taken together, constitute the "process" of becoming a professional.

Your review of the material will help in narrowing the number of schools and types of programs which warrant further investigation and contact. Your decision is generally based upon a variety of factors but should be most strongly influenced by the *vision* that you hold for yourself in the future.

Sport psychology, as a discipline, is the offspring of two strong parents ... psychology and sport/exercise. As part of the maturation process, it has experienced some of the "growing pains" inherent in the development of a profession, and has struggled with a precise definition and uniform agreement of the term itself.

As an example, to date, no universally accepted operational definition of the designation "sport psychologist " exists. The same holds true for: 1) the lack of specific and consistent educational requirements (other than those mandated for AAASP certification), 2) varying degrees of emphasis placed on research versus practical application in different programs, and 3) ultimately, the nature and scope of practice itself. Though there is agreement *in principle*, the discipline exists with a degree of "professional ambiguity" in that the roles and responsibilities of individuals in the field vary based on the chosen educational path and type of degree. Therefore, the term "sport psychologist" should be considered a generic title.

Basically, sport psychologists function in three different roles. Because these roles are not mutually exclusive, a degree of overlap may exist for a given individual and within a given position. Cox (1994) identified the three specialized roles as 1) the research sport psychologist, 2) the educational sport psychologist, and 3) the clinical sport psychologist.

Cox describes the researcher as an individual who is a "scientist and scholar" (p. 9). This person may conduct theoretical and/or applied research, and may teach both undergraduate and graduate courses in sport psychology and related areas. These individuals are generally found in positions at the university level and generally require the Ph.D. degree.

An educational sport psychologist is described as one who "use[s] the medium of education to teach correct principles of sport psychology to athletes and coaches ... develop[s] psychological skills for performance enhancement [and] help[s] athletes ... to enjoy sport and use it as a vehicle for improving their quality of life" (p. 9). This person enjoys a broad spectrum of opportunities in that the use of performance enhancement techniques is not unique to athletes and can be applied to a variety of nonathletic consultation settings (i.e., business and industry, music, and other performing arts). This person is also sometimes called a performance enhancement consultant or sport consultant or other similar term. Training for this position is generally at the master's or doctoral level.

Clinical sport psychologists are "prepared to deal with emotional and personality disorder problems that affect some athletes" (p. 9). This role requires completion of a doctoral degree in clinical or counseling psychology and may lead to licensure as a psychologist. Some individuals with preparation as clinical social workers may have some applicable background in this area. Based on training, these individuals may conduct research and work in educational and/or clinical environments, and may be eligible to receive third-party reimbursement.

Superficially, the distinctions among the three roles may seem an issue of semantics. There is a tremendous amount of educational diversity among sport psychologists. However, the differences are critical to you as an interested student, in that they may strongly impact both your educational focus and training and, eventually, your ability to function within certain environments. There are a myriad of opportunities which may be found if you are willing to invest time and energy exploring the realm of professional opportunities. As a profession we are moving to a point in our development wherein sport psychologists, by virtue of their educational choices, may choose more clearly defined career paths based on interests which may be focused upon one or more of the three areas of academics, performance enhancement, or clinical practice.

As a parallel, consider the model of contemporary medical education. Students apply to either allopathic (MD) or osteopathic (DO) medical schools. In general, their standardized medical education consists of two years in basic sciences and two years in clinical rotations. Following graduation, they may enter research-oriented or clinical specialty programs, which culminate in expertise within a particular area of research, education, or practice. The educational process and requirements are well established, and ultimately lead to a well-articulated terminal goal.

Unlike traditional medical education, sport psychology has not yet matured to the point wherein a uniform curriculum provides a standard foundation and subsequent systematized "practice" opportunities. Furthermore, the precise outcome goals of the educational process are also less clearly distinguished. Choice of a program, especially at the doctoral level, may seriously impact a student's opportunities to work with athletes and to develop expertise in an "applied" practice setting. Traditionally, the non-clinical Ph.D. has been a research degree; therefore, the emphasis of most educational Ph.D. programs in sport psychology remains one of research, not of practice. Students interested in a more "applied" focus should bear this in mind when making program choices for graduate education in sport psychology.

The "Process-Product" Equation

As a general strategy for evaluation, Gould (Daniel Gould, personal communication, May 1, 1995) uses a very simple, yet effective, "process-product" equation that may help guide you in your decisions relative to graduate school and, later, through your educational program. An easy way to conceptualize this equation is to ask the following question: "Is the process congruent with the product (and vice versa)?"

In virtually any situation, the "product" is the anticipated goal or desired outcome. In this case, the product is an identified role as a sport psychologist in education, research, or practice, or some combination of these roles.

The "process" constitutes the *means* by which the outcome is obtained or achieved. In this case, a master's or doctoral program is the educational process by which one is prepared to become a sport psychologist.

The process-product equation is especially helpful in two important ways: 1) it will assist you in clearly *defining* your professional objectives (by asking yourself "What do I hope to achieve as a sport psychology professional?"), and 2) it will assist you in selecting programs which are *congruent* with your goals by helping you determine the type of process that is necessary for your chosen career path.

For example, a student who hopes to work exclusively in the area of sport psychology research would probably be happiest in a nonclinical Ph.D. program with a strong research focus. Alternatively, a student who desires intensive contact with athletes in developing performance enhancement techniques may be best suited to a master's or doctoral program which provides numerous opportunities for actual practice in a supervised environment. In these examples, the tone and focus of the programs are congruent with, and supportive of, the professional goals established by the student.

Training in sport psychology can be completed at the Master's and Doctoral levels. Because of this, it is important, prior to embarking on your educational journey, to determine *which* (or both) of the two degrees will best prepare you to meet your projected goals. In some cases, a "terminal" master's degree (i.e., one which prepares you for a career requiring no further formal education) may prove more useful than further education at the doctoral level, based on your personal career choices.

The "Graduate Training and Career Possibilities" booklet (see Appendix E) states: "Most of the professional employment opportunities in sport psychology require doctoral degrees from accredited colleges and universities ... [Individuals] with master's degrees... compete at a distinct disadvantage for the limited number of full-time positions available in exercise and sport psychology." This statement holds true when "professional employment opportunities" incorporate more traditional university-related, academic, or research positions, and/or individual clinical practice opportunities requiring licensure. However, given the true paucity of traditional sport psychology positions, even doctoral preparation provides no guarantee of gainful employment. It merely strengthens the chances for a position in higher education or satisfies licensure requirements for practice as a psychologist. In this profession, more (i.e., Ph.D. vs. master's preparation) is not necessarily better but merely provides a different focus.

It is also important to note that, given national trends, decreased funding is available to support educational programs in general. Given this trend, in addition to changes in the economic environment for mental health care (which may affect clinical sport psychologists), the complexion of those positions for which doctoral level preparation is required may be significantly altered. Furthermore, "performance enhancement" is seldom, if ever, reimbursed by third-party payers.

Students interested in graduate education in sport psychology should be aware that lucrative *and* exciting positions in research and practice are very difficult to find. Many positions may be exciting, but few, if any, are lucrative. However, the field is dynamic and growing, and there is hope for the future. There is a great need for those whose vision recognizes the importance of current work as a bridge to the almost limitless possibilities for this future. Therefore, both master's and doctoral programs which promote high standards of academic achievement, coupled with creativity, entrepreneurial skills, and flexibility, should be considered to best prepare neophyte professionals for this field.

Sport Psychology Program Focus

One difficulty for aspiring students exists in learning to "read between the lines." Universities do not provide materials which intentionally foster misrepresentations. However, *perceptions* of program orientation may be skewed, or good intentions not made clear, due to the lack of clarity in the use of particular terms. For example, some schools allude to "applied" work. This may be interpreted as "direct contact" with athletes. However, the *intention* of that word may be far different, in that it may be meant to imply *research* that has an "applied" focus. This disparity in perceptions represents quite a significant variation in actual work, and students should be clear about program focus to ensure a mutual understanding that is in everyone's best interest. It is always sad to hear about students who go to programs expecting one focus and find that that focus is not really available, making for an unhappy student and faculty.

A critical difference among sport psychology programs rests in the specific program focus. That is, some programs provide greater concentration in the area of research (whether theoretical or applied), while others are oriented more towards a practice model (often considered an "applied" emphasis). Graphically represented, one could envision a model with four quadrants, wherein emphasis on both research and practice can be evaluated. In this case, a modified Likert scale is incorporated to facilitate the process (Low = 1, High = 5):

Research and Practice Sport Psychology Program Focus Model

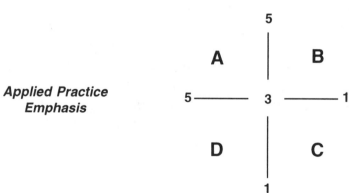

Quadrants: A — High Research/High Practice
            B — High Research/Low Practice
            C — Low Research/Low Practice
            D — Low Research/High Practice

It is critical to determine exactly *where* your interests lie in this model and to *identify a compatibly matched program and advisor.* For those more interested in academic research (and less so in applied/practice work), a program in quadrant B would be most appropriate. Students who desire greater emphasis on consultation and first-hand experiences with athletes in performance enhancement, but less emphasis on research, would probably be most comfortable with a program in quadrant D. Those who wish a mix of the two would find themselves most comfortable with a program in quadrant A. Those most comfortable with a program in quadrant C may be in the wrong field.

This model can be used to conduct a three-fold evaluation. First, use it to identify your own interests relative to research and practice. This can be accomplished by reexamining your outcome goals or projected professional "product" (refer to the "Process-Product Equation" section). By determining what you would like to do, you will be able to identify where you most appropriately fit in the model. This will help you determine the type of program which will best meet your needs.

Second, the model can be beneficial in evaluating prospective programs. As you read materials and assimilate information, use the research/practice scales to rate your program choices. During your conversations with faculty and students, ask *them* to rate their program. Compare their evaluation with your own, based on your reading/information gathering. Importantly, determine the degree to which these are congruent and, if not, why.

Finally, ask your potential advisor to rate his/her research vs. practice focus, because an individual professor may have a somewhat different approach towards these variables than the program as a whole. If this rating varies from *your* desired rating (i.e., your program preference), consider the difference carefully. A good "match" between student, program and advisor is one wherein there is a strong degree of congruence relative to both the educational process and the projected product. If your interests are in contrast with either the program or your advisor, the likelihood exists that no one will be happy. It is best to enter a graduate program which facilitates the possibility of a "win-win" situation, wherein a common purpose and mutually satisfactory approach have been established. By using the model and thinking through the process-product equation, you will have a much stronger chance of completing your program in an effective and satisfying manner!

Developing Awareness

One of the best ways to prepare for entry into the field is to develop an understanding of and familiarity with the issues which challenge our development as a profession. In this way you will be better prepared to ask the questions which will lead to a clear distinction between the programs that ideally represent your interests and those that do not.

The directory, aside from simply listing programs and institutions, provides valuable information for those willing to invest a few hours in reviewing it carefully. Although this requires some time and energy now, it will save a great deal of effort in the future.

Appendix H provides an excellent overview of references which will prove helpful in developing a perspective relative to the field. These will contribute significantly to your global fund of knowledge about sport psychology. However, a number of articles/books on selected topics will prove particularly helpful to you:

1) *Developing an Overview of Sport Psychology*
   (Definitions, roles, history, and current issues.)

   Feltz, D. (1992). The nature of sport psychology. In Horn,
      T. S. (Ed.). *Advances in sport psychology* (pp. 13–22).
      Champaign, IL: Human Kinetics.

   Williams, J. M., & Straub, W. F. (1993). Sport psychology:
      past, present, future. In J. M. Williams (Ed.). *Applied
      sport psychology: Personal growth to peak performance.*
      (pp. 1–10). Mountain View, CA: Mayfield Publishing Company.

2) *Variations in Scope of Practice*
   (Overview of three different roles in which sport psychologists function.)

   Anshel, M. H. (1997). The science of sport psychology. In
      Sport psychology: From theory to practice. (3rd ed.)
      (pp. 11–13). Scottsdale, AZ: Gorsuch Scarisbruck, Publishers.

3) *Career and Future Directions in Applied Sport Psychology*

   Taylor, J. (1991). Career direction, development and
      opportunities in applied sport psychology. *The Sport
      Psychologist, 5*, 266–280.

   Vealey, R. S. (1988). Future directions in psychological
      skills training. *The Sport Psychologist, 2,* 318–336.

4) *Guidelines for Clinical Psychology Graduate Programs*
   (Helpful hints for developing personal essays, successful interviewing, program analysis
   and evaluation. Specific to clinical psychology programs. Provides excellent model for
   sport psychology program evaluation as well. Highly recommended.*)*

   Norcross, J. C., Sayette, M. A., & Mayne, T. J. (1996).
      *Insider's guide to graduate programs in clinical and counseling
      psychology* (1996–1997 edition). New York: The Guilford Press.

When you have completed these readings, the differences in focus, theoretical frameworks, and projected directions of the various programs will have become much more evident. However, to discern the most subtle variations, it is best to spend time in discussion with others, both students and faculty.

Becoming a Wise Consumer

As a prospective student of graduate-level training, you must learn to become a wise consumer. Given your potential investment of time (master's programs—2 years; Ph.D. programs—3–4 years), energy (lots) and financial resources (varies, dependent upon funding, but can be *substantial*), it is critical to learn as much about the program and faculty as possible. Remember, once accepted and with your program initiated, you have established a working relationship which must endure the rigors of the program and the idiosyncrasies of higher education. Though certainly not cast in stone, transfer between graduate programs is much more difficult than at the undergraduate level. In fact, few doctoral programs will consider transfers with advanced standing (most Ph.D. students wishing to transfer must initiate the entire process again from scratch ... some credit for courses taken may be applied, but generally relatively little). Therefore, it is especially important in this situation to thoroughly investigate all aspects of potential programs and choose wisely.

Given all this, it is vital for students to learn to assimilate information. Primary sources of information include:

1. *Written materials* provided by the university (these usually detail particular graduate school requirements) and the specific department (may elaborate on individual program philosophies, options, requirements, electives, etc.). This directory is one place to start, but it is important to get materials from the programs themselves.

2. *On-site visit* to the university—enables first-hand observation of faculty-student interactions, facilities, current research projects, and interviews with students and faculty. This can be very helpful and is strongly encouraged for your top choices. Arrangements should be made to meet with several current graduate students or, at least, be provided with names and telephone numbers for 3–4 current students (and graduates as appropriate) with whom you can talk about the program.

3. *Telephone interviews*—with faculty and current students (when site visits are not possible). This is very helpful, in that you can develop a "flavor" for your ability to speak and interact effectively with a professor. Also, students are generally very forthcoming and will share perceptions of the program, ideas and thoughts about faculty—student interactions, and a host of information not readily evident in brochures. This is often great for establishing the "bottom line."

It is strongly encouraged to contact a program, at least by telephone, before applying. Some faculty have indicated amazement at students who apply to programs, yet have never contacted the faculty or students. Written materials often do not provide enough information on which to make application decisions! Even if on-site visits or meetings at conferences are not possible, you should at least talk with faculty and current students by telephone (the faculty should be happy to give you names of 3–4 students with whom you can talk) to get a feeling for what the people and program are like. This is also helpful in the admissions process, wherein a positive impression that you make over the telephone can be helpful in tilting an admissions decision your way as opposed to your being "just a name" on an application.

Remember that your decision to enter a graduate program will affect the rest of your professional life. Your ability to work with and learn from faculty and other students is dependent upon mutual educational interests and effective communication skills. First-hand knowledge and assessment of these interests/skills cannot be gleaned solely from the directory. The time and money spent talking with faculty and other students is a worthwhile investment in your future.

4. *Conference meetings*—in many cases, your first exposure to particular faculty/students from identified schools may arise at a conference. Take advantage of these opportunities—introductions often anchor positive memories of individuals and may serve you well in the future. These meetings are especially helpful if you have many programs in which you are interested and want to get some information/develop impressions before narrowing your list to a more manageable number.

5. *Networking*—networking with other students in the field is a tremendously valuable resource. Most students enrolled in a sport psychology graduate program have spent a great deal of effort investigating the realm of program possibilities, and may be able to steer you in the right direction, saving you time, energy, and money. In many cases, department secretaries (if not the faculty) will be happy to pass your telephone number or address (including e-mail address) along to current students, who understand the importance of making a well-informed choice of a graduate program.

6. *Literature search*—conduct a literature search through several of the available data bases (e.g., SPORTDISCUS, PSYCH-LIT) to determine the types of publications and work completed by prospective faculty. This information may serve as a springboard to further questions about your potential future advisor, and demonstrates the type of preparation and motivation which is highly valued in prospective students.

Above all, it is important to *ask questions* to clarify specific issues, concerns and thoughts which may arise relative to a program. The following list provides a sample of the types of questions which may facilitate the "process" necessary to make your vision a reality, and incorporates those which appeared previously in the 1995 Directory. Use these questions to develop a "profile" for each program. As you rule out certain options and narrow your list, the answers to these questions may become more critical in helping you make your final decision.

An effective method of initiating this process is to develop an understanding of *your* needs and goals relative to your education and future career aspirations. Self-knowledge/self-awareness is central to our work as sport psychologists. It is especially important, therefore, to take some time for introspection/reflection to help you establish baseline criteria for your search.

Questions for Introspection/Reflection

1. What aspects of the educational process are most important to me?
2. What do I wish to accomplish through my educational experience?
3. Where do I see myself professionally in 5, 10, 15 years?
4. What are my professional goals for teaching, research, and service to the profession and community?
5. What salary range would be acceptable upon graduation?
6. What type of academic/non-academic environment would best suit my needs?
7. What "resources" (other than money) will I need to help me through my education? Are these accessible? If not, how will I develop these?

Note:

It would be helpful to identify a faculty member who can help you "walk through" this process. Ideally, this should be someone who has an excellent grasp of the field and who can advise you accordingly.

General Questions

1. What is the size of the institution?
2. Does the institution operate on a semester or quarter system?
3. What type of grading system is used (i.e., letter grades, pass/fail)?
4. What is the cost per credit hour (for in-state and for out-of-state students)?
5. Where is the institution located (i.e., urban, suburban, or rural setting)?
6. What type of housing is available?
7. Are out-of-state tuition waivers available? If so, is this available for the duration of the program, or for one year only?
8. What types and amount of financial aid are available?

The Program

1. What are the entrance requirements for the university and for the program?
2. How long has the program been in existence? Does the faculty anticipate any major changes in the program in the foreseeable future?
3. What is the usual length of the program for both master's and doctoral work?
4. Is a thesis optional for completion of master's programs? What other options, if any, are available?
5. How "flexible" is the program (i.e., are many electives available)? What is the relationship of the program with others on the university campus? Are students welcomed to join other departments for course work and/or research or applied practice experiences?
6. Are some form of comprehensive exams required for completion of the degree programs? Are these written, oral, or both?
7. What are the strengths and weaknesses of the program? (This question should be asked of <u>both</u> faculty and students.)
8. What is the core curriculum? How is it structured? Are the courses taken in sequence available every year so that the sequence can be followed without interruption? Are these outlined on a semester-by-semester basis? Are these courses taught by graduate students or faculty?
9. What textbooks are used, and in which courses? (This is where your familiarity with books and readings will be quite useful. See Appendix G for a helpful list). For example, the Jean Williams text, *Applied Sport Psychology: Personal Growth to Peak Performance*, is a very "applied" text. If the school indicates a strong preference for applied work but fails to consider this book (or others like it) in any course, you may need to keep this in the back of your mind ... it may serve as a "red flag." Do the text selections represent a broad spectrum of sport science knowledge which embraces both the research and practice areas?
10. What is the prevailing "theoretical framework" of the department? How "open minded" is the department to more creative, less scientific, and less traditional thinking ... would this be welcomed or discouraged?
11. If the department is in psychology or counseling, is the program APA approved? If in these departments, does the program provide good exposure to sport-related coursework and actual practice? The same question can be posed in the opposite direction for those programs housed in departments of exercise and sport science.

12. Describe the department's operational definition of "applied work" as it is provided for students at both the master's and doctoral levels. Rate the program on the Research and Practice Sport Psychology Program Focus Model shown previously.
13. What is the ratio of applied *experience* to research *experience* at both the master's and doctoral levels?
14. What opportunities exist for *structured, consistent, supervised* "hands-on" applied experiences? What types of relationships has the department developed with the athletic department, community, and others to facilitate your exposure to "real world" situations within the learning environment?
15. Do opportunities exist for multicultural and cross-cultural experiences and training? Is there a process/approach taught to develop sensitivity to and awareness of the cultures inherent in different types of sport and exercise populations?
16. What courses address the following topics, and in how much depth: ethics, clinical and counseling issues (if not a clinical/counseling program), communication, professional development, business practices, use of technology, leadership skills, and creative approaches to entrepreneurship.
17. What time of the day/evening are classes generally scheduled?

Practica/Internships

1. Are internships required to complete the program? If so, what are the requirements, and how are these arranged and supervised? Are these readily available, or must they be developed by students? Are they compensated? If not required, what opportunities exist for student internships? When does this contact begin in the program sequence? Who arranges these experiences, how are they supervised, and how often is supervision available? What other opportunities have been designed to facilitate "professional development" activities?
2. Is academic credit available for independently arranged internships?
3. Have collaborative relationships been developed within the community to facilitate a broad spectrum of practicum experiences?

Faculty

1. What research areas are being pursued by faculty and students?
2. How are students involved in the research process? Do all students receive the opportunity to engage in research, or only those that have received student assistantships?
3. What journals do the faculty publish in? What books have they written? What topics do they focus on?
4. What conferences do the faculty attend, and where is their work presented?
5. Authorship: Who is the first author on research projects, papers, book chapters, etc.? Is this a consistent practice, or one which is negotiated "up front," prior to the initiation of research/writing? How often do students appear as coauthors on papers presented at conferences and published in journals, either as first author, or as second, third, etc., author?
6. What are their terminal goals for their students? How would they describe the student's "marketable skills" upon completion of the program?

7. Does the program allow and encourage independent research (other than that done for thesis or dissertation purposes)? Are faculty available on a consistent basis to provide feedback and guidance?
8. What is the faculty's travel schedule? How easily can students make appointments? Do other commitments (committees, etc.) play a major role in the expenditure of faculty time?
9. What types of jobs have the program's recent graduates (at both the master's and doctoral levels) obtained ?

Students

1. In general, how do students like the program?
2. What attracted the students to the school and the program?
3. What do the students see as the strengths and weaknesses of the program?
4. How much flexibility do the students see as existing in the program for: independent and creative thinking, individual and nonmainstream academic efforts, entrepreneurial pursuits, membership on a student's thesis or dissertation committee?
5. What types of hands-on learning experiences are available?
6. Are funds available for student research and travel to conferences?
7. How much independent study work is realistically allowed?
8. What type of relationship exists between students and faculty?
9. What type of relationship exists between students—competitive, cooperative, collaborative?
10. What types of work do student assistants perform?
11. Would the students choose the program again, given their present knowledge and experience?

Some Global Considerations

While no one can prescribe a means to measure the pulse of the profession, there are a few tips, easily applied, which may help create a picture of the field, the players, and the situation as it exists today.

1. Consider that best is a relative term: Good educational experiences result when the seeds of excellence are sowed within a supportive environment. The best program for one student may be anothers nightmare, despite the program's reputation. A best fit occurs when there is congruency in philosophy, focus, and direction between the educational team members, consistent for faculty and students. Be guided by well-informed decisions, not popular opinion.
2. Maximize your educational investment: Make program choices that will provide the greatest potential return on your educational investment. The time, energy, and effort committed to graduate programs in sport psychology should prepare you as a professional with marketable skills applicable to a variety of settings, whether your focus is research or practice. Consider programs which aspire to the Biggest Bang for the Buck Theory.
3. Maximize cross-training opportunities: Many current students and recent graduates have emphasized the importance of using elective opportunities to become well rounded, with

exposure to a multidisciplinary-enriched fund of knowledge. Recommendations, at a minimum, include course work in: counseling, psychopathology, eating disorders, and alcohol and chemical substance abuse. These are especially important for students in nonclinical sport psychology programs. Other excellent recommendations include organizational development, entrepreneurship, and computer technology courses. The demands of the work force are changing much more quickly than the traditional system of education. To be successful, one must be proactive, future focused and willing to take risks.

4. Learn to create your own opportunities: One of the most important tasks in this emerging profession is gaining access to athletes. There are many ways to *create* opportunities for working with athletes of all ages. Consider programs in the community, with little league, park and recreation sessions, and amateur athletic events. Skill development necessary for excellence as both a researcher and practitioner can be enhanced in this way, while increasing your visibility and presence in the athletic community.

5. Become a multimedia and multifaceted consumer: Much valuable information for sport psychologists comes from academically nontraditional sources. A tremendous amount of research and information on teamwork and competitive performance comes from business sources. Anecdotal information gleaned from newspapers, TV news/sport broadcasts, popular sport magazines, and a variety of other sources provide both real life examples and validation for our mission as sport psychologists. An increased awareness of our world and the potential application of our knowledge and experience can only enhance the growth of the profession.

6. Become a sponge and browse the Net: The Internet provides one of the most fertile resources for information gathering. The Sport Psychology Listserve, run by Dr. Michael Sachs at Temple University, is a bulletin board which provides a bird's eye view of the salient issues in the field. This and several other interesting Web site addresses can be found in Appendix O. They will provide food for thought for prospective students and professionals alike.

Putting it All Together

The list provided above is lengthy but is intended to develop your thinking relative to important issues in sport psychology graduate education. You need not ask each question, of course, nor pose the questions exactly as phrased above. However, to get the "big picture," these questions address many concerns which have arisen in the experiences of those who have gone before you.

As a sport psychologist in any of the specialized roles, the use of intuitive skills and tacit knowledge is very important. Developing these skills and learning to trust yourself in using them is a sequential process. This can be accomplished through a firmly established fund of knowledge coupled with a heightened, multisensory awareness of people, places, and dynamic situations.

As you investigate potential programs, begin to practice these intuitive skills and incorporate them in your decision-making process. Learn to assimilate information from several of the sources previously discussed (see the section on "Becoming a Wise Consumer"). Look for *patterns* of consistency in attitudes and responses among faculty and students, and for congruency between verbal responses and printed materials. The important message is often not what is said, but what remains unsaid. Learn to trust your 'gut' level feeling relative to the program, students, and faculty.

Despite all your efforts to "know" a program, this cannot truly happen until you have become a *part* of it. You must live the reality to know the program in its entirety. Your goal is to make the best possible choice, considering all the information available. Recognize that *every* program has benefits and drawbacks. The important issue is to decide which program will work best for _you!_

In Summary

The purpose of this chapter has been to present issues and provide questions for students who are considering graduate education in the field of sport psychology. This chapter has attempted to represent the many issues which you should consider as you enter this dynamic and exciting field. However, there will always be other, perhaps more personal issues, that may be of concern, and your introspection will help you become aware of and sensitive to these needs as you explore the various graduate programs. Remember, like an athlete, your journey to success in this field is determined by your energy and effort in preparation. Best wishes in making your "vision" become your "reality"!

Reference

Cox, R. H. (1994). *Sport psychology: Concepts and applications.* (3rd ed.) Dubuque, IA: Wm. C. Brown, Inc.

Endnote

The author would like to express her thanks to the editors, and especially Michael Sachs, for their assistance and valuable suggestions in preparing this chapter.

HOW TO USE THIS DIRECTORY

This directory, as noted in the introduction, is designed to provide a starting point for students searching for a graduate program in applied sport psychology, or faculty or other individuals interested in a reference work of graduate programs in the field. The basic information provided can guide the individual toward programs in specific geographical areas, with particular faculty involved, with internships available, and/or offering particular degrees.

The information requested from programs was, of necessity, brief and is not intended to provide a basis upon which to make a final selection or rejection of a graduate program! Rather, the directory provides some basic information for a preliminary screening of programs and for contacting the appropriate person for further information. The previous section, "Taking the Next Step: What to Ask as You Review the Directory," will be helpful in directing your search to obtain the additional information necessary to select a graduate program in applied sport psychology.

Please note a number of important points concerning this directory:

1. The information requested for each program in this directory encompassed the following: address, contact person, telephone and fax numbers, electronic mail address, World Wide Web site, faculty substantively involved in the graduate program and their research/applied areas of interest, degrees offered, program information (students in the program, acceptance rates, admissions requirements, financial assistance available), internship information, and special comments concerning the program. However, not all programs provided all the information requested (in some cases the information may not have been available). In cases where information was not provided, that category (such as financial assistance available, or internship information) has simply been omitted from the program entry rather than leaving it blank.

Additionally, new information about financial assistance available has been included. Programs were asked for information about the percentages of current students in the program receiving the following forms of assistance:

Fellowships
Research Assistantships
Teaching Assistantships
Tuition Waivers
Other Forms of Financial Aid

While most programs provided this information, the data should be used with caution. Temple University (home institution for two of your editors) is a perfect example. None of our current students have fellowships, although fellowships are available for qualified students. The information in the directory entry can, therefore, give you a feeling for what students are currently receiving, but it also helps to know what is available and find out about all your options.

Also note that some students receive more than one form of funding at any one point in their programs. Thus, percentages reported may exceed 100.

2. Faculty members substantively involved in each graduate program are listed alphabetically.

3. The degree(s) held by the faculty, such as Ph.D. or other degrees, are *not* indicated. Since this information was not always available, it was thought best to omit it from the listing. However, most of the faculty listed hold a doctoral degree in physical education, psychology, or a related field.

4. Most of the programs listed focus upon applied sport psychology. Some, however, are oriented towards research, with little, if any, applied component. In trying to improve our directory, we reviewed some other publications, including the excellent *Insider's Guide to Graduate Programs in Clinical and Counseling Psychology* (1996/1997 edition), by John Norcross, Michael Sayette, and Tracy Mayne (1996, New York: The Guilford Press). In response to a request from many students for a better way to evaluate programs as to their focus on research, applied work, or both, we asked programs to select one of the seven numbers on the following Likert Scale. Norcross et al. used this scale (with established validity) to have programs self-rate themselves along a clinically oriented to research oriented continuum. We thought that this might be an effective way to address this for our field as well. We asked programs to circle the number that best reflects the emphasis/orientation of their program:

Program Rating:

1	2	3	4	5	6	7
Applied Orientation			Equal Emphasis			Research Orientation

_____ Please check here if your program offers opportunities to pursue an applied orientation OR a research orientation (as opposed to an equal emphasis on both)

We also included the following Note: "At the risk of starting a controversy over definitions, please note that research can be basic and/or applied, but simply indicates a focus upon research during one's program. An applied orientation means that the focus is upon applied/consulting work (which could be focused upon education/performance enhancement AND/OR clinical/counseling), with a requirement/encouragement to do such work in one or more settings. Some programs will have an equal emphasis on both, and are encouraged to note this, but many programs are clearly oriented towards one side or the other, and it will be helpful for students to know this."

Please let your editors know if this information is helpful to you. It can be revised for the next edition to make it as useful to you as possible. Some programs did not respond to this question, and so no self-rating is indicated. In addition, we caution you again to check programs carefully. A program may self-rate as a "1" (very strong applied orientation) when they still do or require a considerable amount of research. The information is useful as a guide and not a definitive rating!

Please also note that some programs in psychology are not applied sport psychology programs per se, but do have faculty interested in the area. This is indicated where appropriate.

5. In some cases the number of students in the program may not seem consistent with the number of students that appear to be admitted each year. Some programs have provided

information on the number of students in the overall department (or admitted to the overall department), as opposed to the number of students in (or admitted to) the sport psychology area specifically. This is a good example of a program feature that you would be wise to check when considering a particular program.

6. The information provided is current as of July, 1997. The user should still check all information when considering a given program. New features of a program may be added,new financial resources may become available, faculty may change, etc.

Key to Abbreviations:

APA—American Psychological Association

Degrees Offered:

C.A.S   — Certificate of Advanced Study
Ed.D.   — Doctor of Education
M.A.   — Master of Arts
M.Ed.   — Master of Education
M. Phil. — Master of Philosophy
M.P.E.   — Master of Physical Education
M.S.   — Master of Science
M.S.Ed. — Master of Science of Education
D.P.E.   — Doctor of Physical Education
Ph.D.   — Doctor of Philosophy
Psy.D.   — Doctor of Psychology

GRADUATE PROGRAMS
IN
APPLIED SPORT PSYCHOLOGY

UNIVERSITY OF ALBERTA

Department of Physical Education and Sport Studies
University of Alberta
Edmonton, Alberta
Canada T6G 2H9

CONTACT PERSON:	Anne Jordan (Faculty Grad. Coord.)	John Hogg
PHONE NUMBER:	(403) 492-3198	(403) 492-5910
FAX NUMBER:		(403) 492-2364
E-MAIL ADDRESS:	Ajordan@PER.ALBERTA.CA	jhogg@PER.ALBERTA.CA

FACULTY AND AREA OF INTEREST

Romeo Chua	Motor learning and motor control
Christine Hanrahan	Learning and performance psychology: applications for the performing arts
John Hogg	Psychology of performance enhancement: applications for athletes and coaches
Wendy Rodgers	Social psychology of exercise, health, and lifestyle behavior
Billy Strean	Sport and exercise psychology: philosophy of naturalistic inquiry, and qualitative methodology
Len Wankel	Social psychology of sport and recreation, health, and well-being

PROGRAM INFORMATION

Degrees offered
- M.A. (thesis)
- M.S. (thesis)
- M.A. (course based)
- Ph.D. (dissertation)

Approx. number of students in program
- 18–22 (eventually)

Approx. number of students in each degree program offered
- 14 Master's/8 Ph.D.

Approx. number of students who apply/are accepted annually by program
- 25–30 apply/8–10 accepted

Admissions requirements
- 4-year degree in physical education (or equivalent)
- Master's degree in a related field

The program has available for qualified students
- Fellowships
- Research Assistantships
- Teaching Assistantships
- Other Forms of Financial Aid

Internship possibility
- Not officially

Internship required for degree completion
- N/A

Number of hours required for internship
- N/A

COMMENTS

Core Graduate Course Offerings:

PESS 540:   The psychology of performance in sport and physical activity
PESS 541:   Psycho-social dimensions in sport and physical activity
PESS 542:   Social science perspectives in physical activity, fitness, and well-being
PESS 543:   Seminar in the learning and memory of movement
PESS 582:   Social cognitive approaches to health promoting behaviors
PESS 642:   Advanced seminar in the psychology of sport and physical activity

ARIZONA STATE UNIVERSITY

Department of Exercise Science and Physical Education
PEBE 112
Arizona State University
Tempe, AZ 85287-0404

Program Rating:

1	2	3	4	**5**	6	7
Applied Orientation			Equal Emphasis			Research Orientation

CONTACT PERSON: Daniel M. Landers
PHONE NUMBER: (602) 965-7664 (Office)
(602) 965-3913 (Secretary)   (602) 965-4676 (Laboratory)
FAX NUMBER: (602) 965-8108
PROGRAM WEB SITE: http://www.asu.edu/clas/espe/

FACULTY AND AREA OF INTEREST

Debra Crews	Psychological benefits of exercise for special populations
Betty Kelley	Stress and burnout among coaches and athletes
Daniel M. Landers	Arousal/anxiety/attention and performance
Darwyn E. Linder	Social perception of athletes, pain and performance
Ellen Williams	Psychological skills with ASU athletic teams

PROGRAM INFORMATION

Degrees offered
- M.S.
- Ph.D.

Approx. number of students in program
- 12

Approx. number of students in each degree program offered
- 75% M.S./25% Ph.D.

Approx. number of students who apply/are accepted annually by program
- 40 apply/6–7 accepted

Admissions requirements
- Minimum of 3.00 Jr./Sr. GPA
- Minimum of 50th percentile GRE (verbal + quantitative)
- Sport or exercise psychology courses
- Letter of intent indicating goals which are consistent with program
- Mentor willing to work with student
- Major research experience (undergraduate honor's thesis or master's thesis) required of Ph.D. applicants

The program has available for qualified students
- Research Assistantships
- Teaching Assistantships
- Other Forms of Financial Aid (including out-of-state tuition waivers)

ARIZONA STATE UNIVERSITY ...

PROGRAM INFORMATION ...

Assistantships
- 0% Fellowships
- 50% Graduate Assistantships
- 50% Teaching Assistantships
- 100% Tuition Waivers (out-of-state)
- 20% Other Forms of Financial Aid (in-state fee waivers)

Internship possibility
- • Yes

Internship required for degree completion
- • No

Number of hours required for internship
- • 10 hours per week for 15 weeks or 20 hours per week for 15 weeks

Description of typical internship experience
- • Graduate students enrolled in programs in exercise science, psychology, or related fields, who are being mentored by one of the listed faculty members, may gain experience in applied sport psychology by assisting with psychological skills training provided to intercollegiate athletes or to other subject populations. Most often, these programs are part of a research effort designed to test the efficacy of interventions or to explore psychological processes that mediate the effectiveness of applied sport psychology interventions. The major focus, therefore, is on the research effort rather than on the acquisition by the student of a broad range of intervention skills.

COMMENTS

The program primarily prepares individuals for *research* in the psychology of exercise and sport. Students are expected to immerse themselves in research and take research credits from their first semester to the conclusion of the program. Two teaching assistants teach several sections of an undergraduate course entitled "Psychological Skills for Optimal Performance." This experience is open to doctoral students in exercise science who are committed to becoming sport researchers.

UNIVERSITY OF ARIZONA

Department of Psychology
University of Arizona
Tucson, AZ 85721

Program Rating:

1	2	3	4	**5**	6	7
Applied Orientation			Equal Emphasis			Research Orientation

CONTACT PERSON:	Jean M. Williams	Peggy Collins
	(Sport Psychology Information)	(Psych. Graduate Secretary)
PHONE NUMBER:	(520) 621-6984	(520) 621-7456

FACULTY AND AREA OF INTEREST

Jean M. Williams	Psychology of injury, group dynamics, relationship of psychological states to performance, performance enhancement

PROGRAM INFORMATION

Degree offered
- Ph.D.

The program has available for qualified students
- Fellowships
- Teaching Assistantships
- Other Forms of Financial Aid

Assistantships
- % Fellowships
- % Research Assistantships
- % Teaching Assistantships
- % Tuition Waivers
- % Other Forms of Financial Aid

Note: Exact percentages are not available, however, 100% of the students receive either fellowships, research assistantships, or teaching assistantships for at least four years.

Internship possibility
- Yes, up to 400 hours in sport psychology

Internship required for degree completion
- No, except for the clinical program

Description of typical internship experience
- Internships are available with community athletes and in the Athletic Department's mental training program, primarily for performance enhancement but also for life skills development. Internships are also available at substance abuse centers, corporations, and fitness/wellness centers; primarily for stress management, general health promotion, and personal development.

COMMENTS

As of fall 1996, the graduate program in sport psychology was transferred from the Department of Exercise and Sport Sciences to the Department of Psychology. The move resulted in the elimination of the former M.S. degree in sport psychology. The Department of Psychology offers only a Ph.D. program with majors in the following areas: clinical psychology, cognitive psychology, developmental psychology, psychobiology, policy and law, and social psychology. Students within these major areas, in addition to fulfilling the requirements for the major, can declare an interest in sport psychology and thereby pursue course work, research, and internships specific to their sport psychology interests. At any given time, funding is available for up to two half-time T.A.'s who have sport psychology interests.

Over the last decade, the department of Psychology has undergone rapid growth and development, adding a number of distinguished scholars as professors. The acquisition of faculty actively continues, with the department fast becoming one of the premier programs in the country. The Department emphasizes research training in order to equip students for both academic and applied careers. It strongly encourages interdisciplinary study for students, which reflects the faculty's own interdisciplinary orientation to scholarship.

AUBURN UNIVERSITY

Motor Behavior Center
Health and Human Performance
HHP, Auburn University
Auburn, AL 36849-5323

CONTACT PERSON:	T. G. Reeve
PHONE NUMBER:	(334) 844-1463
FAX NUMBER:	(334) 844-4025
E-MAIL ADDRESS:	reevetg@mail.auburn.edu

FACULTY AND AREA OF INTEREST

M. G. Fischman	Feedback and practice effects in skill acquisition
T. G. Reeve	Cognitive processes in sport and physical activity

PROGRAM INFORMATION

Degrees offered
- M.S.
- M.Ed.

Approx. number of students in program
- 2–3

Approx. number of students in each degree program offered
- All M.S.

Admissions requirements
- GRE and GPA scores are used in a university formula to determine if criterion for admission is made

The program has available for qualified students
- Teaching Assistantships
- Other Forms of Financial Aid

Internship possibility
- Yes

Internship required for degree completion
- No

Number of hours required for internship
- 2–10

BALL STATE UNIVERSITY

School of Physical Education
Ball State University
Muncie, IN 47306

Program Rating:

1	2	3	**4**	5	6	7
Applied Orientation			Equal Emphasis			Research Orientation

CONTACT PERSON: S. Jae Park
PHONE NUMBER: (317) 285-1458
FAX NUMBER: (317) 285-8254

FACULTY AND AREA OF INTEREST

M. Buck	Teacher education
D. Costill	Exercise physiology
G. Gehlsen	Biomechanics
M. Gray	Sport sociology
J. Reno	Administration and sport management
V. Wayda	Sport psychology

PROGRAM INFORMATION

Degrees offered
- M.A.
- M.S.

Approx. number of students in program
- 100

Approx. number of students in each degree program offered
- 70% M.A./30% M.S.

Approx. number of students who apply/are accepted annually by program
- Depends

Admissions requirements
- 2.75 GPA (out of 4.00)
- GRE recommended

The program has available for qualified students
- Research Assistantships
- Teaching Assistantships

Assistantships

0%	Fellowships
35–40%	Research Assistantships (get tuition waivers)
0%	Teaching Assistantships
0%	Tuition Waivers
0%	Other Forms of Financial Aid

BALL STATE UNIVERSITY ...

PROGRAM INFORMATION ...

Internship possibility
- Yes

Internship required for degree completion
- Not for all of them

Number of hours required for internship
- 3 semester hours

Description of typical internship experience
- Internships provide on the job experiences.

BOISE STATE UNIVERSITY

Department of Health, Physical Education, and Recreation
1910 University Drive
Boise State University
Boise, ID 83725

CONTACT PERSON: Linda M. Petlichkoff
PHONE NUMBER: (208) 385-1231
FAX NUMBER: (208) 385-1894
E-MAIL ADDRESS: lpetli@bsu.idbsu.edu

FACULTY AND AREA OF INTEREST
Bill Kozar — Motor learning
Linda M. Petlichkoff — Competitive anxiety, participation motivation, goal orientation

PROGRAM INFORMATION

Degree offered
- M.S.

Approx. number of students in program
- 4

Approx. number of students in each degree program offered
- 100% M.S.

Approx. number of students who apply/are accepted annually by program
- 40 apply / 8–10 are accepted into the total M.S. program

Admissions requirements
- Minimum 2.75 GPA with an appropriate pattern of classes to provide a foundation in physical education, but 3.00 GPA over the last two years
- No GRE requirement

The program has available for qualified students
- Research Assistantships
- Other Forms of Financial Aid

Assistantships
- 0% Fellowships
- 20% Research Assistantships
- 0% Teaching Assistantships
- 20% Tuition Waivers
- 0% Other Forms of Financial Aid

Internship possibility
- Several possibilities do exist on campus

Internship required for degree completion
- No

Description of typical internship experience
- Possible practicum experiences available with several teams on campus.

BOSTON UNIVERSITY

Department of Developmental Studies and Counseling
605 Commonwealth Avenue
Boston University
Boston, MA 02215

Program Rating:

1	2	3	**4**	5	6	7
Applied Orientation			Equal Emphasis			Research Orientation

CONTACT PERSON: Leonard D. Zaichkowsky
PHONE NUMBER: (617) 353-3378
FAX NUMBER: (617) 353-2909
E-MAIL ADDRESS: sport@acs.bu.edu
PROGRAM WEB SITE: http://www.education.bu.edu/sport psychology/

FACULTY AND AREA OF INTEREST

John Cheffers   Aggression/violence
John Yeager   Performance enhancement—life skill development
Leonard D. Zaichkowsky   Psychophysiology/self-regulation, career transition
Faculty in counseling psychology, human movement, and related areas within Boston University.

PROGRAM INFORMATION

Degrees offered
- M.Ed.
- Ed.D.

Approx. number of students in program
- 9 M.Ed./4 Ed. D.

Approx. number of students in each degree program offered
- 75% M.Ed./25% Ed.D.

Approx. number of students who apply/are accepted annually by program
- 15 M.Ed. apply/10 M.Ed. accepted; 15 Ed.D apply/2 Ed.D. accepted

Admissions requirements
- Undergraduate GPA of 3.00
- Strong GRE or MAT scores
- Strong references
- Strong exercise/sport experience

The program has available for qualified students
- Teaching Assistantships
- Other Forms of Financial Aid

Assistantships
- 0%   Fellowships
- 0%   Research Assistantships
- 20%   Teaching Assistantships
- 0%   Tuition Waivers
- 90%   Other Forms of Financial Aid

BOSTON UNIVERSITY ...

PROGRAM INFORMATION ...

Internship possibility
- Yes

Internship required for degree completion
- Yes (both M.Ed. and Ed.D. degrees)

Number of hours required for internship
- Full-time internship after course work—for the master's degree, two semesters
- For the doctoral degree, one half-time placement during second year. Full-time internship for the third year.

Description of typical internship experiences
- University counseling centers, university athletic departments, Academy for Physical and Social Development, wellness centers, Olympic and professional sports teams

COMMENTS

Boston University has suspended its APA-approved doctoral program in counseling psychology. However, qualified students can obtain a specialization in sport and exercise psychology at the doctoral level. Students accepted into the developmental studies program follow a curriculum that is based on a scientist-practitioner model, emphasizing an integrative view of human development, counseling, research, sport psychology, and sport science (following AAASP certification guidelines). Students are also expected to complete a year-long supervised practicum in a sport psychology environment. Comprehensive examination tasks are required prior to writing the dissertation.

BOWLING GREEN STATE UNIVERSITY

School of HPER
Eppler Complex
Bowling Green State University
Bowling Green, OH 43403

Program Rating:

1	2	3	**4**	5	6	7

Applied Orientation   Equal Emphasis   Research Orientation

CONTACT PERSON:	Vikki Krane	Janet Parks
PHONE NUMBER:	(419) 372-7233	(419) 372-6906
FAX NUMBER:	(419) 372-0383	
E-MAIL ADDRESS:	VKRANE@BGNET.BGSU.EDU	JPARKS@BGNET.BGSU.EDU
PROGRAM WEB SITE:	http://www.bgsu.edu/departments/hper/gp.html	

FACULTY AND AREA OF INTEREST

Vikki Krane   Anxiety, feminism
Faculty in developmental kinesiology

PROGRAM INFORMATION

Degree offered
  - M.Ed.

Approx. number of students in program
  - 2–5 in Sport Psychology/15–20 in developmental kinesiology

Approx. number of students in each program offered
  - 100% M.Ed.

Approx. number of students who apply/are accepted annually by program
  - Developmental kinesiology is a new program, exact number of applicants/students is not yet known.

Admission requirements
  - 2.70 GPA (3.00 GPA required to be eligible for an assistantship)
  - GRE scores
  - 3 letters of recommendation
  - Personal statement
  - Resume

The program has available for qualified students
  - Research Assistantships
  - Teaching Assistantships
  - Other Forms of Financial Aid

Assistantships
  - 0% Fellowships
  - 40%* Research Assistantships
  - 40%* Teaching Assistantships
  - 80% Tuition Waivers
  - 40% Other Forms of Financial Aid

*Graduate Assistantships account for approximately 40% of all graduate students. These assistantships often include both teaching and research possibilities.

BOWLING GREEN STATE UNIVERSITY ...

PROGRAM INFORMATION ...

Internship possibility
- No

COMMENTS

The developmental kinesiology program uses an interdisciplinary approach to exercise science. Sport psychology is one of several concentrations within the program. Course requirements include completing 4 of 7 classes in the flexible core. Upon completion of core requirements, the remainder of the academic experience is developed in consultation with the student's mentor/advisor. The sport psychology concentration places equal importance on theory, research, and applied sport psychology skills. A thesis or a directed project is required for a capstone experience.

BROOKLYN COLLEGE

Department of Physical Education
Brooklyn College
Brooklyn, NY 11210

Program Rating:

1	2	**3**	4	5	6	7
Applied Orientation			Equal Emphasis			Research Orientation

CONTACT PERSON: Vivian Acosta
PHONE NUMBER: (718) 951-5879
FAX NUMBER: (718) 951-4541

FACULTY AND AREA OF INTEREST

Vivian Acosta	Women in sport and exercise
Stuart Levitt	Psychological factors in performance
Charles Tobey	Social psychology of sport and exercise

PROGRAM INFORMATION

Degree offered
- M.S.
- The Department offers master's specializations in four areas:
  (1) Psychosocial Aspects of Physical Activity
  (2) Physical Education Teaching and Athletics
  (3) Exercise Science and Rehabilitation
  (4) Sports Management

Approx. number of students in program
- 10–12 in psychosocial program/75–100 in department

Approx. number of students in each degree program offered
- 15% Psychosocial Aspects of Physical Activity
- 45% Physical Education Teaching and Athletics
- 15% Exercise Science and Rehabilitation
- 25% Sports Management

Approx. number of students who apply/are accepted annually by program
- 8–10 apply/7–9 accepted for the Psychosocial program
- 50–60 apply/40–50 accepted for the department

Admissions requirements
- GPA of 3.00
- 12 undergraduate credits in physical education, with one course each in
  (a) philosophy/history of physical education, (b) motor learning, sport psychology, or sociology of sport, (c) kinesiology or biomechanics, and (d) human physiology

The program has available for qualified students
- Other Forms of Financial Aid

Assistantships
0% Fellowships
0% Research Assistantships

BROOKLYN COLLEGE ...

PROGRAM INFORMATION ...

0% Teaching Assistantships
0% Tuition Waivers
20% Other Forms of Financial Aid

Internship possibility
- No, not at the present time (please note that an internship has been available in the past and may be available again at some point in the future)
- An internship is available, however, in the sports management and exercise science and rehabilitation areas

COMMENTS

The program in the psychosocial aspects of physical activity area includes 21 credits in the Physical Education Department. Required courses in physical education include 12 credits: (1) sport psychology; (2) psychology of physical activity; exercise science and sports medicine; (3) sociology of sport; and (4) research seminar. In addition, students complete 9 credits in the Psychology and Sociology Departments for a total of 30 credits for the degree.

CALIFORNIA STATE UNIVERSITY, FULLERTON

Division of Kinesiology and Health Promotion
800 North State College Boulevard
California State University
Fullerton, CA 92634

Program Rating:

1	2	**3**	4	5	6	7
Applied Orientation			Equal Emphasis			Research Orientation

CONTACT PERSON: Carol A. Weinmann (KHP Division Chair & Graduate Coordinator)
PHONE NUMBER: (714) 278-3316
FAX NUMBER: (714) 278-5317
PROGRAM WEB SITE: http://www.fullerton.edu/hdcs/322kines.html

FACULTY AND AREA OF INTEREST

Patricia Laguna	Performance enhancement/attention control
Kenneth Ravizza	Performance enhancement/peak performance
Carol A. Weinmann	Self-concept/self-confidence/performance enhancement

PROGRAM INFORMATION

Degree offered
- M.S.

Approx. number of students in program
- 25

Approx. number of students in each degree program offered
- 100% M.S.

Approx. number of students who apply/are accepted annually by program
- 40 apply/25 accepted

Admissions requirements
- GPA of 3.20 in major (2.50 in last 60 units)
- GRE
- Essay

The program has available for qualified students
- Graduate Assistantships
- Teaching Associateships
- Other Forms of Financial Aid

Assistantships
- 0% Fellowships
- 15% Graduate Assistantships
- 85% Teaching Associateships
- 0% Tuition Waivers
- 0% Other Forms of Financial Aid

Internship possibility
- Yes

CALIFORNIA STATE UNIVERSITY, FULLERTON ...

PROGRAM INFORMATIOM ...

Internship required for degree completion
- No

Number of hours required for internship
- 10 hours per week plus one-hour weekly conference

Description of typical internship experiences
- Using applied sport psychology techniques/interventions with university athletic teams.

COMMENTS

The individual involved in this area of study is grounded in the theoretical, research, and practical aspects of motivation and human behavior in relationship to sport and exercise for all ages and ability levels. The program is designed to prepare students for (1) a doctoral program in sport psychology, (2) an effective approach to performance enhancement in a multitude of settings, (3) consultation with athletes, coaches, and group and personal clients, and (4) a more effective approach to coaching and teaching. Three faculty serve the students in this emphasis area.

CALIFORNIA STATE UNIVERSITY, LONG BEACH

Department of Kinesiology and Physical Education
1250 Bellflower Boulevard
California State University
Long Beach, CA 90840

Program Rating: Program offers opportunities to pursue an applied orientation OR a research orientation (as opposed to an equal emphasis on both)

CONTACT PERSON: Michael Lacourse (Graduate Coordinator)
PHONE NUMBER: (562) 985-4558
FAX NUMBER: (562) 985-8067
E-MAIL ADDRESS: mlacours@csulb.edu
PROGRAM WEB SITE: http://www.csulb.edu/~kpe/

FACULTY AND AREA OF INTEREST

Sharon Guthrie	Clinical applications and research in eating disorders
William Husak	Research in activation and coaching education
Dale Toohey	Education in coaching
Michael Lacourse	Psychophysiology of imagery/brain imaging

PROGRAM INFORMATION

Degree offered
- M.S.

Approx. number of students in program
- 100

Approx. number of students in each degree program offered
- 100% M.S.

Approx. number of students who apply/are accepted annually by program
- 50 apply/30 accepted

Admissions requirements
- Ask for graduate handbook

The program has available for qualified students
- Research Assistantships

Assistantships
- 0% Fellowships
- 10% Research Assistantships
- 5% Teaching Assistantships
- 5% Tuition Waivers
- 0% Other Forms of Financial Aid

Internship possibility
- Yes

Internship required for degree completion
- Yes

Number of hours required for internship
- Will vary

Description of typical internship experience
- Working with university teams.

CALIFORNIA STATE UNIVERSITY, LONG BEACH ...

COMMENTS

The M.S. program allows the student to complete an individualized program in sport psychology.

CALIFORNIA STATE UNIVERSITY, SACRAMENTO

Department of Health and Physical Education
6000 J Street
California State University
Sacramento, CA 95819

Program Rating:

1	2	3	**4**	5	6	7
Applied Orientation			Equal Emphasis			Research Orientation

CONTACT PERSON: Karen L. Scarborough
PHONE NUMBER: (916) 278-7309
FAX NUMBER: (916) 278-7664
E-MAIL ADDRESS: scarboro@csus.edu
PROGRAM WEB SITE: http://www.hhs.csus.edu/

FACULTY AND AREA OF INTEREST

Karen L. Scarborough   Psychological skills training

PROGRAM INFORMATION

Degree offered
- M.S.

Approx. number of students in program
- 10

Approx. number of students in each degree program offered
- 100% M.S.

Approx. number of students who apply/are accepted annually by program
- 5 apply/3 accepted

Admissions requirements
- 2.80 GPA overall or 3.00 in last 60 units
- Undergraduate physical education degree (major or minor)

The program has available for qualified students
- Teaching Assistantships/Graduate Assistantships

Assistantships
- 0% Fellowships
- 0% Research Assistantships
- 60% Teaching Assistantships
- 0% Tuition Waivers
- 0% Other Forms of Financial Aid

Internship possibility
- Yes

Internship required for degree completion
- No

Number of hours required for internship
- 3–10 hours per week

CALIFORNIA STATE UNIVERSITY, SACRAMENTO ...

PROGRAM INFORMATION ...

Description of typical internship experience
- Individualized mental training for California State University, Sacramento, athletes.
- Administer psychological skills program for a CSUS team.
- Administer psychological rehabilitation program for injured athletes.

COMMENTS

The master of science degree in physical education provides a concentration in sport performance for those interested in sport psychology, sport sociology, and teaching/coaching. Flexible use of electives provides specific focus opportunities.

UNIVERSITY OF CALIFORNIA, BERKELEY

Division of Social Science
200 Hearst Gymnasium
University of California
Berkeley, CA 94720

CONTACT PERSON: Brenda Jo Light Bredemeier
PHONE NUMBER: (510) 530-1225 (office)
(510) 642-3288 (message)   (510) 886-3018 (home)
FAX NUMBER: (510) 642-7241
E-MAIL ADDRESS: BRENDA@UCLINK2.BERKELEY.EDU

FACULTY AND AREA OF INTEREST

Brenda Bredemeier   Psycho-social development in physical activity contexts; moral development and behavior, including aggression, gender, and other cultural influences; children at risk

PROGRAM INFORMATION

Degrees offered
- M.S.
- Ph.D.

Approx. number of students in program
- 8

Approx. number of students in each degree program offered
- 20–30% M.S./70–80% Ph.D.

Approx. number of students who apply/are accepted annually by program
- 20–25 apply/2 accepted

Admissions requirements
- Good GRE scores
- Statement of purpose
- Grades in previous courses
- Quality of previous program
- Letters of recommendation

The program has available for qualified students
- Fellowships
- Research Assistantships (depending on grants)
- Teaching Assistantships

Internship possibility
- Yes (practicum possibility)

Internship required for degree completion
- No

Number of hours required for internship
- Flexible, depending on individual cases and programs

Description of typical internship experience
- Supervised work with youth sport, high school or intercollegiate athletes, elementary or middle school physical education students, community sport participants.

UNIVERSITY OF CALIFORNIA, BERKELEY ...

COMMENTS

Emphasis on praxis, integrating theory, research, and practice (including teaching and consulting).

UNIVERSITY OF CALIFORNIA, LOS ANGELES

Department of Psychology
Attn.: UCLA Ph.D. Program in Social Psychology
1285 Franz Hall/Box 951563
University of California
Los Angeles, CA 90095-1563

CONTACT PERSON: Graduate Program Director
PHONE NUMBER: (310) 825-2617
FAX NUMBER: (310) 206-5895

FACULTY AND AREA OF INTEREST

Robert Bjork — Cognitive psychology, memory

Tara K. Scanlan — Professor and Director of the *International Center for Talent Development*. Motivation and emotion regarding youth sport through elite athletes, as well as performers in other talent domains (e.g., art, music, education). Includes developmental and significant other issues, and an integration of quantitative and qualitative research approaches. Currently, developing a model of sport commitment and examining the role of enjoyment within this framework. The model is to be investigated and applied across talent domains. Also interested in effective parenting, teaching, and coaching for the gifted and talented.

Bernard Weiner — Cognitive approaches to motivations, applications to education, achievement motivation, and emotion

Additional course work and faculty expertise is available within the cognitive, developmental, and health psychology areas in psychology, as well as in the School of Education and other cross campus units.

PROGRAM INFORMATION

Degree offered
- Ph.D. only (no M.S.)

Approx. number of students who apply/are accepted annually by program
- 100–120 apply/5–10 accepted

Admissions requirements
- Three letters of recommendation (preferably from research psychologists)
- The GRE General Test and Subject Test in Psychology
- All <u>admitted</u> students must have taken the following courses:
  - Statistics
  - Two of the following: learning, physiological, or perception/information processing
  - Two of the following: developmental, social, or personality/abnormal
  - One course in either biology or zoology
  - Two courses in physics or chemistry
  - At least one mathematics course, preferably calculus or probability
  - Although it is possible to gain admission with deficiencies in these requirements, they must be remedied within the first four quarters of graduate study.

UNIVERSITY OF CALIFORNIA, LOS ANGELES ...

PROGRAM INFORMATION ...

The program has available for qualified students
- Post Doctoral Fellowships
- Fellowships
- Research Assistantships
- Teaching Assistantships
- Other Forms of Financial Aid

Internship possibility
- Outreach: see comments

COMMENTS

Sport psychology is offered within the Department of Psychology's social psychology area and is central to the newly founded *International Center for Talent Development (ICTD)*. The *ICTD* is multidisciplinary and includes research, instruction, and outreach components. Post doctoral fellowships and research assistantships are available.

The *ICTD* focuses on understanding and facilitating the development of talent across a diverse range of domains (e.g., sport, music, art, education) and skill levels (e.g., youth sport through world-class athletes). Talent development is viewed broadly to include such issues as the development of expertise, motivation and emotion, development (cognitive, motoric, and social), significant other influences (family, coaches, teachers, peers), and the sociology involved in establishing talent domains.

UNIVERSITY OF CANBERRA

Centre for Sports Studies
University of Canberra
PO Box 1
Belconnen ACT 2616, Australia

Program Rating:

1	**2**	3	4	5	6	7
Applied Orientation			Equal Emphasis			Research Orientation

CONTACT PERSON: John B. Gross
PHONE NUMBER: (06) 2012009
FAX NUMBER: (06) 2015999
E-MAIL ADDRESS: gross@science.canberra.edu.au
PROGRAM WEB SITE: http://science.canberra.edu.au/sportstud/

FACULTY AND AREA OF INTEREST

John B. Gross   Coaching behaviors—attributions and sports performance

PROGRAM INFORMATION

Degree offered
- Graduate diploma in Applied Psychology

Approx. number of students in program
- 3

Approx. number of students in each degree program offered
- 100% Graduate Diploma

Approx. number of students who apply/are accepted annually by program
- 10 apply/3 accepted

Admissions requirements
- Graduate Diploma—three years of psychology plus a sports science major

Assistantships
- 0% Fellowships
- 0% Research Assistantships
- 0% Teaching Assistantships
- 0% Tuition Waivers
- 0% Other Forms of Financial Aid

Internship possibility
- Yes

Internship required for degree completion
- No

Number of hours required for internship
- None

Description of typical internship experience
- Graduate Diploma—two weeks attendance at an academy or institute of sport

COMMENTS

The graduate diploma in applied psychology involves one year of course work, including a major research project and a two-week placement at an academy or institute of sport. Fees per year for the graduate diploma are approximately $12,000 (Australian).

CLEVELAND STATE UNIVERSITY

Department of Health, Physical Education, and Recreation
Physical Education Building 223
Cleveland State University
Cleveland, OH 44115

CONTACT PERSON: Susan Ziegler
PHONE NUMBER: (216) 687-4876
FAX NUMBER: (216) 687-9290

FACULTY AND AREA OF INTEREST
Susan Ziegler   Performance enhancement

PROGRAM INFORMATION

Degree offered
- M.Ed.*

Approx. number of students in program
- 30

Approx. number of students in each degree program offered
- 100% M.Ed.

Approx. number of students who apply/are accepted annually by program
- 5–10 apply/7–8 accepted

Admissions requirements
- 2.75 GPA

The program has available for qualified students
- Teaching Assistantships

Assistantships
- 0% Fellowships
- 0% Research Assistantships
- 0% Teaching Assistantships
- 0% Tuition Waivers
- 0% Other Forms of Financial Aid

Internship possibility
- No

COMMENTS

*The program is currently on hold due to Dr. Ziegler's shift to administration. This is likely to last for a few years. Please contact Dr. Ziegler if interested in the program.

UNIVERSITY OF COLORADO

Department of Kinesiology
Campus Box 354
University of Colorado
Boulder, CO 80309-0354

Program Rating:

1	2	3	4	5	**6**	7

Applied Orientation   Equal Emphasis   Research Orientation

CONTACT PERSON: Penny McCullagh
PHONE NUMBER: (303) 492-8021
FAX NUMBER: (303) 492-4009
E-MAIL ADDRESS: MCCULLAGH@COLORADO.EDU
PROGRAM WEB SITE: http://www.colorado.edu/kines/

FACULTY AND AREA OF INTEREST

Penny McCullagh   Observational learning (modeling); psychological factors and injury; modeling and rehabilitation; motivation

Tom Raedeke   Stress, burnout

PROGRAM INFORMATION

Degrees offered
- M.S.
- Ph.D. approved, spring 1998 (limited enrollment, limited support)

Approx. number of students in program
- 8

Approx. number of students in each degree program offered
- 100% M.S.

Approx. number of students who apply/are accepted annually by program
- 15 apply/3 accepted

Admissions requirements
- B.S. degree in kinesiology/psychology
- Minimum GPA of 2.75
- Minimum GRE combined of 1000

The program has available for qualified students
- Teaching Assistantships
- Other Forms of Financial Aid

Assistantships
- 0% Fellowships
- 10% Research Assistantships
- 10% Teaching Assistantships
- 0% Tuition Waivers
- 0% Other Forms of Financial Aid
- 80% None

Internship possibility
- Yes (minimal)

UNIVERSITY OF COLORADO ...

PROGRAM INFORMATION ...

Internship required for degree completion
   • No

Description of typical internship experience
   • There is no typical intern program. If an internship were completed, it would need to be arranged by the student and approved by the program.

COMMENTS

The program is a research-oriented program. The primary research areas currently being pursued include:

1. *Modeling*—the primary emphasis here is how we modify motor and psychological skills as a function of observation. Recently we have been examining the use of observational learning as a technique for modifying anxiety and self-efficacy in exercise testing and rehabilitation situations;

2. *Psychological Factors and Athletic Injuries*—the emphasis here is examining social psychological factors that may impact injuries in both sport and exercise settings;

3. *Motivation*—the emphasis here has been on motivational factors related to youth sport and exercise.

DEAKIN UNIVERSITY, RUSDEN CAMPUS

Department of Physical Education
662 Blackburn Road
Deakin University, Rusden Campus
Clayton 3168, Victoria, Australia

CONTACT PERSON: Rob Sands   Sue South (School Administrator)
PHONE NUMBER: 03 9244 7244   03 9244 7244
FAX NUMBER: 03 9244 7407
E-MAIL ADDRESS: rsands@deakin.edu.au

FACULTY AND AREA OF INTEREST
Faculty in health and behavioral sciences (School of Human Movement)

PROGRAM INFORMATION

Degrees offered
- Master's in Applied Science (Research) in which students must have a 10-unit undergrad sequence of psychology courses; then proceed to a fourth-year Honours course within the School of Psychology
- Ph.D.
- Graduate Diploma in Sport Science and Graduate Diploma in Psychology as pathways to master by course work
- Master's preliminary program

Approx. number of students in program
- 20

Approx. number of students in each degree program offered
- 80% Master's/20% Ph.D. (currently small but growing numbers)

Approx. number of students who apply/are accepted annually by program
- 30 apply

The program has available for qualified students
- Graduate Assistantships (limited at this stage)
- Other Forms of Financial Aid (only for Australian students)

Internship possibility
- No, not yet

COMMENTS

Human Movement students have to fully load their three years with psychology units to enroll within the School of Psychology Honours year. We are currently negotiating with the School of Psychology to jointly develop a number of undergraduate and graduate units for students of both schools (Human Movement and Psychology). We also have to be mindful that the new Professional Association of Sport Science requires 1000 hours of undergraduate study to become a qualified sport scientist, while the College of Sport Psychology (within the APS; [Australian Psychology Society]) requires a master's degree in psychology for registration as a practising member. It seems we are moving to the position of having to fulfill both sets of professional criteria before an individual can be qualified as a sport psychologist.

DeMONTFORT UNIVERSITY BEDFORD

School of Physical Education, Sport & Leisure
DeMontfort University Bedford
37 Lansdowne Road
Bedford MK 40 2BZ, England

Program Rating:

1	2	3	4	5	6	**7**
Applied Orientation			Equal Emphasis			Research Orientation

CONTACT PERSON: Howard K. Hall
PHONE NUMBER: (01234) 793316
FAX NUMBER: (01234) 350833
E-MAIL ADDRESS: HKHall@DMU.AC.UK
PROGRAM WEB SITE: http://www.dmu.ac.uk/dept/schools/pesl/spob/research_psych.html

FACULTY AND AREA OF INTEREST

Paul Carpenter	Commitment, peer relations, children's sport
Howard K. Hall	Motivation, stress
Alistair Kerr	Stress
Steve Kozub	Team cohesion and player leadership
Ken Roberts	Movement timing and coincident-anticipation timing in children
Daniel Weigand	Psychosocial development via sport, mental skills training, goal setting

PROGRAM INFORMATION

Degrees offered
- M.Phil. and Ph.D. are attained through research
- M.S. is attained through a taught course

Approx. number of students in program
- 7

The program has available for qualified students
- Research Assistantships
- Teaching Assistantships

Assistantships
- 0% Fellowships
- 0% Research Assistantships
- 0% Teaching Assistantships
- 0% Tuition Waivers
- 0% Other Forms of Financial Aid

Internship possibility
- No

Internship required for degree completion
- No

DeMONTFORT UNIVERSITY BEDFORD ....

COMMENTS

M.Phil./Ph.D. degrees are by research only. The program currently has 7 students enrolled for M.Phil/Ph.D. degrees. We also offer a taught M.S. in sport studies with a specialization in sport psychology. We offer both teaching and research assistantships to support graduate students studying for M.Phil./Ph.D. or M.S. degrees.

UNIVERSITY OF EXETER

School of Health Sciences
University of Exeter
Heavitree Road
Exeter EX1 2LU
United Kingdom

Program Rating:

1	2	3	**4**	5	6	7

Applied Orientation   Equal Emphasis   Research Orientation

CONTACT PERSON: Stuart Biddle
PHONE NUMBER: +44 (0) 1392 264751
FAX NUMBER: +44 (0) 1392 264792
E-MAIL ADDRESS: S.J.H.BIDDLE@EXETER.AC.UK
PROGRAM WEB SITE: http://www.exeter.ac.uk/education/

FACULTY AND AREA OF INTEREST

Stuart Biddle	Sport and exercise motivation, attitudes, emotion
Sue Bock	Coaching psychology, children in sport, mental training
Steve Boutcher	Psychophysiology, stress, health
Ken Fox	Exercise and public health, self-esteem and exercise, body image, weight management
Geoff Meek	Attitude and motivation, special needs
Andrew Sparkes	Interpretive paradigm, body and self, innovation and change

Also a range of modules in research methods taught in psychology faculty

PROGRAM INFORMATION

Degrees offered
- M.S. and M.S. (European) in exercise and sport psychology
- M.Phil. by supervised research
- Ph.D. by supervised research

Approx. number of students in program
- 15 M.S., 2 M.S. (European)/8–10 Research

Approx. number of students who apply/are accepted annually by program
- 40–50 apply (M.S.)/30 accepted

Admissions requirements
- Good honours degree (2.1) or B average usually in psychology or exercise and sport sciences

Assistantships:
- 7% Fellowships
- 0% Research Assistantships
- 0% Teaching Assistantships
- 0% Tuition Waivers
- 0% Other Forms of Financial Aid

Internship possibility
- Yes

Internship required for degree completion
- No

UNIVERSITY OF EXETER ...

COMMENTS

In the exercise and sport Psychology group at Exeter, expertise exists in psychometrics and instrument development, and data analysis using structural equation modelling, hierarchical class analysis, and meta-analysis. Qualitative data analysis is relatively new to exercise and sport psychology, and Exeter has the foremost authority on the topic in European exercise and sport sciences in Dr. Sparkes.

63

FLORIDA STATE UNIVERSITY

Department of Educational Research
Program in Educational Psychology, B-197
Florida State University
Tallahassee, FL 32306

Program Rating:

1	2	3	**4**	5	6	7
Applied Orientation			Equal Emphasis			Research Orientation

CONTACT PERSON: David Pargman
PHONE NUMBER: (904) 644-6058
FAX NUMBER: (904) 644-8776
E-MAIL ADDRESS: Pargman@SY2000.cet.fsu.edu

FACULTY AND AREA OF INTEREST

David Pargman — Health psychological issues (stress, injury), perceptual cognitive factors, motivation, learning

PROGRAM INFORMATION

Degrees offered
- M.S.
- Ph.D.

Approx. number of students in program
- 25–30

Approx. number of students in each degree program offered
- 50% M.S./50% Ph.D.

Approx. number of students who apply/are accepted annually by program
- 40 apply/10 accepted

Admissions requirements (minimum requirements for consideration)
- Minimum GPA of 3.00
- Minimum GRE score of 1000

The program has available for qualified students
- Teaching Assistantships
- Other Forms of Financial Aid

Assistantships
- 10% Fellowships
- 10% Research Assistantships
- 10% Teaching Assistantships
- 10% Tuition Waivers
- 10% Other Forms of Financial Aid

Internship possibility
- Yes

Internship required for degree completion
- Yes, for the Ph.D. degree

FLORIDA STATE UNIVERSITY ...

PROGRAM INFORMATION ...

Number of hours required for Internship
- A minimum of 8 semester hours

Description of typical internship experience
- Assignment to one of Florida State University's varsity athletic teams.
- Assignment to one of Tallahassee's mental health or wellness clinics.

COMMENTS

Psychological processes and conditions associated with athletics and sports situations are studied in the graduate program. Although the academic side (research, theory) of sport psychology is emphasized, students are offered practical (clinical, analytical) experiences in various sport programs. Students can be prepared to teach at the university level, to conduct research, and to serve as consultants to athletes, sport organizations, and those who participate in sport.

UNIVERSITY OF FLORIDA

Department of Exercise and Sport Sciences
College of Health and Human Performance
305 Florida Gymnasium
University of Florida
Gainesville, FL 32611

Program Rating:

1	2	3	4	5	6*	7

Applied Orientation   Equal Emphasis   Research Orientation

*Program offers opportunities to pursue an applied orientation OR a research orientation (as opposed to an equal emphasis on both).

CONTACT PERSON:	Robert N. Singer
PHONE NUMBER:	(352) 392-0584
FAX NUMBER:	(352) 392-5262
E-MAIL:	RSINGER@HHP.UFL.EDU

FACULTY AND AREA OF INTEREST

James Cauraugh	Processes, variables, and mechanisms involved in skill acquisition and control
Chris Janelle	Attention, visual search, arousal, and expertise
Milledge Murphey	Psychological factors in high-risk and combative sport
Robert N. Singer	Information processing and cognitive operations involved in self-paced and dynamic settings; factors contributing to motivation and achievement
Keith Tennant	Learning strategies in skill development

PROGRAM INFORMATION

Degrees offered
- M.S.
- Ph.D. (motor behavior specialization)

Approx. number of students in program
- 25

Approx. number of students in each degree program offered
- 40% M.S./60% Ph.D.

Approx. number of students who apply/are accepted annually by program
- 40 apply/8 accepted

Admissions requirements
- 1000 GRE (the higher the better)
- 3.00 GPA (minimum)

The program has available for qualified students
- Teaching Assistantships
- Other Forms of Financial Aid

Assistantships
- 3%   Fellowships
- 5%   Research Assistantships
- 50%   Teaching Assistantships

UNIVERSITY OF FLORIDA ...

PROGRAM INFORMATION ...

    0%   Tuition Waivers
   20%   Other Forms of Financial Aid

Internship possibility
   • Yes

Internship required for degree completion
   • No

Number of hours required for internship
   • To be negotiated

Description of typical internship experience
   • Flexible.

COMMENTS

Emphasis is on the study of cognitive, psychological, and psychobiological factors contributing to learning and performance excellence, as well as on psychological factors associated with exercise and fitness performance. The orientation is to the scholarly aspects of the specialization, with research conducted in laboratory or in field settings. Students can be involved in applied settings. Students at the master's level are primarily prepared for doctoral work, and doctoral graduates are primarily prepared for university positions and secondarily for applied settings.

FURMAN UNIVERSITY

Department of Health and Exercise Science
Furman University
Greenville, SC 29613

Program Rating:

1	2	3	4 *	5	6	7
Applied Orientation			Equal Emphasis			Research Orientation

*Program offers opportunities to pursue an applied orientation OR a research orientation (as opposed to an equal emphasis on both)

CONTACT PERSON: Frank M. Powell
PHONE NUMBER: (803) 294-3418
FAX NUMBER: (803) 294-2942
E-MAIL ADDRESS: frank.powell@furman.edu
PROGRAM WEB SITE: http://www.furman.edu/

FACULTY AND AREA OF INTEREST

Frank M. Powell   Anxiety, Arousal, Aging
Paul Rasmussen   Clinical intervention

PROGRAM INFORMATION

Degree offered
- M.A. in exercise science, 30 hours required.

Approx. number of students in program
- 45 students in M.A. program, 1–2 focus on sport psychology

Approx. number of students in each degree program offered
- 100% M.A.

Approx. number of students who apply/are accepted annually by program
- 1 apply/1 accepted

Admissions requirements
- B.A. or B.S. degree from an accredited school
- Two letters of recommendation

Assistantships:
- 0% Fellowships
- 0% Research Assistantships
- 30% Teaching Assistantships
- 60% Tuition Waivers
- 10% Other Forms of Financial Aid

Internship possibility
- Yes

Description of typical internship experience
- Performance enhancement and/or stress management intervention with senior athletes (55 years and over).

UNIVERSITY OF GEORGIA

Department of Exercise Science
Exercise Psychology Laboratory
University of Georgia
Athens, GA 30602-3654

Program Rating:

1	2	3	4	5	6	**7**
Applied Orientation			Equal Emphasis			Research Orientation

CONTACT PERSON:	Rod K. Dishman	Patrick J. O'Connor
PHONE NUMBER:	(706) 542-9840	(706) 542-4382
FAX NUMBER:	(706) 542-3148	(706) 542-3148
E-MAIL ADDRESS:	rdishman@uga.cc.uga.edu	poconnor@uga.cc.uga.edu
PROGRAM WEB SITE:	http://www.coe.uga.edu/exs	

FACULTY AND AREA OF INTEREST

Rod K. Dishman	Psychophysiological and neurobiological/immunological effects of acute and chronic exercise; exercise adherence
Patrick O'Connor	Circadian rhythms and sleep; eating disorders; overtraining; pain; mood responses to exercise

PROGRAM INFORMATION

Degrees offered
- M.A.
- Ph.D.

Approx. number of students in program
- 8–10

Approx. number of students in each degree program offered
- 50% M.A./50% Ph.D.

Approx. number of students who apply/are accepted annually by program
- Approximately 10 apply/approximately 2–3 accepted

Admissions requirements (minimum requirements)
- 1000 GRE
- Undergraduate GPA of 3.00 (2.60 for M.A.)
- Graduate GPA of 3.50
- A TOEFL score of 600 is required for foreign students
- A student with a B.A. or B.S. degree can be admitted to the Ph.D. program if the following formula is satisfied: Undergraduate GPA x 1000 + GRE verbal + GRE quantitative > 4300.
- Preference is given to students who have strong backgrounds in biopsychology and exercise science, and who have research interests compatible with ongoing research in the program

The program has available for qualified students
- Research Assistantships
- Teaching Assistantships

UNIVERSITY OF GEORGIA ...

PROGRAM INFORMATION ...

Assistantships
- 29% Fellowships
- 29% Research Assistantships
- 42% Teaching Assistantships
- 0% Tuition Waivers
- 0% Other Forms of Financial Aid

Internship possibility
- No

COMMENTS

The Ph.D. and M.A. specializations in exercise psychology are research programs designed for advanced study and research related to the behavioral and biopsychological responses and adaptations to acute and chronic physical activity. The Ph.D. degree prepares individuals for careers in universities, government, private industry, or the health sciences. The M.A. degree program prepares individuals for additional graduate work at the doctoral level and may lead to careers in allied health occupations, adult fitness/wellness, teaching, and research.

Prerequisites for the M.A. include a background in the behavioral or biological sciences, including chemistry, biology, physiology, and psychology. Undergraduate course work in exercise science is desirable. Prerequisites for the Ph.D. include a background in the behavioral and biological sciences, including biopsychology, chemistry (through organic), biology, and physiology. Students are expected to have an undergraduate or master's degree in exercise science or an appropriate related field, e.g., psychology.

Programs of study are developed by the student and major professor (three person advisory committee for M.A.; five person advisory committee for Ph.D.) based on the student's background, interests, and career goals.

The Department of Exercise Science has a well-equipped exercise psychology laboratory for assessing psychophysiological phenomena including GSR, ECG, EMG, and EEG recorders and beat-to-beat blood pressures under laboratory conditions. Ambulatory measures of blood pressure, heart rate variability, and polysomnography are also made while people live outside the laboratory setting. Collaboration with laboratories in pharmacology, biopsychology, and medical microbiology permit studies of psychopharmacologic, neuroendocrine, and psychoimmunologic responses to exercise and behavioral stressors. The exercise physiology and muscle biology laboratories permit cross-disciplinary research in exercise science. A separate fitness center conducts adult fitness, cardiac rehabilitation, and senior adult programs for university faculty/staff and the Athens community.

GEORGIA SOUTHERN UNIVERSITY

Department of Health and Kinesiology
P.O. Box 8076
Georgia Southern University
Statesboro, Georgia 30460-8076

Program Rating:

1	**2**	3	4	5	6	7
Applied Orientation			Equal Emphasis			Research Orientation

CONTACT PERSON:	Jim McMillan (Graduate Prog. Coord.)	Kevin L. Burke
PHONE NUMBER:	(912) 681-0495	(912) 681-5267
	(912) 681-0200 (Dept. Office)	
FAX NUMBER:	(912) 681-0381	
E-MAIL ADDRESS:	McMillan@GVSMS2.CC.GASOU.EDU	
	KevBurke@gsaix2.cc.GASOU.edu	
PROGRAM WEB SITE:	http://www.gasou.edu	

FACULTY AND AREA OF INTEREST

Kevin L. Burke	Performance enhancement, momentum, optimism, humor
Charles J. Hardy	Social influence processes
Barry Joyner	Performance prediction, data analysis
W. Kent Guion	Activity epidemiology
Bart Buxton	Psychology of injury, sports medicine, athletic training
Jim McMillan	Psychophysiological aspects of performance

PROGRAM INFORMATION

Degree offered
- M.S. with a major in kinesiology, sport psychology emphasis

Approx. number of students in program
- 10

Admissions requirements
- 2.75 or greater GPA on all undergraduate work
- A score of 450 or greater on the verbal section *and* a total score of 1450 or greater on the combined three sections (verbal, quantitative, and analytical) of the GRE.
- If the GRE verbal score is 400–449, then a combined three-score total of 1500 or greater must be met.
- Students who do not meet these admission requirements may be granted provisional admission status if they have a 2.5 or greater GPA, a GRE verbal score of 350–399, and a three-score total of 1350 or greater.
- Resume with at least 3 references listed

The program has available for qualified students
- Research Assistantships
- Teaching Assistantships

Assistantships
0%   Fellowships
10%   Research Assistantships
70%   Teaching Assistantships

GEORGIA SOUTHERN UNIVERSITY ...

PROGRAM INFORMATION ...

80% Tuition Waivers
0% Other Forms of Financial Aid

Internship possibility
- Yes

Internship required for degree completion
- Yes

Number of hours required for internship
- 3 semester hours

Description of typical internship experience
- Students enroll in a practicum course where they receive supervision from an Association for the Advancement of Applied Sport Psychology certified consultant while structuring and applying intervention/performance enhancement techniques with teams and/or individual athletes/exercise participants.

COMMENTS

The master of science program in Kinesiology with an emphasis in sport psychology is based on the integration of science and application in performance enhancement. This foundation gives students the opportunity to be well grounded in the fundamentals of the scientific process as well as involved in supervised individual and group/team interventions. The program consists of 36 semester credit hours, including course work in research methods, data analysis, individual and team interventions, team dynamics, the psychological aspects of elite performance, and the psychology of youth sports. All students are required to complete both a sport psychology practicum and a research thesis.

KINESIOLOGY CORE (9 semester hours)

Course Title	Semester Hours
Research Design in Kinesiology	3
Data Analysis in Kinesiology	3
Seminar in Kinesiology	3

SPORT PSYCHOLOGY EMPHASIS (27 semester hours)

Course Title	Semester Hours
Psychology of Peak Performance	3
Team Dynamics	3
Psychology of Youth Sports	3
Sport Psychology Interventions	3
Practicum in Sport Psychology	
Guided Elective	3
Free Elective	3
Thesis	6
	Total = 36 Semester Hours

GEORGIA SOUTHERN UNIVERSITY ...

COMMENTS ...

Typical Course Sequence*

Fall Semester #1
Psychology of Peak Performance
Research Design in Kinesiology
Elective

Fall Semester #2
Sport Psychology Interventions
Seminar in Kinesiology
Thesis

Spring Semester #1
Team Dynamics
Data Analysis in Kinesiology
Elective

Spring Semester #2
Psychology of Youth Sports
Practicum in Sport Psychology
Thesis

*Summer semester course offerings may alter this course sequence.

UNIVERSITY OF HOUSTON

Department of Health, Physical Education, and Recreation
123 Melcher Gym
University of Houston
Houston, TX 77204-5331

Program Rating:

1	2	3	4	5	6*	7
Applied Orientation			Equal Emphasis		Research Orientation	

*Program offers opportunities to pursue an applied orientation OR a research orientation (as opposed to an equal emphasis on both).

CONTACT PERSON: Dale G. Pease
PHONE NUMBER: (713) 743-9838
FAX NUMBER: (713) 743-9860
E-MAIL: DPEASE@UH.EDU
PROGRAM WEB SITE: http://www.coe.uh.edu

FACULTY AND AREA OF INTEREST

Dale G. Pease	Sport psychology, motor learning, leadership, psychophysiology
Charles Layne	Motor learning, motor control

PROGRAM INFORMATION

Degrees offered
- M.Ed.
- M.S. (emphasis area within motor behavior track)
- Ed.D. (emphasis area within psychological bases of human movement track)

Approx. number of students in program
- 20

Approx. number of students in each degree program offered
- 66% M.Ed. and M.S./34% Ed.D.

Approx. number of students who apply/are accepted annually by program
- 15 apply/10 accepted

Admissions requirements
- M.Ed.: 900 GRE (verbal + quantitative)
- M.S.: 1000 GRE (verbal + quantitative)
- Ed.D.: 1000 GRE (verbal + quantitative)

The program has available for qualified students
- Research Assistantships
- Teaching Assistantships

Assistantships
- 0% Fellowships
- 10% Research Assistantships
- 70% Teaching Assistantships
- 0% Tuition Waivers
- 0% Other Forms of Financial Aid

Internship possibility
- No (although one is currently being formalized)

THE UNIVERSITY FOR HUMANISTIC STUDIES

380 Stevens Ave., Suite 210
Solona Beach, California 92075

Program Rating:

1	**2**	3	4	5	6	7
Applied Orientation			Equal Emphasis			Research Orientation

CONTACT PERSON: Cristina Bortoni Versari
PHONE NUMBER: (619) 259-9733, (619) 635-0204 (Voicemail)
FAX NUMBER: (619) 259-9755
E-MAIL ADDRESS: cversari@aol.com

FACULTY AND AREA OF INTEREST

Cristina Bortoni Versari   Executive coaching, personality profile of athletes, career transition/athletic retirement, performance enhancement

PROGRAM INFORMATION

Degrees offered
- M.A. in sport counseling
- Ph.D. in sport psychology

Assistantships
- 0% Fellowships
- 10% Research Assistantships
- 0% Teaching Assistantships
- 0% Tuition Waivers
- 80% Other Forms of Financial Aid

Internship possibility
- Yes

Internship required for degree completion
- Yes, for Ph.D.

COMMENTS

The sport psychology program at the University for Humanistic Studies consists of an 18-month degree in sports counseling and a 36–48 month Ph.D. program in sport psychology. Both programs have been designed to meet the needs of professionals who are dedicated to helping and preparing athletes to be more effective in sports and their personal lives during and after their athletic careers.

A unique humanistic approach considering individual dimensions of mind, body, and spirit in their social, cultural, and environmental contexts is combined with personal development, technical, and professional skills.

Graduates in sport psychology consult with individual athletes, teams, athletic organizations, committees, and national and international governing bodies. Graduates are also able to effectively teach, coach, and develop programs tailored for this unique population. Through

COMMENTS ...

intensive training and internships, graduates enhance their competence and professional skills to better serve others. Individuals who wish to pursue licensing as an MFCC or psychologist will have the opportunity to add courses that are required for the State of California.

The faculty of the sport psychology program consists of experienced professionals who have proven results in applying psychology to such areas as performance enhancement, substance abuse, athletic career transition, retirement, testing and evaluation, individual and family counseling, crisis intervention, group techniques, communication and relationship skills, and gender issues. Leaders in the field of sport psychology enhance the quality of the program as guest lecturers; they guarantee the diversity of approaches in working with clients in the field of sports.

HUMBOLDT STATE UNIVERSITY

Department of Health and Physical Education
Forbes Complex—Physical Education Department
Humboldt State University
Arcata, CA 95521

CONTACT PERSON: Chris Hopper
PHONE NUMBER: (707) 826-4536
FAX NUMBER: (707) 826-5446

FACULTY AND AREA OF INTEREST

Al Figone — Coaching education
Chris Hopper — Health psychology with families, social psychological aspects of sports for persons with disabilities

PROGRAM INFORMATION

Degree offered
- M.A.

Approx. number of students in program
- 40

Approx. number of students in each degree program offered
- 100% M.A.

Approx. number of students who apply/are accepted annually by program
- 15 apply/12 accepted

Admissions requirements
- 3.00 GPA

The program has available for qualified students
- Research Assistantships
- Teaching Assistantships
- Other Forms of Financial Aid

Internship possibility
- Yes

Internship required for degree completion
- No

Number of hours required for internship
- Nine credit hours

Description of typical internship experience
- Work with: (1) community sport organizations; (2) involvement with college athletic programs; (3) exercise psychology opportunities in Wellness Institute; (4) school based/family based/community based health psychology.

COMMENTS

The M.A. program has four areas of emphasis: adapted; athletic training; exercise physiology/wellness; and teaching/coaching. Students can pursue an applied exercise/sport psychology area of specialization within each emphasis area. Students are encouraged to complete their thesis in exercise/sport psychology. The Humboldt campus is located on the northwest coast of California, 250 miles north of San Francisco. The quality of life is exceptional.

UNIVERSITY OF IDAHO

Division of Health, Physical Education, Recreation, and Dance
107 PEB
University of Idaho
Moscow, ID 83844-2401

Program Rating:

1	2	3	**4**	5	6	7

Applied Orientation   Equal Emphasis   Research Orientation

CONTACT PERSON: Damon Burton
PHONE NUMBER: (208) 885-2186
FAX NUMBER: (208) 885-5929
E-MAIL ADDRESS: dburton@uidaho.edu

FACULTY AND AREA OF INTEREST

Damon Burton   Motivation/goal setting, stress/anxiety, coaching education, PST program evaluation, exercise adherence

PROGRAM INFORMATION

Degrees offered
- M.S.
- Ph.D.

Approx. number of students in program
- M.S. program: 3–4 full-time/1–2 part-time
- Ph.D. program: 2–3 full-time/1–2 part-time

Approx. number of students in each degree program offered
- 67% M.S.
- 33% Ph.D.

Approx. number of students who apply/are accepted annually by program
- M.S. program: 18–20 apply/1–2 accepted
- Ph.D. program: 6–10 apply/maximum of 1 accepted

Admissions requirements
- M.S. program: Minimum of 3.00 GPA, 1000 GRE scores
- Ph.D. program: 3.00 GPA undergraduate, 3.50 GPA masters, 1050 GRE scores

The program has available for qualified students
- Teaching Assistantships

Assistantships

Master's (4)		Ph.D. (2)	
0%	Fellowships	0%	Fellowships
0%	Graduate Assistantships	50%	Graduate Assistantships
75%	Teaching Assistantships	50%	Teaching Assistantships
0%	Tuition Waivers	0%	Tuition Waivers
25%	Other Forms of Financial Aid	0%	Other Forms of Financial Aid

Internship possibility
- Yes—M.S. and Ph.D.

UNIVERSITY OF IDAHO ...

PROGRAM INFORMATION ...

Internship required for degree completion
- Yes—M.S. and Ph.D.

Number of hours required for internship
- 6–9 credit hours

Description of typical internship experience
- Previous students have conducted internships with teams in such sports as basketball, golf, volleyball, tennis, gymnastics, and track and field, all at the university level (except for gymnastics). These internships involve developing, implementing and evaluating a PST program for that sport. Additionally, doctoral internships will be supervised by the licensed psychologist employed by the Athletic Department at Washington State University.

COMMENTS

Our two year master's program is designed to develop good researchers and good applied consultants. Students typically use their degree as a stepping stone into such career fields as: (a) coaching/teaching, (b) exercise and wellness, or (c) Ph.D. work in educational or clinical sport psychology. The program has reasonably good flexibility in both curriculum and internship possibilities that help prepare students to meet AAASP certification requirements. Course requirements emphasize a solid background in the sport sciences and elective course work in psychology and counseling. With Washington State University only eight miles away in Pullman, master's internship possibilities are available to work with many types of sports, including consulting through our new Vandal Sport Psychology Services Program, allowing students to develop and implement "psychological skills training" programs and evaluate their effectiveness. At the master's level, the internship and thesis may be combined so that the student's thesis involves testing an applied sport psychology question or evaluating the effectiveness of a PST program with the team they are working with. However, many students also select traditional thesis topics in such areas as motivation, exercise adherence, goal setting, stress/coping, and anxiety.

Our new doctoral program carries a similar focus to the master's program but most elective course work will be taken at Washington State University. Students take 23–24 credits, which includes 6 credits of doctoral practicum, in WSU's APA-approved counseling psychology program as well as 12 credits of psychology foundation courses. Starting fall 1997, doctoral students will get the opportunity to get consulting experience through work with Vandal Sport Psychology Services, a joint program with the UI Athletic Department, to provide sport psychology services to coaches and athletes. This Ph.D. program emphasizes research and application skills equally, with significant practical experience available in both areas.

ILLINOIS STATE UNIVERSITY

5000 CAST Dean's Office
Illinois State University
Normal, IL 61790-5000

Program Rating:

1	2	3	4	5	6	7
Applied Orientation			Equal Emphasis			Research Orientation

CONTACT PERSON: Sally A. White   Bill Vogler (Graduate Coordinator)
PHONE NUMBER: (309) 438-2809   (309) 438-5782
FAX NUMBER: (309) 438-5037
E-MAIL ADDRESS: swhite@ilstu.edu
PROGRAM WEB SITE: link to Dr. White's page: swhite@ilstu.edu

FACULTY AND AREA OF INTEREST

Sally A. White   Achievement motivation theory, parent-child relationships, athletes with disabilities

PROGRAM INFORMATION

Degree offered
- M.S.

Approx. number of students in program
- 3–5

Approx. number of students in each degree program offered
- 100% M.S.

Approx. number of students who apply/are accepted annually by program
- 40 apply/3 accepted

Admissions requirements
- 3.20 GPA
- 1100 GRE

The program has available for qualified students
- Teaching Assistantships
- Other Forms of Financial Aid (including tuition waivers)

Assistantships
- 0%   Fellowships
- 0%   Research Assistantships
- 100%   Teaching Assistantships
- varies   Tuition Waivers (some available)
- 0%   Other Forms of Financial Aid

Internship possibility
- Yes

Internship required for degree completion
- No

Number of hours required for internship
- Up to 8 credit hours are possible; no more than 6 may apply toward fulfillment of degree requirements.

Description of typical internship experience
- Open for students to arrange.

UNIVERSITY OF ILLINOIS

Department of Kinesiology
University of Illinois
205 Freer Hall
906 South Goodwin Avenue
Urbana, IL 61801

CONTACT PERSON: Glyn Roberts
PHONE NUMBER: (217) 333-6563
FAX NUMBER: (217) 244-7322

Jim Misner (Graduate Coordinator)
(217) 333-1083

FACULTY AND AREA OF INTEREST

Les Carlton	Motor learning
Edward McAuley	Motivation, exercise behavior
Karl Newell	Motor learning
Steven Petruzzello	Psychophysiology of movement
Glyn Roberts	Motivation, children in sport

PROGRAM INFORMATION

Degrees offered
- M.S.
- Ph.D.

Approx. number of students in program
- 20

Approx. number of students in each degree program offered
- 40% M.S./60% Ph.D.

Approx. number of students who apply/are accepted annually by program
- 30–40 apply/4–5 accepted

Admissions requirements
- GPA of 4.50 on a 5.00 scale
- GRE score of 1200 (verbal + quantitative)

The program has available for qualified students
- Fellowships
- Research Assistantships
- Teaching Assistantships
- Other Forms of Financial Aid

Internship possibility
- Yes

Internship required for degree completion
- No

Number of hours required for internship
- One unit (3–4 hours)

Description of typical internship experience
- Working with University of Illinois teams as a consultant.

INDIANA UNIVERSITY

Department of Physical Education
Indiana University
HPER 168
Bloomington, IN 47405

Program Rating:

1	2	3	4	5	6	**7**
Applied Orientation			Equal Emphasis			Research Orientation

CONTACT PERSON: John S. Raglin
PHONE NUMBER: (812) 335-0682
FAX NUMBER: (812) 855-6778
E-MAIL ADDRESS: raglinj@indiana.edu
PROGRAM WEB SITE: http://www.indiana.edu/~kines/

FACULTY AND AREA OF INTEREST

John S. Raglin — Anxiety and athletic performance, personality, overtraining, exercise and mental health, psychobiology of sport, exercise adherence

PROGRAM INFORMATION

Degree offered
   • M.S. in applied sport science with a specialization in sport psychology
Approx. number of students in program
   • 5
Approx. number of students in each degree program offered
   • 100% M.S.
Admissions requirements
   • GPA 2.80 or higher on a 4.00 scale
   • GRE minimum total of 800 for verbal and quantitative
The program has available for qualified students
   • Teaching Assistantships
Assistantships
   0% Fellowships
   0% Research Assistantships
   75% Teaching Assistantships
   0% Tuition Waivers
   0% Other Forms of Financial Aid
Internship possibility
   • No
Description of typical internship experience
   • Previous students have conducted research projects with varsity athletic teams or with participants in summer youth sport camps. There are no internships per se available.

INDIANA UNIVERSITY ...

COMMENTS

The program is a master of science in human performance, with specialization in sport psychology. The degree emphasizes research in issues related to exercise and mental health as well as sport, rather than application. The program is intended to serve as preparation for the student interested in pursuing a doctorate in sport psychology with a specialization in psychobiological aspects of sport.

IOWA STATE UNIVERSITY

Department of Physical Education and Leisure Studies
Iowa State University
Ames, IA 50010

Program Rating:

1	2	3	**4**	5	6	7
Applied Orientation			Equal Emphasis			Research Orientation

CONTACT PERSON: Sharon Mathes
PHONE NUMBER: (515) 294-8766
FAX NUMBER: (515) 294-8740
E-MAIL ADDRESS: SMATHES@iastate.edu
PROGRAM WEB SITE: http://www.iastate.edu

FACULTY AND AREA OF INTEREST

Sharon Mathes — Sport psychology
Deborah Rhea — Sport psychology/pedagogy

PROGRAM INFORMATION

Degree offered
- M.S.

Approx. number of students in program
- 5 active/5 part-time

Approx. number of students in each degree program offered
- 100% M.S.

Approx. number of students who apply/are accepted annually by program
- 5 apply/3 accepted

Admissions requirements
- 3.00 GPA
- GRE general test recommended

The program has available for qualified students
- Teaching Assistantships

Assistantships
- 0%   Fellowships
- 0%   Graduate Assistantships
- 10%   Teaching Assistantships
- 0%   Tuition Waivers
- 0%   Other Forms of Financial Aid

Internship possibility
- Yes

Internship required for degree completion
- No

Number of hours required for internship
- 3–6 credit hours

Description of typical internship experience
- Several general areas are possible: (1) audit undergraduate sport psychology

PROGRAM INFORMATION ...

class, develop and deliver lectures, develop test questions, grade test questions; (2) observe, and assist where appropriate, Psychological Skills Training with teams and individual athletes; (3) work individually, where appropriate, with individual athletes; (4) performance analysis employing Interpersonal Process Recall (IPR).

UNIVERSITY OF IOWA

Department of Sport, Health, Leisure and Physical Studies
E102 Fieldhouse
University of Iowa
Iowa City, IA 52242

Program Rating:

1	2	3	4	5	6	7
Applied Orientation			Equal Emphasis			Research Orientation

CONTACT PERSON: Dawn E. Stephens
PHONE NUMBER: (319) 335-9348   (319) 335-9335 (Main Office)
FAX NUMBER: (319) 335-6669
E-MAIL ADDRESS: DAWN-E-STEPHENS@UIOWA.EDU
PROGRAM WEB SITE: http://www.uiowa.edu/~shlps/grad.htm

FACULTY AND AREA OF INTEREST

Dawn E. Stephens   Social psychology of sport, motivational issues, moral atmosphere

PROGRAM INFORMATION

Degrees offered
- M.A.
- Ph.D.

Approx. number of students in program
- 10

Approx. number of students in each degree program offered
- 60% M.A./40% Ph.D.

Approx. number of students who apply/are accepted annually by program
- 12 apply/4 accepted

Admissions requirements
- GRE: 1500 (verbal + Quantitative + Analytical)
- 3.00 GPA
- Three letters of recommendation
- Transcripts

The program has available for qualified students
- Fellowships
- Research Assistantships
- Teaching Assistantships

Assistantships
varies   Fellowships
  25%   Research Assistantships
  75%   Teaching Assistantships
   0%   Tuition Waivers
   0%   Other Forms of Financial Aid

UNIVERSITY OF IOWA ...

PROGRAM INFORMATION ...

Internship possibility
- No

Internship required for degree completion
- No

COMMENTS

The program's emphasis is on theoretical research in sport and physical activity contexts, with a particular emphasis on female and youth participants.

ITHACA COLLEGE

Department of Graduate Studies in Exercise and Sport Sciences
Ithaca College
Ithaca, NY 14850

Program Rating:

1	**2** *	3	4	5	6	7
Applied Orientation			Equal Emphasis			Research Orientation

*Program offers opportunities to pursue an applied orientation OR a research orientation (as opposed to an equal emphasis on both).

CONTACT PERSON: Craig Fisher
PHONE NUMBER: (607) 274-3112
FAX NUMBER: (607) 274-1943
E-MAIL ADDRESS: cfisher@ithaca.edu
PROGRAM WEB SITE: http://www.ithaca.edu/grad/grad1/

FACULTY AND AREA OF INTEREST

Craig Fisher	Sport psychology, self-confidence, personality, rehabilitation adherence
Gary Sforzo	Psychophysiology
Ellen Staurowsky	Gender issues in sport, leadership and sport
Greg Shelley	Counseling student athletes
Deb Wuest	Stress management

PROGRAM INFORMATION

Degree offered
- M.S.

Approx. number of students in program
- 6–10

Approx. number of students in each degree program offered
- 100% M.S.

Approx. number of students who apply/are accepted annually by program
- 10–20 apply/6–15 accepted

Admissions requirements
- 3.00 GPA from accredited institution
- Successful completion of certain core courses
- GRE required

The program has available for qualified students
- Teaching Assistantships

Assistantships
- 0% Fellowships
- 0% Research Assistantships
- 75% Teaching Assistantships
- 0% Tuition Waivers
- 0% Other Forms of Financial Aid

Internship possibility
- None in sport psychology

Description of typical internship experience
- Only in exercise physiology area.

ITHACA COLLEGE ...

COMMENTS

Sport psychology is a concentration along with exercise physiology and sport pedagogy in a 30-credit M.S. program with thesis and a 36-credit M.S. program without thesis.

KANSAS STATE UNIVERSITY

Department of Kinesiology
Natatorium 8
Kansas State University
Manhattan, KS 66506

CONTACT PERSON: David Dzewaltowski
PHONE NUMBER: (913) 532-0708
FAX NUMBER: (913) 532-6486
E-MAIL ADDRESS: DADX@KSU.KSU.EDU

FACULTY AND AREA OF INTEREST

David Dzewaltowski — Motivation, exercise adherence
Mary McElroy — Sociocultural, qualitative methods
A faculty search is in progress to fill an exercise psychology position

PROGRAM INFORMATION

Degree offered
- M.S.

Approx. number of students in program
- 5–10

Approx. number of students in each degree program offered
- 100% M.S.

Approx. number of students who apply/are accepted annually by program
- variable apply/variable accepted

Admissions requirements (minimum requirements to be considered for admission)
- GRE scores
- 3.00 GPA
- Three letters of reference

The program has available for qualified students
- Research Assistantships
- Teaching Assistantships

Internship possibility
- Yes

Internship required for degree completion
- No

Number of hours required for internship
- 3–6 credit hours

Description of typical internship experience
- Practicum/internship experiences are available in exercise settings (corporate, cardiac rehabilitation, adult) through the Kinesiology Department's Center for Exercise Research. Practicum/internship experiences with athletic teams are possible.

COMMENTS

The Department of Kinesiology, located in the College of Arts and Sciences, is strongly committed to graduate education and research. Kinesiology faculty study human movement from several perspectives, including biomechanical, physiological, neurological, psychological, and sociocultural. The psychology emphasis draws on faculty's strengths in exercise and health psychology to develop students' understanding of elite and non elite (youth, older adults, etc.) populations.

UNIVERSITY OF KANSAS

Department of Health, Sport, and Exercise Sciences
161 Robinson
University of Kansas
Lawrence, KS 66045

Program Rating:

1	2	3	4	5	6	7
Applied Orientation			Equal Emphasis			Research Orientation

CONTACT PERSON: David Templin
PHONE NUMBER: (913) 864-0778
FAX NUMBER: (913) 864-3343
PROGRAM WEB SITE: http://www.soe.ukans.edu/courses/hper892

FACULTY AND AREA OF INTEREST

Jim LaPoint   Social psychology of sport
David Templin   Applied psychology of sport

PROGRAM INFORMATION

Degrees offered
- M.S.
- Ed.D.
- Ph.D.

Approx. number of students in program
- 10 M.S./10 Ph.D.

Approx. number of students in each degree program offered
- 50% M.S./50% Ph.D.

Approx. number of students who apply/are accepted annually by program
- 30 M.S. apply/10–15 M.S. accepted
- 20 Ph.D. apply/3 Ph.D. accepted

Admissions requirements
- M.S.: Undergraduate degree in Physical Education
  - GPA of 3.00
- Ph.D.: Undergraduate or master's degree in physical education
  - Master's GPA of 3.50
  - Undergraduate GPA of 3.00
  - GRE verbal + quantitative > or = 1000
  - Coaching or playing background in sport

The program has available for qualified students
- Teaching Assistantships (Ph.D.)

Assistantships
- 0% Fellowships
- 0% Research Assistantships
- 25% Teaching Assistantships
- 25% Tuition Waivers
- 50% Other Forms of Financial Aid

UNIVERSITY OF KANSAS ...

PROGRAM INFORMATION ...

Internship possibility
- Yes (Ph.D.)

Internship required for degree completion
- Yes (Ph.D.)

Number of hours required for internship
- One season or semester required, 2 years possible

Description of typical internship experience
- Several options are available. First, one can work as a sport psychology consultant for a high school district (with five high schools). Second, one can spend consulting time in the University of Kansas Peak Performance Clinic, working with individual athletes and doing high school team seminars. Third, one can work as a sport psychology consultant with one of the 16 teams at the university.

COMMENTS

The program offers course work and opportunities which are applied in nature. Students are prepared in the doctoral program to pursue a career in higher education as an applied sport psychologist or work as an applied sport psychology consultant in private practice. The program includes a Peak Performance Clinic and an internship program involving the University of Kansas Athletic Department and Kansas City High School athletic programs. Students who are accepted must have a strong sporting background (playing and/or coaching), a background in physical education or related field, and strong interpersonal skills. An interview is suggested at the doctoral level. This program *does not* lead to licensure.

JOHN F. KENNEDY UNIVERSITY

Graduate School of Professional Psychology
John F. Kennedy University
12 Altarinda Road
Orinda, CA 94563

Program Rating:

1	**2** *	3	4	5	6	7

Applied Orientation   Equal Emphasis   Research Orientation

*Program offers opportunities to pursue an applied orientation OR a research orientation (as opposed to an equal emphasis on both).

CONTACT PERSON:	Gail Solt (Director)
PHONE NUMBER:	(510) 254-0110
FAX NUMBER:	(510) 254-4870
PROGRAM WEB SITE:	http://www.jfku.edu

FACULTY AND AREA OF INTEREST

Mark Clementi	Optimal performance
Lesleigh Franklin	Women in sport
Vince Granito	Ethics in sport psychology, injury
Keith McConnell	Group process, optimal performance
David Shields	Moral development
Gail Solt	Children and sports, optimal performance
Betty Wenz	Ethics in sport psychology, optimal performance

PROGRAM INFORMATION

Degrees offered
- M.A. The M.A. degree is offered in both sport psychology and in counseling psychology with a specialization in sport psychology.
- Psy.D. (as of January 1996)

Approx. number of students in program
- 50

Approx. number of students in each degree program offered
- 80% M.A. in sport psychology/20% M.A. in counseling psychology

Approx. number of students who apply/are accepted annually by program
- 40–50 apply/20+ accepted

Admissions requirements
- An interview and/or three letters of recommendation
- Strong interest in the field
- Appropriate prerequisites

The program has available for qualified students
- Other Forms of Financial Aid

Assistantships
- 0% Fellowships
- 0% Research Assistantships
- 0% Teaching Assistantships
- 1% Tuition Waivers
- 45% Other Forms of Financial Aid

JOHN F. KENNEDY UNIVERSITY ...

PROGRAM INFORMATION ...

Internship possibility
- Yes

Internship required for degree completion
- Yes

Number of hours required for internship
- 12 units for M.A. in Sport Psychology
- 18 units for M.A. in Counseling Psychology
- Psy.D. units to be determined

Description of typical internship experience
- An 11-week experience at a local college, meeting 11 hours per week with a team or individuals. Supervised by an individual supervisor and by attending a counseling case seminar. Internship may include education, optimal performance consulting, and support.

COMMENTS

Sport psychology students have many options for internships, including working with college teams, youth sport teams, sport organizations, mental health treatment facilities, and private sport clubs. Students serve as "counselors" in JFK's summer sport camps as part of fulfilling their internship requirement. They help design, create, and conduct the camps, which use sport as a vehicle for enhancing self-esteem, building cooperative groups, and developing skills. The sport psychology program has also established a number of on-going internships which are staffed each year by students. These programs include support groups for injured athletes, sport psychology programs at local high schools, and various intercollegiate teams and athletes in the San Francisco Bay area.

Students may choose to pursue an M.A. degree in sport psychology, which enables them to work as applied sport consultants or prepares them for doctoral work in clinical or consulting psychology. Students may also choose to pursue an M.A. degree in counseling psychology, which may qualify them for the marriage, family, and child counselor (MFCC) License in California.

JFK also offers a certificate program. It consists of 18 units, typically 4–5 quarters in duration. Individuals already in a related field typically pursue this option.

LAKEHEAD UNIVERSITY

Department of Physical Education
Lakehead University Fieldhouse
Lakehead University
Thunder Bay, Ontario,
Canada   P7B 5E1

Program Rating:

1	2	3	**4**	5	6	7
Applied Orientation			Equal Emphasis			Research Orientation

CONTACT PERSON: Jane Crossman
PHONE NUMBER: (807) 343-8642
FAX NUMBER: (807) 343-8944
E-MAIL ADDRESS: Jane.Crossman@lakeheadu.ca
PROGRAM WEB SITE: http://www.lakeheadu.ca/ (click admissions, and then click Arts & Sciences)

FACULTY AND AREA OF INTEREST

Jane Crossman	Psychological rehabilitation from athletic injury, mental training
Jocelyn Farrell	Motivation and goal setting

PROGRAM INFORMATION

Degrees offered
- M.A.
- M.S.

Approx. number of students in program
- 15

Approx. number of students in each degree program offered
- 100% M.S.

Approx. number of students who apply/are accepted annually by program
- N/A apply/13–15 accepted

Admissions requirements
- Honors degree, minimum 70% standing
- If degree is not in physical education, a qualifying year may be necessary

The program has available for qualified students
- Fellowships
- Research Assistantships
- Teaching Assistantships
- Other Forms of Financial Aid

Assistantships
- 0%   Fellowships
- 0%   Research Assistantships
- 0%   Teaching Assistantships
- 0%   Tuition Waivers
- 0%   Other Forms of Financial Aid

Internship possibility
- Yes—guaranteed

LAKEHEAD UNIVERSITY ...

PROGRAM INFORMATION ...

Internship required for degree completion
- Yes

Number of hours required for internship
- 10 hours per week

Description of typical internship experience
- Students may assist in the teaching of undergraduate courses or teach activity courses. Other possible tasks include assisting in research, supervising our micro-computer laboratory or assisting with the coaching of our varsity teams.

COMMENTS

Lakehead University provides the opportunity for qualified students to obtain either an M.A. or M.S. in applied sport science and coaching. The program of courses focuses on four areas in sport science: (1) psychology, (2) physiology, (3) biomechanics, and (4) sports medicine. The primary focus of the sport psychology course offerings involves the study of a variety of mental training procedures designed to improve athletic performance. Students are required to complete a master's thesis.

MANCHESTER METROPOLITAN UNIVERSITY

Crewe & Alsager Faculty
Manchester Metropolitan University
Hassall Road
Alsager ST 7 2HL, England

CONTACT PERSON: Dave Collins
PHONE NUMBER: (44) 161-247-5429
FAX NUMBER: (44) 161-247-6375
E-MAIL ADDRESS: D.COLLINS@MMU.AC.UK

FACULTY AND AREA OF INTEREST

Dave Collins	Psychophysiology, imagery and modeling, drugs in sport, decision making
Keith Davids	Ecological psychology, motor control, and skill acquisition
Francois Xavier-Li	Ecological psychology
Nick Smith	Psychophysiology, stress and coping, health psychology

PROGRAM INFORMATION

Degrees offered
- M.Sc.
- M.Phil.
- Ph.D.

Approx. number of students in program
- 20

Approx. number of students in each degree program offered
- 5% M.S./70% M.Phil. (with upgrade to Ph.D. possible)/25% Ph.D.

Approx. number of students who apply/are accepted annually by program
- 12 apply/3–4 accepted

Admissions requirements
- Write for specifics. Decisions are based on profiles.

The program has available for qualified students
- Research Assistantships
- Teaching Assistantships
- Other Forms of Financial Aid

Internship possibility
- No

COMMENTS

The programme is a traditional British university model, with substantial emphasis on research, but placed within a vibrant and rapidly developing department. In addition, the department has plans for a part-time taught master's degree (much closer to the usual U.S. programme) in applied sport and exercise psychology. The department currently hosts over 25% of the government-funded sport science support programmes with elite athletes. Major projects in stress/performance, coach education, and match analysis are also features of the department's research portfolio.

UNIVERSITY OF MANITOBA

Department of Psychology
St. Paul's College, University of Manitoba
Winnipeg, Manitoba, Canada R3T 2M6
or
Faculty of Physical Education and Recreation Studies
Frank Kennedy Building, University of Manitoba
Winnipeg, Manitoba, Canada R3T 2N2

Program Rating:

1	2	3	**4**	5	6	7
Applied Orientation			Equal Emphasis			Research Orientation

CONTACT PERSON:	Garry Martin (Psychology)	Dennis Hrycaiko (Physical Education)
PHONE NUMBER:	(204) 474-8589	(204) 474-8764
FAX NUMBER:	(204) 275-5421	(204) 275-5122

FACULTY AND AREA OF INTEREST

Garry Martin	Research and applied, various aspects of sport performance enhancement
Dennis Hrycaiko	Research/applied performance enhancement
Henry Janzen	Applied performance enhancement

PROGRAM INFORMATION

Degrees offered
- M.A.
- M.S.
- Ph.D.

Note: The M.A. and Ph.D. degrees are in clinical psychology (an APA-approved program). Sport psychology is a sub-speciality within clinical psychology. The M.Sc. degree in physical education has a specialization in sport psychology.

Approx. number of students in program
- 55 in clinical psychology
- 37 in M.Sc. in physical education

Approx. number of students in each degree program offered
- 30% M.A./70% Ph.D. in clinical psychology
- 6 students in sport psychology

Approx. number of students who apply/are accepted annually by program
- 10 apply/1–2 accepted in clinical psychology
- 10 apply/5–6 accepted in sport psychology

Admissions requirements
- Must meet Department of Psychology requirements for clinical psychology program
- Check with programs for specific admissions requirements

The program has available for qualified students
- Teaching Assistantships

PROGRAM INFORMATION ...

Assistantships

- 5% Fellowships
- 5% Research Assistantships
- 10% Teaching Assistantships
- 0% Tuition Waivers
- 0% Other Forms of Financial Aid

Internship possibility

- Yes

Internship required for degree completion

- Yes—Ph.D. students in clinical psychology must complete an APA-approved internship in Canada or the U.S.A.

Number of hours required for internship

- The APA-accredited internship is for one academic year (September to May) and does not specify a number of hours

Description of typical internship experience

- Students who work with Dr. Martin are required to take 1 (of 4) practica in the area of sport psychology. One possibility is to assist in consultation with the provincial figure skating team, including administering behavioral assessments to individual athletes, designing and implementing treatment programs for individual athletes, and teaching athletes a variety of performance enhancement and coping strategies.

COMMENTS

Physical Education offers a master of science degree program with the opportunity to specialize in sport psychology. The program has considerable flexibility and can be tailored to meet interests of individual students. In the clinical psychology program, students apply to 1 of 2 streams, a generalist stream or a behavior modification stream. Students who select the behavior modification stream have the option of receiving specialized training in sport psychology. Training includes readings courses in sport psychology, thesis research in sport psychology, and sport psychology practica with Dr. Martin, working with a provincial sport team. Training is very behaviorally oriented.

MANKATO STATE UNIVERSITY

Department of Psychology/Clinical Psychology
Box 35
Mankato State University
Mankato, MN 56001

CONTACT PERSON: Wayne C. Harris
PHONE NUMBER: (507) 389-1818

FACULTY AND AREA OF INTEREST
Michael Fatis
Wayne C. Harris
Dan Sachan

PROGRAM INFORMATION

Degrees offered
- M.A. (predoctoral in clinical psychology)
- M.A. (predoctoral in industrial/organizational [I/O])

Approx. number of students in program
- 20 clinical/6 I/O

Approx. number of students in each degree program offered
- 100% M.A.

Approx. number of students who apply/are accepted annually by program
- 50 apply/15 accepted

Admissions requirements
- Undergraduate GPA > or = 3.00
- GRE scores

The program has available for qualified students
- Fellowships (minority fellowship)
- Research Assistantships (second-year student)
- Teaching Assistantships
- Other Forms of Financial Aid (work-study)

Internship possibility
- Yes

Internship required for degree completion
- Yes, required for the M.A. degree in clincial psychology
- In industrial/organizational, an internship is not required but is encouraged

Number of hours required for internship
- A minimum of 700 hours

MANKATO STATE UNIVERSITY ...

COMMENTS

Training in applied sport psychology is within the context of a predoctoral program in clinical psychology. The clinical program emphasizes behavior therapy/analysis and commitment to scientific psychology. Existing research programs can be found in the following areas: behavioral medicine, child behavior disorders, developmental disabilities, behavioral gerontology, and performance enhancement. Students are encouraged to participate in research and practice. Graduates of the program are regularly admitted to APA-approved doctoral programs in clinical psychology. Human performance is one emphasis area in the industrial/organizational M.A. Assessment of performance, training, and motivation are included in the human performance emphasis.

UNIVERSITY OF MARYLAND, COLLEGE PARK

Department of Kinesiology
HLHP Building
University of Maryland
College Park, MD 20742

Program Rating:

1	2	3	4	5	**6**	7
Applied Orientation			Equal Emphasis		Research Orientation	

CONTACT PERSON:	Donald H. Steel (Coordinator)	Brad D. Hatfield
PHONE NUMBER:	(301) 405-2490	(301) 405-2489
	(301) 405-2450 (Office)	
FAX NUMBER:	(301) 314-9167	
E-MAIL ADDRESS:	BH5@UMAIL.UMD.EDU	

FACULTY AND AREA OF INTEREST

Elizabeth Y. Brown	Sport vision
Brad D. Hatfield	Psychophysiology
Seppo Iso-Ahola	Social psychology and mental training
Donald H. Steel	Anxiety

PROGRAM INFORMATION

Degrees offered
- M.A.
- Ph.D.

Approx. number of students in program
- 40

Approx. number of students in each degree program offered
- 20 M.A. (50%)/20 Ph.D (50%)

Admissions requirements
- 3.00 GPA
- GRE

The program has available for qualified students
- Teaching Assistantships

Assistantships
- 10% Fellowships
- 0% Research Assistantships
- 90% Teaching Assistantships
- 0% Tuition Waivers
- 0% Other Forms of Financial Aid

Internship possibility
- No

UNIVERSITY OF MARYLAND, COLLEGE PARK ...

COMMENTS

The program is oriented towards the social psychology and the psychophysiological aspects of exercise and sport psychology. There is collaborative laboratory support with the Exercise Physiology Lab at the University of Maryland as well as other federal research institutions and at the Naval Medical Research Institute at the Bethesda Naval Hospital. The clinical aspects of sport psychology are currently limited to academic coverage with the graduate course work.

McGILL UNIVERSITY

Department of Physical Education
McGill University
475 Pine Avenue West
Montreal, Quebec, Canada H2W 1S4

CONTACT PERSON: Graham Neil
PHONE NUMBER: (514) 398-4188
FAX NUMBER: (514) 398-4186
E-MAIL ADDRESS: Neil@EDUCATION.MCGILL.CA

FACULTY AND AREA OF INTEREST

M. Downey	Psychology of motor learning/pedagogy
D. Q. Marisi	Sport psychology
G. I. Neil	Social psychology of sport and physical activity

PROGRAM INFORMATION

Degree offered
- M.A. (in psychology of motor performance)

Approx. number of students in program
- 15

Approx. number of students in each degree program offered
- 100% M.A.

Approx. number of students who apply/are accepted annually by program
- 12 apply/6 accepted

Admissions requirements
- Undergraduate degree in physical education
- Cumulative GPA above a 3.00 on a 4.00 scale

The program has available for qualified students
- Fellowships
- Research Assistantships
- Teaching Assistantships
- Other Forms of Financial Aid

Internship possibility
- No

UNIVERSITY OF MEMPHIS

Department of Human Movement Sciences and Education
Field House 1069
The University of Memphis
Memphis, TN 38152

Program Rating:

1	2	3	4	5	**6**	7
Applied Orientation			Equal Emphasis		Research Orientation	

CONTACT PERSON:	Mary Fry
PHONE NUMBER:	(901) 678-4986
	(901) 678-4316 (Department)
FAX NUMBER:	(901) 678-3591
E-MAIL ADDRESS:	fry.mary@coe.memphis.edu
PROGRAM WEB SITE:	http://www.hmse.memphis.edu/gopher.hmse.memphis.edu

FACULTY AND AREA OF INTEREST

Mary Fry — Motivation to participate in physical activity across the life span; developmental sport psychology; achievement motivation research; motivational climate

PROGRAM INFORMATION

Degree Offered
- M.S. in exercise and sport science

Approximate number of students in program
- 20–25

Approximate number of students who apply/are accepted annually by program
- 50 apply/25 accepted

Admissions requirements
- GRE or MAT scores
- Undergraduate degree with acceptable GPA
- Letters of recommendation
- Application with written statement of goals

Assistantships
- 0% Fellowships
- 40% Research Assistantships
- 10% Teaching Assistantships
- 50% Tuition Waivers
- 10% Other Forms of Financial Aid

Internship possibility
Yes

Internship required for degree completion
No

UNIVERSITY OF MEMPHIS

Department of Psychology
University of Memphis
Memphis, TN 38152

Program Rating:

1	2	3	4	5	**6**	7

Applied Orientation   Equal Emphasis   Research Orientation

CONTACT PERSON: Andrew Meyers
PHONE NUMBER: (901) 678-2146
FAX NUMBER: (901) 678-2579
E-MAIL ADDRESS: AMEYERS@MEMPHIS.EDU
PROGRAM WEB SITE: http://www.memphis.edu/psych.htm

FACULTY AND AREA OF INTEREST

Robert Klesges	Health psychology, performance enhancement
Andrew Meyers	Performance enhancement, exercise and health
Robert Neimeyer	Exercise and mental health
James Whelan	Performance enhancement, ethics in sport psychology

PROGRAM INFORMATION (Clinical Program)

Degrees offered
- M.A.
- M.S.
- Ph.D.

Approx. number of students in program
- 65

Approx. number of students in each degree program offered
- 100% of clinical students in Ph.D.

Approx. number of students who apply/are accepted annually by program
- 300 apply/12 accepted

Admissions requirements
- 1100 GRE
- 3.00 GPA
- Average student scores are 1300 GRE and 3.50 GPA

The program has available for qualified students
- Research Assistantships
- Teaching Assistantships
- Clinical Placements

Assistantships
- 0% Fellowships
- 60% Research Assistantships
- 20% Teaching Assistantships
- 100% Tuition Waivers (ll students receive waiver of tuition and fees)
- 20% Other Forms of Financial Aid (clinical placements)

UNIVERSITY OF MEMPHIS ...

PROGRAM INFORMATION ...

Internship possibility
- No (all students must complete a one-year clinical internship for the Ph.D. degree, but there is no formal sport internship experience available per se)

COMMENTS

No formal program in sport psychology is available. The department offers master's and Ph.D. degrees in clinical, experimental, and school psychology, and a master's in general psychology. Within the clinical program there are behavioral medicine and community health, child and family and psychopathology and psychotherapy research specialties where sport psychology work can take place. The program is essentially a clinical one with sport psychology as a subspecialty emphasis.

MIAMI UNIVERSITY

Department of Physical Education, Health, and Sport Studies
Phillips Hall
Miami University
Oxford, OH 45056

Program Rating:

1	2	3	**4**	5	6	7
Applied Orientation			Equal Emphasis			Research Orientation

CONTACT PERSON: Robert Weinberg
PHONE NUMBER: (513) 529–2700
FAX NUMBER: (513) 529–5006
E-MAIL ADDRESS: WEINBERG_R@MIAMIU.MUOHIO.EDU

FACULTY AND AREA OF INTEREST

Thelma S. Horn	Children's perceived competence, coaching behavior, stress reactivity
Jay Kimiecik	Exercise psychology, motivation, peak experience
Robin S. Vealey	Anxiety, self-confidence, psychological skills training, coaching behavior
Robert Weinberg	Cognitive strategies, goal setting, anxiety, mental training

PROGRAM INFORMATION

Degree offered
- M.S.

Approx. number of students in program
- 15

Approx. number of students in each degree program offered
- 100% M.S.

Approx. number of students who apply/are accepted annually by program
- 30 apply/8 accepted

Admissions requirements
- 3.00 minimum undergraduate GPA
- Three letters of recommendation
- GRE

The program has available for qualified students
- Teaching Assistantships

Assistantships
- 0% Fellowships
- 10% Research Assistantships
- 50% Teaching Assistantships
- 0% Tuition Waivers
- 20% Other Forms of Financial Aid

Internship possibility
- Yes

MIAMI UNIVERSITY ...

PROGRAM INFORMATION ...

Internship required for degree completion
- No

Description of typical internship experience
- Psychological skills intervention with university teams and individual athletes.
- Collegiate, high school, and/or youth sport coaching.
- Editorial assistant for sport psychology journals.
- Academic counseling for university student-athletes.
- Coaching education.

COMMENTS

Students may select either the thesis (30 total credits required) or nonthesis (34 total credits required) option. Nonthesis students may complete their degree in one calendar year. Thesis students should plan on two years to complete the degree. A comprehensive oral exit examination is required of all students. The curriculum is based on a cross-disciplinary perspective with required course work in psychological, sociocultural, motoric, and physiological foundations of sport and/or exercise. Electives may include courses in counseling and psychology as well as independent study and research with faculty in the area. An ongoing sport and exercise psychology seminar is attended by students and faculty in which professional and research issues are discussed and group research projects are coordinated. The program emphasizes knowledge of theory, research, and practice in sport psychology. Opportunities for collaborative research with faculty and psychological intervention with athletes are available for students, and every attempt is made to match student interests with faculty expertise. Selected faculty research interests include goal setting, confidence, coaching behaviors, imagery, motivation, exercise motivation, and optimal experience. Both quantitative and qualitative methodologies are encouraged. The program has been successful in placing students in sport/exercise psychology doctoral programs as well as coaching, academic counseling, and corporate fitness positions.

MICHIGAN STATE UNIVERSITY

Department of Physical Education and Exercise Science
201 IM Sports Circle
Michigan State University
East Lansing, MI 48824

Program Rating:

1	2	3	**4**	5	6	7

Applied Orientation   Equal Emphasis   Research Orientation

CONTACT PERSON: John Haubenstricker
PHONE NUMBER: (517) 355–4741
FAX NUMBER: (517) 353–2944
PROGRAM WEB SITE: http://www.educ.msu.edu/units/dept/pees/

FACULTY AND AREA OF INTEREST

Martha Ewing	Achievement motivation, anxiety, youth in sports, goal setting
Deborah Feltz	Self-efficacy, collective efficacy
Lynnette Overby	Mental imagery

PROGRAM INFORMATION

Degrees offered
- M.S.
- Ph.D.

Approx. number of students in program
- 35

Approx. number of students in each degree program offered
- 60% M.S./40% Ph.D.

Approx. number of students who apply/are accepted annually by program
- 10–15 apply/2–3 accepted

Admissions requirements
- Minimum score of 1000 on GRE (verbal + quantitative or verbal + analytic or quantitative + analytic)
- Major or minor in Physical Education
- Thesis in master's program

The program has available for qualified students
- Fellowships
- Research Assistantships
- Teaching Assistantships
- Other Forms of Financial Aid (Dean's Scholars, Dissertation Grants, etc.)

Assistantships
- 20% Fellowships
- 5% Research Assistantships
- 40% Teaching Assistantships
- 45% Tuition Waivers
- 5% Other Forms of Financial Aid

Intership possibility
- Yes

111

MICHIGAN STATE UNIVERSITY ...

PROGRAM INFORMATION ...

Practicum required for degree completion
- No

Number of hours required for practicum
- None required

Description of typical practicum experience
- Each doctoral student receives the opportunity to do applied work with a college, high school, or club sport team in a supervised experience.

COMMENTS

An interdepartmental master's degree with urban studies is also available for interested students.

UNIVERSITY OF MINNESOTA

School of Kinesiology and Leisure Studies
220 Cooke Hall
University of Minnesota
Minneapolis, MN 55455

Program Rating:

1	2	3	**4**	5	6	7
Applied Orientation			Equal Emphasis			Research Orientation

CONTACT PERSON:	March L. Krotee	Diane Wiese-Bjornstal
PHONE NUMBER:	(612) 625–0538	(612) 625–6580
FAX NUMBER:	(612) 626–7700	(612) 626–7700
E-MAIL ADDRESS:	Krote001@tc.umn.edu	dwiese@ZX.CIS.UMN.EDU
PROGRAM WEB SITE:	http://www.coled.umn.edu/kls/	

FACULTY AND AREA OF INTEREST

Bruce Anderson	Skill and performance
William Bart	Cognition
David Johnson	Cooperative learning
Roger Johnson	Cooperative learning
Mary Jo Kane	Psychosocial dimensions, women in sport
March L. Krotee	Psychosocial dimensions, performance of elite athletes, systems management
John Romano	Stress management, counseling
Michael G. Wade	Performance effects, human factors
Richard Weinberg	Performance effects
Diane Wiese-Bjornstal	Psychosocial dimensions, youth sport, injury

PROGRAM INFORMATION

Degrees offered
- M.Ed.
- M.A.
- Ph.D.

Approx. number of students in program
- 20

Approx. number of students in each degree program offered
- 50% master's/50% Ph.D.

Approx. number of students who apply/are accepted annually by program
- 50 apply/5 accepted

Admissions requirements
- GRE
- MAT
- TOEFL
- GPA—3.00 undergraduate, 3.50 graduate

The program has available for qualified students
- Fellowships

UNIVERSITY OF MINNESOTA ...

PROGRAM INFORMATION ...

- Research Assistantships
- Teaching Assistantships
- Other Forms of Financial Aid (doctoral dissertation grants, graduate school scholarships, grants, and minority fellowships)

Assistantships

- 0% Fellowships
- 0% Research Assistantships
- 0% Teaching Assistantships
- 0% Tuition Waivers
- 0% Other Forms of Financial Aid

Internship possibility

- Yes

Internship required for degree completion

- No

Number of hours required for internship

- Arranged

Description of typical internship experience

- Self-directed and cooperatively planned between student, faculty, and cooperating unit, agency, or federation.

COMMENTS

A cooperatively designed graduate program is arranged to meet the individual needs of the graduate student.

UNIVERSITY OF MISSOURI, COLUMBIA

Department of Educational & Counseling Psychology
16 Hill Hall
University of Missouri, Columbia
Columbia, MO 65211

Program Rating:

1	2	3	**4**	5	6	7
Applied Orientation			Equal Emphasis			Research Orientation

CONTACT PERSON: Richard H. Cox
PHONE NUMBER: (573) 882–7602
FAX NUMBER: (573) 884–5989
E-MAIL ADDRESS: rhcox@showme.missouri.edu
PROGRAM WEB SITE: http://tiger.coe.missouri.edu/~ecp/

FACULTY AND AREA OF INTEREST

Richard H. Cox — Anxiety/performance relationships
Rick McGuire — Motivation

PROGRAM INFORMATION

Degrees offered
- M.A.
- Ph.D.

Approx. number of sport psychology students in program
- 3–10

Approx. number of students in each degree program offered
- 85% M.A./15% Ph.D.

Approx. number of students who apply/are accepted annually by program
- Admission into Counseling Psychology program is very competitive

Admissions requirements
- GPA
- GRE/MAT
- Letters of support
- Research experience

The program has available for qualified students
- Research Assistantships
- Teaching Assistantships

Assistantships
- % Fellowships
- % Research Assistantships
- % Teaching Assistantships
- % Tuition Waivers
- % Other Forms of Financial Aid

Note: Exact percentages are not available, however, Ph.D. candidates can expect some financial support in the form of an assistantship, scholarship, and/or fellowship.

PROGRAM INFORMATION ...

Internship/practicum possibility
- Yes

Internship/practicum required for degree completion
- Yes

Number of hours required for internship/practicum
- 9 semester hours of practicum required for M.A. candidates
- 400 hours of practicum, and the full-time equivalent of one year of internship is required for Ph.D. candidates

COMMENTS

The Ph.D. program in counseling psychology at MU is APA approved and is consistently ranked among the top 3 programs nationally. Both the master's and doctoral programs are organized as a joint program between the Department of Educational and Counseling Psychology and the Department of Psychology. Sport psychology is a subspecialty in counseling psychology, offered through the Department of Educational and Counseling Psychology. Counseling psychology students with a strong interest in sport psychology graduate with degrees in counseling psychology with support work in sport psychology. The doctorate in counseling psychology, with a subspecialty in sport psychology, is designed to qualify the recipient to become AAASP certified as an applied counseling sport psychologist. Recipients of the master's and/or doctorate in counseling psychology may apply to become licensed to practice in the state of Missouri.

UNIVERSITY OF MISSOURI, KANSAS CITY

Department of Physical Education
5100 Rockhill Road
University of Missouri, Kansas City
Kansas City, MO 64110-2499

Program Rating:

1	2	3	4	5	6	**7**
Applied Orientation			Equal Emphasis			Research Orientation

CONTACT PERSON: Cynthia Pemberton
PHONE NUMBER: (816) 235–2751
FAX NUMBER: (816) 235–5521
E-MAIL ADDRESS: CPEMBERTON@smtpgate.umkc.edu
PROGRAM WEB SITE: http://www.CCTR.UMKC.EDU/DEPT/PHYSED/

FACULTY AND AREA OF INTEREST

Patricia McSwegin	Aspects of fitness and exercise
Cynthia Pemberton	Motivation in sport and exercise
Mary Phyl Dwight	Coaching education

PROGRAM INFORMATION

Degrees offered
- M.A.
- Ph.D. (interdisciplinary)

Approx. number of students in program
- 20

Approx. number of students in each degree program offered
- 90% M.A./10% Ph.D.

Admissions requirements
- M.A.: Baccalaureate degree
- GPA of 2.75
- Ph.D.: 1500 on GRE (500 verbal minimum + quantitative + specialized area)
- Other specified requirements identified by coordinating discipline and co-discipline

The program has available for qualified students
- Fellowships
- Teaching Assistantships
- Other Forms of Financial Aid

Assistantships
- 0% Fellowships
- 10% Research Assistantships
- 0% Teaching Assistantships
- 15% Tuition Waivers
- 75% Other Forms of Financial Aid

Internship possibility
- Yes

Internship required for degree completion
- No

UNIVERSITY OF MISSOURI, KANSAS CITY ...

PROGRAM INFORMATION ...

Number of hours required for internship
- 3–6 credit hours

Description of typical internship experience
- Working with intercollegiate, potential Olympic, high school, and mature athletes.
- Working in a sportsmedicine setting.
- Consulting with school districts on physical education and sport (interscholastic or youth) programs.
- Working in fitness centers and exercise testing situations.

COMMENTS

The M.A. and interdisciplinary Ph.D. are designed to prepare students to become AASP certified sport psychology consultants.

THE UNIVERSITY OF MONTANA

Department of Health and Human Performance
McGill 220 A
The University of Montana
Missoula, MT 59812

Program Rating:

1	**2** *	**3** *	4	5	6	7

Applied Orientation　　　　　　　Equal Emphasis　　　　　　　Research Orientation

*Program offers opportunities to pursue an applied orientation OR a research orientation (as opposed to an equal emphasis on both).

CONTACT PERSON: Lewis A. Curry
PHONE NUMBER: (406) 243–5242
FAX NUMBER: (406) 243–4536
E-MAIL ADDRESS: curry58@selway.umt.edu

FACULTY AND AREA OF INTEREST

Lewis A. Curry — Applied exercise and sport psychology, optimal performance, life-skills training and performance enhancement intervention and strategies

PROGRAM INFORMATION

Degree offered
- M.S.
- Ed.D. in counselor education—Program is in process of adopting sport counseling track—Contact Lewis Curry for information

Approx. number of students in program
- 6

Approx. number of students in each degree program offered
- 100% M.S.

Approx. number of students who apply/are accepted annually by program
- 20–25 apply/10–12 accepted

Admissions requirements
- GRE 900 (verbal + quantitative)
- 3.00 GPA in health and human performance or related field (such as psychology)
- Official copies of transcripts
- Three letters of recommendation

The program has available for qualified students
- Teaching Assistantships
- Other Forms of Financial Aid

Assistantships
- 0% Fellowships
- 0% Research Assistantships
- 20–30% Teaching Assistantships
- 0% Tuition Waivers
- 0% Other Forms of Financial Aid

UNIVERSITY OF MONTANA ...

PROGRAM INFORMATION ...

Internship possibility
- Yes

Internship required for degree completion
- No

Number of hours required for internship
- 6 semester credits

Description of typical internship experience
- Flexible, but limited, with some students having worked with athletic teams in high school/college settings. Internships/practicum experiences may be possible in the H.H.P. Education Center, recently established to provide life-skills training and sport perfomance enhancement consulting.

COMMENTS

The University of Montana has a strong psychology program (Ph.D. program). A strong point is that students take cognate courses in the psychology department.

UNIVERSITE de MONTREAL

Département d'Education Physique
CP 6128, Succursale "A"
Université de Montréal
Montréal, Québec
Canada H3C 3J7

CONTACT PERSON: Wayne R. Halliwell
PHONE NUMBER: (514) 343–7008
FAX NUMBER: (514) 343–2181

FACULTY AND AREA OF INTEREST

Claude Alain	Information processing, preparation to react
Wayne R. Halliwell	Motivation, mental preparation
Luc Proteau	Learning, movement control, individual differences
Claude Sarrazin	Decision making, intervention

PROGRAM INFORMATION

Degrees offered
- M.S.
- Ph.D.

Approx. number of students in program
- 40

Approx. number of students in each degree program offered
- 70% M.S./30% Ph.D.

Approx. number of students who apply/are accepted annually by program
- 20 apply/10 accepted

Admissions requirements
- B.A. or B.Sc. or B.P.E. (usually in physical education or psychology)

The program has available for qualified students
- Research Assistantships
- Teaching Assistantships
- Other Forms of Financial Aid

Internship possibility
- No

COMMENTS

The program is currently an academically oriented, research program. However, a licensed psychologist is on staff and teaches two graduate courses in clinical psychology. Courses are given in French, but the majority of readings are in English and theses may be written in English.

UNIVERSITY OF NEW HAMPSHIRE

Department of Kinesiology
University of New Hampshire
209 New Hampshire Hall
Durham, NH 03824

Program Rating:

1	2	3	**4**	5	6	7
Applied Orientation			Equal Emphasis			Research Orientation

CONTACT PERSON: Heather Barber
PHONE NUMBER: (603) 862–2058
FAX NUMBER: (603) 862–0154
E-MAIL ADDRESS: HB@CHRISTA.UNH.EDU

FACULTY AND AREA OF INTEREST

Heather Barber	Motivation, coaching education
Ron Croce	Neuropsychology

PROGRAM INFORMATION

Degree offered
- M.S.

Approx. number of students in program
- 7–10

Approx. number of students in each degree program offered
- 100% M.S.

Approx. number of students who apply/are accepted annually by program
- 15 apply/8 accepted

Admissions requirements
- GRE (average student scores 1050)
- GPA (average student has 3.25 on 4.00 scale)

The program has available for qualified students
- Teaching Assistantships
- Other Forms of Financial Aid
- Coaching Assistantships

Assistantships
- 0% Fellowships
- 0% Graduate Assistantships
- 45% Teaching Assistantships/Coaching
- 15% Tuition Waivers
- 5–10% Other Forms of Financial Aid

Internship possibility
- Yes

Internship required for degree completion
- No

UNIVERSITY OF NEW HAMPSHIRE ...

PROGRAM INFORMATION ...

Number of hours required for internship
- 8 credit hours

Description of typical internship experience
- Experiential learning in a setting appropriate to the student's objectives. Sport psychology students can either work on campus with the University of New Hampshire athletic program, or off campus in approved sport organizations.

COMMENTS

The University of New Hampshire offers a master of science in sports studies with a concentration in sport psychology. The concentration includes an optional internship with one of the university athletic teams, as well as required courses and a thesis.

UNIVERSITY OF NEW MEXICO

Department of Health, Physical Education, and Recreation
University of New Mexico
Albuquerque, NM 87131

CONTACT PERSON: Joy Griffin
PHONE NUMBER: (505) 277–3360
FAX NUMBER: (505) 277–7601

FACULTY AND AREA OF INTEREST

Joy Griffin   Multicultural issues, eating disorders, biofeedback
Vonda Long   Self-concept development, experiential learning *
Wayne Maes   Cognitive therapy

*Dr. Long is the main contact person in the counselor education program. There are six other faculty involved

PROGRAM INFORMATION

Degrees offered
- M.S.
- Ed.D.
- Ph.D.

Approx. number of students in program
- 186**

Approx. number of students in each degree program offered
- 75% M.S./25% Doctoral**

Approx. number of students who apply/are accepted annually by program
- 50** apply/5–6 accepted

Admissions requirements
- Bachelor's or master's degree in physical education, exercise science, health, psychology, counseling (other degrees will be evaluated by department)
- Undergraduate GPA of 3.00 or better
- Three letters of recommendation
- Written statement of career goals and areas of interest
- History of prospective student's sport background
- Completed application form including transcripts

The program has available for qualified students
- Teaching Assistantships

Internship possibility
- Yes

Internship required for degree completion
- Yes

Number of hours required for internship
- 6 credit hours

UNIVERSITY OF NEW MEXICO ...

PROGRAM INFORMATION ...

Description of typical internship experience
- Internship experiences available to work with high school, collegiate, semi-professional teams, and other possibilities with faculty approval.

Note: *Numbers are for counselor education program-separate numbers specific to sport psychology are unavailable.

COMMENTS

Health promotion, physical education and leisure programs and counselor education at the University of New Mexico offer specialization in the area of sport counseling at the doctoral level (Ed.D. or Ph.D.). An interdisciplinary approach capitalizes on the strengths of several excellent programs to meet the current needs of the sport counseling specialist. Two different doctoral options exist. Option 1 is recommended for professionals who wish to teach, conduct research, and work with athletes at a college or university. Option 2 is recommended for professionals who wish to enter private practice. Graduate programs in sport counseling at the University of New Mexico have been designed to meet criteria for AAASP certification.

UNIV. OF NORTH CAROLINA, CHAPEL HILL

Department of Physical Education
University of North Carolina at Chapel Hill
203 Fetzer Gymnasium, CB# 8700
Chapel Hill, NC 27599–8700

Program Rating:

1	2	3	**4**	5	6	7
Applied Orientation			Equal Emphasis			Research Orientation

CONTACT PERSON: John M. Silva
PHONE NUMBER: (919) 962–5176
FAX NUMBER: (919) 962–0489
E-MAIL ADDRESS: Silva@UNC.edu
PROGRAM WEB SITE: http://www.unc.edu/depts/exercise/SP_cover.html

FACULTY AND AREA OF INTEREST

John M. Silva — Elite athlete, intervention, psychometrics
Diane Stevens — Social psychological aspects of sport, self-presentation, gender, performance Enhancement

PROGRAM INFORMATION

Degree offered
- M.A.

Approx. number of students in program
- 8–11

Approx. number of students in each degree program offered
- 100% M.A.

Approx. number of students who apply/are accepted annually by program
- 30–40 apply/5–7 accepted

Admissions requirements: (minimum)
- 1000 GRE
- 3.00 GPA
- Three letters of reference are the minimum requirements

The program has available for qualified students
- Fellowships
- Internships
- Research Assistantships
- Teaching Assistantships
- Other Forms of Financial Aid

Assistantships

20–25%	Fellowships (merit scholarships—competitive)
25%	Research Assistantships
75%	Teaching Assistantships
75–100%	Tuition Waivers
0%	Other Forms of Financial Aid

UNIV. OF NORTH CAROLINA, CHAPEL HILL ...

PROGRAM INFORMATION ...

Internship possibility
- Yes

Internship required for degree completion
- Yes

Number of hours required for intership
- 200 observational hours and 200 contact hours required

Description of typical intership experience
- Students work under direct supervision structuring, applying a complete intervention in two supervised practicum experiences with an athlete in a one-on-one setting. Students also work under direct supervision in a group practicum with intact teams on cohesion, player-coach dynamics, goal setting, and stress management issues.

COMMENTS

The UNC program operates on a scientist/practitioner model and offers students the opportunity to become involved in basic or applied research and supervised individual/group-oriented interventions with university athletes. Research, theory, and applied skills are equally considered in a comprehensive educational and training program in sport psychology. A data-based research thesis is required for the M.A. with specialization in sport psychology. The program is interdisciplinary in nature, and excellent educational opportunities exist with the departments of psychology, counseling, and rehabilitation counseling.

UNC–Chapel Hill offers a program designed for the student who is interested in pursuing a Ph.D. with specialization in sport psychology. Students are fully integrated into the sport psychology program and are considered and interacted with as young professionals.

UNIV. OF NORTH CAROLINA, GREENSBORO

Department of Exercise and Sport Science
University of North Carolina
Greensboro, NC 27412–5001

Program Rating:

1	2	3	4*	5	6	7

Applied Orientation   Equal Emphasis   Research Orientation

*Program offers opportunities to pursue an applied orientation OR a research orientation (as opposed to an equal emphasis on both).

CONTACT PERSON: Diane L. Gill   Daniel Gould   David L. Rudolph

PHONE NUMBER: (910) 334–5573 (Dept. Main Office) (910) 334–3037 (910) 334–3694

FAX NUMBER: (910) 334–3238

E-MAIL ADDRESS:
Gill: diane_gill@uncg.edu
Gould: GOULDD@iris.uncg.edu
Rudolph: dlrudolph@homans.uncg.edu

PROGRAM WEB SITE: http://www.uncg.edu/

FACULTY AND AREA OF INTEREST

Diane L. Gill	Social psychology of sport and exercise
Daniel Gould	Applied sport psychology; youth sports
David L. Rudolph	Exercise psychology

PROGRAM INFORMATION

Degrees offered
- M.S.
- Ph.D.

Approx. number of students in program
- 15

Approx. number of students in each degree program offered
- 60% M.S./40% Ph.D.

Approx. number of students who apply/are accepted annually by program
- 60 apply/8 accepted

Admissions requirements
- Admission is based on previous academic performance (GPA)
- GRE scores
- Letters of reference
- Statement of career goals and objectives
- Past experience and accomplishments
- Visit to campus is strongly recommended for Ph.D. candidates

The program has available for qualified students
- Research Assistantships
- Teaching Assistantships

Assistantships
10% Fellowships
25% Research Assistantships
25% Teaching Assistantships
50% Tuition Waivers (out-of-state waiver only; usually awarded with RA & TA)
0% Other Forms of Financial Aid

UNIV. OF NORTH CAROLINA, GREENSBORO ...

PROGRAM INFORMATION ...

Internship possibility
- Yes

Internship required for degree completion
- No

Number of hours required for internship
- 3 credit hours

Description of typical internship experience
- Students serve as an educational sport psychology specialist with a university athletic team. Both group presentations and individual athletic consultations are involved. Opportunities also exist for internships in nonuniversity sport and exercise programs.

COMMENTS

The UNCG graduate program in sport and exercise psychology offers M.S. and Ph.D. degrees and prepares students for careers as teachers, researchers, coaches, exercise leaders, or sport and exercise psychology consultants. The UNCG program is staffed by three full-time specialists with expertise in three complementary aspects of the field: social psychology, exercise psychology, and intervention/performance enhancement, providing both depth and breadth of knowledge in sport and exercise psychology. Extensive research training and experience are provided with the goal of developing top-flight sport and exercise psychology scholars. In addition, students have the opportunity to develop excellent applied sport and exercise psychology consulting competencies, via work with athletic teams, and based on a scientist-practitioner model.

The Ph.D. degree enables students to pursue in-depth, research-oriented study in sport and exercise psychology, and the program is designed to meet each individual student's career goals and needs. A variety of graduate sport and exercise psychology courses are offered on a regular basis, including a graduate-level introduction to sport and exercise psychology; advanced courses in exercise psychology, social psychology, and applied sport psychology; and a consulting practicum. Also, special topics courses and independent studies are often offered. In addition to sport and exercise psychology courses, the department offers excellent support courses in exercise physiology, pedagogy, motor behavior, and sociocultural sport studies. Many students supplement their sport and exercise psychology programs with courses offered through the psychology and counseling departments.

UNIVERSITY OF NORTH DAKOTA

Department of Health, Physical Education, and Recreation
University Station, Box 8235
University of North Dakota
Grand Forks, ND 58202

CONTACT PERSON: Robert Eklund
PHONE NUMBER: (701) 777–3230
FAX NUMBER: (701) 777–3650
E-MAIL ADDRESS: REKLUND@BADLANDS.NODAK.EDU

FACULTY AND AREA OF INTEREST

Robert C. Eklund   Sport psychology
Jim Whitehead   Exercise psychology

PROGRAM INFORMATION

Degree offered
- M.S.

Approx. number of students in program
- 25

Approx. number of students in each degree program offered
- 100% M.S.

Approx. number of students who apply/are accepted annually by program
- 20 apply/6 accepted

Admissions requirements
- GRE
- Undergraduate GPA 2.75 overall or 3.00 (last two years)
- Minimum of 20 credits in undergraduate physical education

The program has available for qualified students
- Teaching Assistantships

Internship possibility
- Yes

Internship required for degree completion
- No

Number of hours required for internship
- Four hours

Description of typical internship experience
- Teaching undergraduate performance enhancement class; assisting in coaching minor program; supervising coaching practicums; supervising fitness lab.

UNIVERSITY OF NORTH TEXAS

Center for Sport Psychology and Performance Excellence

Department of Kinesiology,
Health Promotion and Recreation
University of North Texas
Box 13857
Denton, TX 76203

Department of Psychology, *
University of North Texas,
Box 311280,
Denton, TX 76203

Program Rating: Program offers opportunities to pursue an applied orientation OR a research orientation (as opposed to an equal emphasis on both).

CONTACT PERSON:	Peggy Richardson	Scott Martin
PHONE NUMBER:	(817) 565–3427	(817) 565–3427
FAX NUMBER:	(817) 565–4904	(817) 565–4904
E-MAIL ADDRESS:	RCHRDSN@COEFS.COE.UNT.EDU	SMARTIN@COEFS.COE.UNT.EDU
PROGRAM WEB SITE:	http://www.coe.unt.edu/	

FACULTY AND AREA OF INTEREST

Karen Cogan	Gender issues in sport and performance enhancement
Scott Martin	Sport and exercise psychology, goal attainment and attitudes toward sport psychology
Trent Petrie	Eating disorders, athletic injuries, sport psychology counseling and life skills training
Peggy Richardson	Women in sport, motivation, Sport psychology consulting, psychological

PROGRAM INFORMATION ...

Degrees offered
- M.S.
- Ph.D.

Approx. number of students in program
- 10–15 (master's)
- 10 (Ph.D.) are admitted to the Department of Psychology (2–4 are interested in sport psychology)

Approx. number of students in each degree program offered
- 80% M.S./20% Ph.D. (from Department of Psychology, etc.)

Admissions requirements
- Master's—800 GRE (375 minimum on Verbal and Quantitative)
- PhD.—1000 GRE (500 minimum on Verbal and Quantitative)
- M.S.—2.80 GPA; Ph.D.—3.0 GPA

The program has available for qualified students
- Research Assistantships
- Teaching Assistantships
- Other Forms of Financial Aid

Assistantships
- 15% Fellowships/Scholarships
- 15% Research Assistantships
- 40% Teaching Assistantships
- 15% Tuition Waivers (partial tuition waivers for out-of-state students)

UNIVERSITY OF NORTH TEXAS ...

PROGRAM INFORMATION ...

     60%   Other Forms of Financial Aid

Internship possibility
- Yes

Internship required for degree completion
- No—M.S.; Yes—Ph.D.

Number of hours required for internship
- 3–6 credit hours

Description of typical internship experience
- Develop a psychological skills intervention program with one of the university's teams.

COMMENTS

The University of North Texas Center for Sport Psychology and Performance Excellence is a multidisciplinary center devoted to offering sport psychology interventions, research, and training. The M.S. degree is offered through Kinesiology, Health Promotion, and Recreation. The Ph.D. degree is offered through the Counseling Psychology program (APA approved program).

* Contact persons for the Department of Psychology are Karen Cogan and Trent Petrie.

Karen Cogan	Trent Petrie
(940)565–2671	(940)565–4718
fax: (940)565–4682	fax: (940)565–4682
e-mail: COGAN@DSA.UNT.EDU	e-mail: PETRIET@UNT.EDU

UNIVERSITY OF NORTHERN COLORADO

Department of Kinesiology
University of Northern Colorado
Greeley, CO 80639

Program Rating:

1	2	3	4	5	6 *	7
Applied Orientation			Equal Emphasis			Research Orientation

*Program offers opportunities to pursue an applied orientation OR a research orientation (as opposed to an equal emphasis on both)

CONTACT PERSON: Robert Brustad
PHONE NUMBER: (303) 351–1737
FAX NUMBER: (303) 351–1762
E-MAIL ADDRESS: bbrustad@hhs.UnivNorthCo.edu
PROGRAM WEB SITE: http://www.hhs.univnorthco.edu/

FACULTY AND AREA OF INTEREST

Robert Brustad — Social psychology of sport, psychosocial aspects of children's sport and physical activity, exercise psychology, coaching effectiveness, motivation

Michelle Ritter-Taylor — Social-cultural influences, group processes, issues related to eating disorders and athletic identity

PROGRAM INFORMATION

Degrees offered
- M.A.
- Ed.D.

Approx. number of students in program
- 10

Approx. number of students in each degree program offered
- 70% M.S./30% Ed.D.

Approx. number of students who apply/are accepted annually by program
- Master's: 10 apply/3 accepted
- Doctoral: 8 apply/1 accepted

Admissions requirements
- GPA and GRE scores operate on a sliding scale
- Minimum GPA of 3.00 for M.S.
- Minimum GPA of 3.50 for Ed.D.
- GRE of 1500 for Ed.D. (verbal + quantitative + analytical)

The program has available for qualified students
- Research Assistantships
- Teaching Assistantships
- Other Forms of Financial Aid

Assistantships
20% Fellowships
0% Research Assistantships
30% Teaching Assistantships
30% Tuition Waivers
10% Other Forms of Financial Aid

UNIVERSITY OF NORTHERN COLORADO ...

PROGRAM INFORMATION ...

Internship possibility
- Yes

Internship required for degree completion
- No

Number of hours required for internship
- 6 credit hours

Description of typical internship experience
- Work with university athletic teams; work in health and exercise settings.

COMMENTS

The program focus at the University of Northern Colorado is on the social psychology of sport and physical activity. It is expected that students will develop an excellent background in social psychological theory and will apply this knowledge to the study of sport and exercise behavior. Particular areas of interest of current faculty and students include the study of motivation, exercise behavior and adherence, children's sport and physical activity involvement, and coaching effectiveness. Master's and doctoral students are expected to supplement their departmental course work with courses from the departments of psychology and sociology. There is not a major emphasis upon applied sport psychology within this program. However, some course work is available in the applied (intervention) area.

NORTHERN ILLINOIS UNIVERSITY

Department of Physical Education
Northern Illinois University
Anderson Hall
DeKalb, IL 60115-2854

Program Rating:

1	2	3	**4**	5	6	7
Applied Orientation			Equal Emphasis			Research Orientation

CONTACT PERSON: Keith Lambrecht
PHONE NUMBER: (815) 758–1738
FAX NUMBER: (815) 753–1413
PROGRAM WEB SITE: http://www.niu.edu/acad/phed

FACULTY AND AREA OF INTEREST

Judith Bischoff   Gender issues, sport governance
Lavon Williams   Motivation of youth sport participants and physical education students

PROGRAM INFORMATION

Degree offered
- M.S.Ed.

Approx. number of students in program
- 125 (the entire graduate program)

Approx. number of students in each degree program offered
- 100% M.S.Ed.

Approx. number of students who apply/are accepted annually by program
- 250 apply/100 accepted (Approximately 100 are accepted but not all attend)

Admissions requirements
- GPA of 2.75 (4.00 scale)
- GRE of 400 minimum in each area
- Transcripts
- Two letters of recommendation
- Goal statement

The program has available for qualified students
- Fellowships
- Research Assistantships
- Teaching Assistantships
- Other Forms of Financial Aid

Assistantships
    <1%   Fellowships
    5%   Research Assistantships
    25%   Teaching Assistantships
    <5%   Tuition Waivers
unknown   Other Forms of Financial Aid

NORTHERN ILLINOIS UNIVERSITY ...

PROGRAM INFORMATION ...

Internship possibility
- Yes, but not guaranteed

Description of typical internship experience
- The student would be assigned to a university, high school, or club team for approximately a semester.

COMMENTS

The M.S.Ed. degree offers specializations or options in sport and exercise psychology, exercise physiology/fitness leadership; adapted physical education; coaching; and sport management. Programs include work in exercise and health psychology. Students who wish to do so may be involved in ongoing research projects.

OREGON STATE UNIVERSITY

Exercise and Sport Science Department
Langton Hall
Oregon State University
Corvallis, OR 97331

Program Rating:

1	2	3	4	5	**6**	7
Applied Orientation			Equal Emphasis			Research Orientation

CONTACT PERSON: Vicki Ebbeck
PHONE NUMBER: (541) 737–6800 (Office)
FAX NUMBER: (541) 737–2788
E-MAIL ADDRESS: EBBECKV@CCMAIL.ORST.EDU
PROGRAM WEB SITE: http://www.orst.edu/dept/hhp/

FACULTY AND AREA OF INTEREST

Bradley J. Cardinal — Exercise psychology, exercise behavior change, professional issues
Vicki Ebbeck — Life-span social psychology, motivation, self-concept development

PROGRAM INFORMATION

Degrees offered
- M.S.
- Ph.D.

Approx. number of students in program
- 5

Approx. number of students in each degree program offered
- 40% M.S./60% Ph.D.

Approx. number of students who apply/are accepted annually by program
- 20 apply/1 Ph.D. and 1 master's thesis accepted. There is an open number of master's comprehensive exam applicants accepted.

Admissions requirements
- Letters of recommendation
- GRE scores
- Satisfactory GPA
- Transcripts
- Letter of intent

The program has available for qualified students
- Teaching Assistantships
- Other Forms of Financial Aid

Assistantships
- 0% Fellowships
- 0% Research Assistantships
- 75% Teaching Assistantships (including a tuition waiver)
- 0% Tuition Waivers (via teaching assistantships)
- 0% Other Forms of Financial Aid

Internship possibility
- No

OREGON STATE UNIVERSITY ...

COMMENTS

The emphasis of the graduate program is on research that addresses social psychological aspects of sport and exercise. There are three graduate courses offered in sport psychology, as well as seminars and independent readings. Thesis project or comprehensive exam options are available for master's students. Doctoral students are provided professional opportunities beyond required course work, such as teaching sport psychology classes, collaborating on research projects, and presenting at conferences. The average time to complete a degree is two years at the master's level and four years at the doctoral level.

UNIVERSITY OF OTTAWA

School of Human Kinetics
University of Ottawa
125 University, Ottawa, Ontario
Canada KIN 6N5

Program Rating:

1	**2** *	3	4	5	6	7

Applied Orientation   Equal Emphasis   Research Orientation

*Program offers opportunities to pursue an applied orientation OR a research orientation (as opposed to an equal emphasis on both).

CONTACT PERSON: John Salmela
PHONE NUMBER: (613) 562–5800, ext. 4261
FAX NUMBER: (613) 562–5149
E-MAIL ADDRESS: JSALMELA@UOTTAWA.CA
PROGRAM WEB SITE: http://www.uottawa.ca/academic/health/sportstudies-etudes/

FACULTY AND AREA OF INTEREST

Terry Orlick	Excellence in performance, mental training with children
Michelle Fortier	Motivation, exercise adherence, gender
John Salmela	Coach expertise, qualitative analysis
Diane Ste. Marie	Cognitive processes in judging
Pierre Trudel	Coaching and intervention

PROGRAM INFORMATION

Degrees offered
- M.A.
- M.S.
- Ph.D.

Approx. number of students in program
- 35

Approx. number of students in each degree program offered
- 33.3% M.A./33.3% M.S./33.3% Ph.D.

Approx. number of students who apply/are accepted annually by program
- 45 apply/25 accepted

Admissions requirements
- B+ in sport science or related area

The program has available for qualified students
- Research Assistantships
- Teaching Assistantships
- Other Forms of Financial Aid

Assistantships
- 5%   Fellowships
- 70% Research Assistantships
- 100% Teaching Assistantships
- 10% Tuition Waivers
- 0%   Other Forms of Financial Aid

139

UNIVERSITY OF OTTAWA ...

PROGRAM INFORMATION ...

Internship possibility
- Yes

Internship required for degree completion
- Yes, for M.A. in sport psychology, intervention/consultation option

Number of hours required for internship
- 360 hours for credit, unlimited hours noncredit

Description of typical internship experience
- Working with intercollegiate or local teams; working as a consultant with intercollegiate and national teams, local athletes, etc.

COMMENTS

A research master's degree in sport psychology (M.Sc.) is offered through the Department of Human Kinetics. A nonthesis master's degree (M.A.) in sport psychology intervention/consultation was offered beginning in 1992. A Ph.D. degree with a specialization in sport psychology is offered through the faculty of the Education Psycho-Pedagogy Department.

Along with the option of doing more conventional quantitative research in motivation and cognitive processes, there is the possibility of carrying out qualitative research on exceptional performers, coaches, and parents. Courses are given in English, French, and bilingually.

THE PENNSYLVANIA STATE UNIVERSITY

Department of Kinesiology
146 Recreation Building
The Pennsylvania State University
University Park, PA 16802

Program Rating:

1	2	3	4	5	**6**	7
Applied Orientation			Equal Emphasis		Research Orientation	

CONTACT PERSON:	Shannon L. Mihalko*	Sam Slobounov	David Yukelson
PHONE NUMBER:	(814) 865–1326 (Office)	(814) 865–3146	(814) 865–0407
	(814) 863–4493 (Dept.)		
FAX NUMBER:	(814) 863–7360	(814) 863–7360	(814) 863–1539
E-MAIL ADDRESS:		SMS18@PSU.EDU	Y39@PSU.EDU

*Note: Inquiries should be directed to the secretary in the Department of Kinesiology (Amy Bierly) at 814–863–0847. Ms. Bierlys e-mail address is: ALB1@OAS.PSU.EDU

FACULTY AND AREA OF INTEREST

Shannon L. Mihalko	Exercise and health psychology, social-cognitive and behavioral determinants and consequences of physical activity, epidemiology of physical activity across the life span
Sam Slobunov**	Psychology of diving, computer simulations, human postural dynamics, motor control
David Yukelson***	Applied sport psychology, group processes and team building, individual and group motivation, life-skill development and student-athlete welfare, psychology of injury

Faculty in psychology

**Sam Slobounov's web site: http://www.personal.psu.edu/sms18/

***Dr. Yukelson is an applied sport psychologist who works with all athletic teams at Penn State. Dr. Yukelson is also an affiliate assistant professor in the Department of Kinesiology where he teaches undergraduate courses in mental training; The Psychology of Coaching; and the social psychology of sport. In addition, he has graduate faculty status to serve on doctoral or thesis committees.

PROGRAM INFORMATION

Degrees offered
- M.S.
- Ph.D.

Approx. number of students in program
- 4

The program has available for qualified students
- Research Assistantships
- Teaching Assistantships
- Other Forms of Financial Aid

Assistantships
- 0% Fellowships
- 0% Research Assistantships
- 0% Teaching Assistantships

THE PENNSYLVANIA STATE UNIVERSITY ...

PROGRAM INFORMATION ...

0%   Tuition Waivers
0%   Other Forms of Financial Aid

Internship possibility
- Yes

Internship required for degree completion
- No

Description of typical internship experience
- Possibilities exist to work with Dr. Yukelson and the Academic Support Center for Student Athletes in an applied intercollegiate athletic setting.

COMMENTS

The graduate program's emphasis is on research that covers exercise psychology, motor behavior/motor control, social psychology of sport, and psychophysiology.

PURDUE UNIVERSITY

Department of Health, Kinesiology, and Leisure Studies
Lambert 113
Purdue University
West Lafayette, IN 47907

CONTACT PERSON: Joan L. Duda
PHONE NUMBER: (765) 494–3172 or 494–3178
FAX NUMBER: (765) 496–1239
E-MAIL ADDRESS: LYNNE@VM.CC.PURDUE.EDU

FACULTY AND AREA OF INTEREST

Melissa Chase	Sport and exercise psychology, self-efficacy
Joan L. Duda	Sport and exercise psychology, motivatio, coach and parental influences

PROGRAM INFORMATION

Degrees offered
- M.S.
- Ph.D.

Approx. number of students in program
- 8

Approx. number of students in each degree program offered
- 40% M.S./60% Ph.D.

Approx. number of students who apply/are accepted annually by program
- 30 apply/1–2 accepted

The program has available for qualified students
- Research Assistantships
- Teaching Assistantships
- Other Forms of Financial Aid

Internship possibility
- One-quarter appointment for a doctoral student with the Athletic Department.

COMMENTS

The department also offers course work/field experiences in the areas of health promotion, health psychology, marketing, and management besides the other subdisciplines of kinesiology. The program has a research emphasis but students do have applied experiences working with athletes and exercise groups.

UNIVERSITE du QUEBEC à TROIS-RIVIERES

Département des Sciences de l'Activité Physique
Université du Québec à Trois-Rivières
C.P. 500, Trois-Rivières, Quebec,
Canada G9A 5H

CONTACT PERSON: Pierre Lacoste
PHONE NUMBER: (819) 376–5128, poste 3780
FAX NUMBER: (819) 376–5092

FACULTY AND AREA OF INTEREST

Pierre Lacoste   Intervention strategies
Denis Methot   Training and performance

PROGRAM INFORMATION

Degree offered
- M.S.

Approx. number of students in program
- 24

Approx. number of students in each degree program offered
- 100% M.S.

Approx. number of students who apply/are accepted annually by program
- 23 apply/21 accepted

Admissions requirements
- Bachelor's degree
- 3.2 GPA

The program has available for qualified students
- Research Assistantships
- Teaching Assistantships

Internship possibility
- Yes

Internship required for degree completion
- No

Number of hours required for internship
- 45 hours (3 credits)

COMMENTS

The program offers two options: (a) professional and (b) research.

QUEEN'S UNIVERSITY

School of Physical and Health Education
Queen's University
Kingston, Ontario
Canada K7L 3N6

CONTACT PERSON: John Albinson
PHONE NUMBER: (613) 545–2666
FAX NUMBER: (613) 545–2009
E-MAIL ADDRESS: ALBINSON@QUCDN.QUEENSU.CA

FACULTY AND AREA OF INTEREST

John Albinson — Stress/hassles of elite athletes, eating disorders, athlete counseling, exercise counseling for non-athletes

David Pashevich — Collective efficacy, group cohesion, self presentation

PROGRAM INFORMATION

Degree offered
- M.A.

Approx. number of students in program
- 6

Approx. number of students in each degree program offered
- 100% M.A.

Approx. number of students who apply/are accepted annually by program
- 12 apply/2–3 accepted

Admissions requirements
- Minimum high B average from a four-year degree in physical education/ kinesiology, etc., or in Psychology with a background in sport involvement
- TOEFL of 600 for students with English as a second language

The program has available for qualified students
- Fellowships
- Research Assistantships
- Teaching Assistantships

Internship possibility
- Yes

Internship required for degree completion
- No

Number of hours required for internship
- One-half course—3 semester hours

Description of typical internship experience
- Students may do a supervised internship/practicum with intercollegiate athletes (university has 46 varsity teams) or in exercise counseling.

QUEEN'S UNIVERSITY ...

COMMENTS

The program offers the opportunity to focus upon applied sport psychology as it relates to consultation with elite athletes and as it relates to exercise counseling with nonelite populations. Students are expected to take a course in a cognate department, normally psychology, business (organizational behavior), or education (counseling). Students interested in exercise counseling may take courses from the Exercise Rehabilitation Program in the school. Normally all students accepted will receive funding.

THE UNIVERSITY OF QUEENSLAND

Departments of Human Movement Studies and Psychology
The University of Queensland
Queensland 4072
Australia

Program Rating:

1	2	3	**4** *	5	6	7
Applied Orientation			Equal Emphasis			Research Orientation

*Program offers opportunities to pursue an applied orientation OR a research orientation (as opposed to an equal emphasis on both).

CONTACT PERSON: Sue Jackson   Stephanie Hanrahan Trish Gorely
PHONE NUMBER: (61) 73–365–6845   (61) 73–365–6453   (61) 73–365–6985
(61) 73–365–6240 (Main Office)
FAX NUMBER: (61) 73–365–6877
E-MAIL ADDRESS: Jackson: suejac@hms.uq.edu.au
Hanrahan: steph@hms.uq.edu.au
Gorely: tgorely@hms.uq.edu.au
PROGRAM WEB SITE: http://www.uq.edu.au/hms/

FACULTY AND AREA OF INTEREST

Trish Gorely	Exercise and health behavior change, evaluation of mental skills training programs
Stephanie Hanrahan	Mental skills training, attributions/motivation, pedagogy in sport psychology
Sue Jackson	Optimal psychological states, quality of experience in sport and exercise

PROGRAM INFORMATION

Degrees offered
- Research Master's (M.A.; M.S.)
- Course work Master's (including Master of Sport and Exercise Psychology)
- Ph.D.

Approx. number of students in program
- 10–20

Approx. number of students in each degree program offered
- 10% Research Master's/60% Course work Master's/30% Ph.D.

Approx. number of students who apply/are accepted annually by program
- 25 apply/10 accepted

Admissions requirements
- Different requirements for different degrees—consult faculty

The program has available for qualified students
- Fellowships
- Research Assistantships
- Teaching Assistantships
- Other Forms of Financial Aid

Assistantships
0% Fellowships

THE UNIVERSITY OF QUEENSLAND ...

PROGRAM INFORMATION ...

30%   Research Assistantships
70%   Teaching Assistantships
10%   Tuition Waivers
10%   Other Forms of Financial Aid

Internship possibility
- Yes

Internship required for degree completion
- Yes, for Course work Master's

Number of hours required for internship
- 1000 (for Master's of Sport and Exercise Psychology)

Description of typical internship experience
- University sports clubs/sport associations.
- Working with private practitioners.
- Community sport clubs.

COMMENTS

All faculty members involved in the sport and exercise psychology program have joint appointments in the Departments of Human Movement Studies and Psychology. Traditionally, master's and doctoral programs in Australia have been predominantly research based. The Course work Master's programs offered at the University of Queensland are professionally oriented training programs and include course work, research, and practicum (internship) components.

SAN DIEGO STATE UNIVERSITY

Department of Exercise and Nutritional Sciences
San Diego State University
San Diego, CA 92182

Program Rating:

1	2	3	**4**	5	6	7
Applied Orientation			Equal Emphasis			Research Orientation

CONTACT PERSON: Dennis J. Selder
PHONE NUMBER: (619) 594–1920
FAX NUMBER: (619) 594–6553
E-MAIL ADDRESS: DSELDER@MAIL.SDSU.EDU

FACULTY AND AREA OF INTEREST

Thomas L. McKenzie	Applied behavior analysis, performance enhancement
Robert Mechikoff	Psychology of coaching, social psychology
Dennis J. Selder	Performance enhancement, motivation

PROGRAM INFORMATION

Degree offered
- M.A.

Approx. number of students in program
- 18

Approx. number of students in each degree program offered
- 100% M.A.

Approx. number of students who apply/are accepted annually by program
- 20 apply/15 accepted

Admissions requirements
- 950 GRE
- 3.00 GPA last 60 units

The program has available for qualified students
- Research Assistantships
- Teaching Assistantships
- Other Forms of Financial Aid

Assistantships
- 0% Fellowships
- 0% Research Assistantships
- 0% Teaching Assistantships
- 0% Tuition Waivers
- 0% Other Forms of Financial Aid

Internship possibility
- Yes

Internship required for degree completion
- Yes, for the M.A. degree

Number of hours required for internship
- Depends upon the student's situation

SAN DIEGO STATE UNIVERSITY ...

PROGRAM INFORMATION ...

Description of typical internship experience
- Serve as consultant to intercollegiate teams, involving assessment, development of mental skills training programs, team building, research reports.

COMMENTS

The study of the psychology of sport and physical activity ranges from theoretical sport psychology to applied sport psychology. Students are able to select their course of studies to reflect their own interests and background. A core of courses is required of all students so that they may appreciate the expanse of the area of study. Further courses are elected to meet each student's specific interests. The main strength of this sport psychology specialization is its emphasis on laboratory and practical experiences. It is designed to reflect the extensive resources in sport psychology which are available in the San Diego region.

An additional program of interest at San Diego State University is the joint Ph.D. degree in behavioral medicine between the Department of Psychology at SDSU and the Department of Psychiatry at the University of California at San Diego.

SAN FRANCISCO STATE UNIVERSITY

Physical Education Department
San Francisco State University
1600 Holloway Avenue
San Francisco, CA 94132

CONTACT PERSON: Andrea B. Schmid
PHONE NUMBER: (415) 338–1786 or (415) 338–1258
FAX NUMBER: (415) 338–1967

FACULTY AND AREA OF INTEREST
Bobbie Bennett	Kinesiology/motor learning
Andrea B. Schmid	Sport psychology
Gail Whitaker	Sport sociology

PROGRAM INFORMATION

Degrees offered
- M.A.
- Coaching Certificate

Approx. number of students in program
- 10

Approx. number of students in each degree program offered
- 100% M.A.

Approx. number of students who apply/are accepted annually by program
- 4–6 apply/3–5 accepted

Admissions requirements
- Undergraduate degree from an accredited institution
- 2.75 GPA in the last 60 semester units attempted
- Students who do not hold an appropriate B.A. degree must complete a 24-unit major in physical education

The program has available for qualified students
- Other Forms of Financial Aid

Internship possibility
- Yes

Description of typical internship experience
- Part-time temporary teaching and coaching assignment in the department.

COMMENTS

Students who wish to focus on sport psychology take our graduate sport psychology and sport sociology courses augmented by courses outside the department (e.g., motivation theory, psychology of biofeedback, etc.).

SAN JOSE STATE UNIVERSITY

Department of Human Performance
San Jose State University
One Washington Square
San Jose, CA 95192–0054

Program Rating:

1	2	3	4	5	6*	7

Applied Orientation   Equal Emphasis   Research Orientation

*Program offers opportunities to pursue an applied orientation OR a research orientation (as opposed to an equal emphasis on both).

CONTACT PERSON: David M. Furst
PHONE NUMBER: (408) 924–3039
FAX NUMBER: (408) 924–3053
E-MAIL: furstd@sjsuvm1.sjsu.edu
PROGRAM WEB SITE: http://www.sjsu.edu/depts/casa/dept/hup.html

FACULTY AND AREA OF INTEREST

David M. Furst   Endurance athletes, disabled athletes, association/dissociation, peak experience

Keith Johnsgard   Sensation seekers
Jill Steinberg   Women and sport

PROGRAM INFORMATION

Degree offered
- M.A.

Approx. number of students in program
- 8

Approx. number of students in each degree program offered
- 100% M.A.

Approx. number of students who apply/are accepted annually by program
- 3 apply/3 accepted

Admissions requirements (Classified standing)
- Baccalaureate degree with a major or minor in physical education
- Minimum GPA of 3.00 in last 60 semester units (or minimum of 2.75 and on probation)
- No undergraduate course deficiencies
- Students are encouraged but not required to submit GRE scores
- NonPE majors can come in as "conditionally classified"

The program has available for qualified students
- Teaching Assistantships
- Other Forms of Financial Aid

Assistantships
- 0%   Fellowships
- 0%   Research Assistantships
- 20%   Teaching Assistantships
- 0%   Tuition Waivers

SAN JOSE STATE UNIVERSITY ...

PROGRAM INFORMATION ...

30% Other Forms of Financial Aid

50% No Financial Aid

Internship possibility

- Yes

Internship required for degree completion

- No

Description of typical internship experience

- Depending on the clinical/applied work being done with the various teams and athletic departments, the student will work with these teams under the direction of one of the clinical sport psychologists.

COMMENTS

Professors at San Jose State University have been involved with sport psychology as long, or longer, than any other university in the United States. Professors Bruce Ogilvie and Thomas Tutko have achieved national and international recognition for their applied work with athletes on every level from Olympic to professional to youth sport. Currently, the sport psychology program is housed within the Human Performance Department. Courses available to students are undergraduate and graduate sport psychology, exercise and mental health, motivation, personality, nutrition and sport, and other courses. Two of the three faculty involved in the applied sport psychology program have Ph.D.s in clinical psychology.

UNIVERSITE de SHERBROOKE

Département de Kinanthropologie
Université de Sherbrooke
2500 Boulevard de l'Université
Sherbrooke, Quebec, Canada JIK 2RI

Program Rating:

1	2	3	4	**5**	6	7

Applied Orientation   Equal Emphasis   Research Orientation

CONTACT PERSON: Paul Deshaies
PHONE NUMBER: (819) 821–8000, ext. 2730
FAX NUMBER: (819) 821–7970
E-MAIL ADDRESS: PDESHAIES@FEPS.USHERB.CA

FACULTY AND AREA OF INTEREST

Marc Belisle	Motives for involvement, stress management
Pierre Demers	Sociology of physical education
Paul Deshaies	Daily physical education for elementary schools, psychobiological analysis of performance
Georges B. Lemieux	Learning, observation

PROGRAM INFORMATION

Degree offered
- M.S.

Approx. number of students in program
- 25

Approx. number of students in each degree program offered
- 100% M.S.

Approx. number of students who apply/are accepted annually by program
- 20 apply/15 accepted

Admissions requirements
- Bachelor's degree in movement science or physical education or equivalent

The program has available for qualified students
- Research Assistantships
- Teaching Assistantships
- Other Forms of Financial Aid

Assistantships
- 10% Fellowships
- 10% Research Assistantships
- 10% Teaching Assistantships
- 0% Tuition Waivers
- 60% Other Forms of Financial Aid

Internship possibility
- No

UNIVERSITE de SHERBROOKE ...

COMMENTS

The program is not specifically in applied sport psychology but in kinanthropology. The program emphasizes a systematic approach applied to contexts such as athletic competition, physical fitness, and adapted physical activity. Within this framework, classes are offered in areas such as sport psychology, sport sociology, and environmental factors. Research activities count for 24 credits of the 45 credits required, and it is here that the student can concentrate on a specific area of interest.

SOUTHEASTERN LOUISIANA UNIVERSITY

Department of Kinesiology and Health Studies
Southeastern Louisiana University
Hammond, LA 70402

Program Rating:

1	2	3	4	5	**6**	7

Applied Orientation   Equal Emphasis   Research Orientation

CONTACT PERSON:	Edmund O. Acevedo
PHONE NUMBER:	(504) 549–2130
FAX NUMBER:	(504) 549–5119
E-MAIL ADDRESS:	eacevedo@selu.edu
PROGRAM WEB SITE:	http:/www.selv.edu/

FACULTY AND AREA OF INTEREST

Edmund O. Acevedo	Psychophysiology, exercise physiology, psychological skills training
Eddie Hebert	Self-talk, videotape feedback, imagery

PROGRAM INFORMATION

Degree Offered
- M.A.

Approximate number of students in program
- 2 in sport psychology
- 42 in overall program

Approximate number of students who apply/are accepted annually by program
- 1 applies/1 accepted in Sport Psychology program
- 15 apply/13 accepted in overall program

Admissions requirements
- Undergraduate GPA of 2.5 (or 3.0 in last two years)
- GRE of 800

Assistanstantships
- 50%   Fellowships (5% in overall program)
- 50%   Research Assistantships (10% in overall program)
- 0%   Teaching Assistantships (5% in overall program)
- 100%   Tuition Waivers (25% in overall program)
- 0%   Other Forms of Financial Aid

Internship possibility
- Yes

Internship required for degree completion
- No

Number of hours required for internship
- Students concentrating in counseling have a greater opportunity to participate in internship experiences than those concentrating in exercise science.

Description of typical internship experience
- Educational sport psychology with individual or team sport athletes and various opportunities in the athletic training room with injured athletes.

UNIVERSITY OF SOUTHERN CALIFORNIA

Department of Exercise Science
University of Southern California
Los Angeles, CA 90089–0652

Program Rating:

1	2	3	4	5	**6**	7
Applied Orientation			Equal Emphasis		Research Orientation	

CONTACT PERSON: John Callaghan
PHONE NUMBER: (213) 740–2479
FAX NUMBER: (213) 740–7909
E-MAIL: callagha@mizar.usc.edu
PROGRAM WEB SITE: http://www.usc.edu/dept/LAS/exsci/

FACULTY AND AREA OF INTEREST

John Callaghan — Personality, motivation, attributions, perceived competence and anxiety, psychological skills

PROGRAM INFORMATION

Degrees offered
- M.A.
- Ph.D.

Approx. number of students in program
- 3–8

Approx. number of students in each degree program offered
- 50% M.A./50% Ph.D.

Approx. number of students who apply/are accepted annually by program
- 2–3 accepted

Admissions requirements
- Undergraduate GPA of 3.00
- 1100 minimum GRE score (verbal + quantitative)

The program has available for qualified students
- Fellowships
- Research Assistantships
- Teaching Assistantships
- Other Forms of Financial Aid

Assistantships
- 0% Fellowships
- 40% Research Assistantships
- 0% Teaching Assistantships
- 40% Tuition Waivers
- 0% Other Forms of Financial Aid

Internship possibility
- No

UNIVERSITY OF SOUTHERN CALIFORNIA ...

COMMENTS

The department has three tracks: exercise physiology, biomechanics, and sport psychology. These three specializations are at the graduate level. Sport psychology is offered for both the M.A. and Ph.D. degrees in the Department of Exercise Science.

SOUTHERN CONNECTICUT STATE UNIVERSITY

Human Performance Laboratory
Moore Fieldhouse
Southern Connecticut State University
501 Crescent Street
New Haven, CT 06515

Program Rating:

1	2	3	4*	5	6	7

Applied Orientation   Equal Emphasis   Research Orientation

*Program offers opportunities to pursue an applied orientation OR a research orientation (as opposed to an equal emphasis on both).

CONTACT PERSON:	David S. Kemler
PHONE NUMBER:	(203) 392–6040
FAX NUMBER:	(203) 392–6020
E-MAIL ADDRESS:	Kemler@scsu.ctstateu.edu
PROGRAM WEB SITE:	http://scsu.ctsstateu.edu/

FACULTY AND AREA OF INTEREST

Robert S. Axtell	Exercise physiology
Joan E. Barbarich	Motor learning
Joan A. Finn	Psychophysiology
David S. Kemler	Sport psychology, health psychology
David W. Martens	Biomechanics
Karl F. Rinehart	Exercise physiology

PROGRAM INFORMATION

Degree offered
- M.S. (Human Performance)

Approx. number of students in program
- 70

Approx. number of students in each degree program offered
- 100% M.S.

Approx. number of students who apply/are accepted annually by program
- 25 apply/15 accepted

Admissions requirements
- 2.50 GPA

The program has available for qualified students
- Graduate Assistantships
- Other Forms of Financial Aid

Assistantships
- 0% Fellowships
- 4% Research Assistantships
- 0% Teaching Assistantships
- 0% Tuition Waivers
- 0% Other Forms of Financial Aid

Internship possibility
- Yes

SOUTHERN CONNECTICUT ST. UNIVERSITY ...

PROGRAM INFORMATION ...

Internship required for degree completion
- No

Number of hours required for internship
- 150 hours

Description of typical internship experience
- See comments

COMMENTS

The human performance/exercise science program provides the opportunity for in-depth study, practical experience and research. Areas of concentration include sport psychology, exercise physiology, cardiac rehabilitation, fitness testing, and biomechanical analysis. The interested sport psychologist can apply sport psychology theories and ideas in courses such as: exercise psychology, youth and sport, motor learning, adaptations to endurance training, and adult fitness and cardiac rehabilitation. This background will prepare students for advanced study, hospital wellness programs, corporate and commercial fitness centers, community agencies, or other related fields of study. Graduate assistantships are available for qualified applicants. Further information related to curriculum and research assistantships may be obtained by contacting Dr. David Kemler.

SOUTHERN ILLINOIS UNIVERSITY, CARBONDALE

Department of Physical Education
Southern Illinois University
Carbondale, IL 62901

CONTACT PERSON: Elaine Blinde
PHONE NUMBER: (618) 453–3119
FAX NUMBER: (618) 453–3329
E-MAIL ADDRESS: Blinde@SIUCVMB.EDU

FACULTY AND AREA OF INTEREST

Elaine M. Blinde   Gender issues in sport; sport retirement; disability
Sarah McCallister   Drug use in sport; coaching attitudes; teaching effectiveness

PROGRAM INFORMATION

Degree offered
- M.S.

Approx. number of students in program
- 8

Approx. number of students in each degree program offered
- 100% M.S.

Approx. number of students who apply/are accepted annually by program
- 12 apply/4 accepted

Admissions requirements
- GRE
- Three current letters of recommendation
- Undergraduate and graduate transcripts

The program has available for qualified students
- Fellowships
- Research Assistantships
- Teaching Assistantships
- Other Forms of Financial Aid

Internship possibility
- No, a full internship is not available, but practicum experiences in applied sport psychology, working directly with athletes and/or exercisers, are available

Description of typical practicum experience
- Individual and team consultation experiences; independent study practicums; practical experience through applied sport psychology graduate courses.

SOUTHERN ILLINOIS UNIVERSITY, CARBONDALE ...

COMMENTS

A wide range of teaching and research opportunities are available to graduate students through departmental assistantships and faculty grants. Students are provided opportunities to engage in both quantitative and qualitative research projects, as well as teach classes in the applied sport psychology area (e.g., relaxation). In addition to the many courses offered by the Department of Physical Education in the social psychological domain, students are encouraged to take courses in counseling, psychology, and sociology. Excellent relationships have been established with related departments on campus. A sport psychology laboratory provides students with computers, office space, a seminar room, and facilities and equipment for consultation and interviewing.

SOUTHERN ILLINOIS UNIVERSITY, EDWARDSVILLE

Department of Health, Recreation, and Physical Education
Box 1126
Vadalabene Center
Southern Illinois University at Edwardswille
Edwardsville, IL 62026–1126

Program Rating:

1	2	3	4	**5**	6	7
Applied Orientation			Equal Emphasis			Research Orientation

CONTACT PERSON:	Curt L. Lox	Darren C. Treasure
PHONE NUMBER:	(618) 692–5961	(618) 692–2306
FAX NUMBER:	(618) 692–3369	(618) 692–3369
E-MAIL ADDRESS:	clox@siue.edu	dtreasu@siue.edu
WEB SITE:	http://www.siue.edu/HRPE/	

FACULTY AND AREA OF INTEREST

Curt L. Lox — Exercise psychology in special populations, sport psychology, coaching

Darren C. Treasure — Motivation in sport, exercise and physical education

PROGRAM INFORMATION

Degree Offered
• M.S.

Approximate number of students in program
• 10

Approximate number of students who apply/are accepted annually by program
• This is a new program, so information is not currently available

Admissions requirements
Undergraduate GPA of 2.5

Assistantships
% Fellowships
% Research Assistantships
% Teaching Assistantships
% Tuition Waivers
% Other Forms of Financial Aid

Note: Because this is a new program, information is not currently available. However, all of these forms of assistance are available for qualified students.

Internship possibility
• Yes

Internship required for degree completion
• No

Number of hours required for internship
• 3 credit hours

Description of typical internship experience
• Working with university athletic teams. Opportunities also exist for internships in exercise and wellness settings.

COMMENTS

The emphasis of the graduate sport and exercise psychology program is on research and academic sport and exercise psychology. Applied sport psychology issues are included, however, and opportunities exist for an individual to gain experience developing and implementing educational psychological skills programs. Opportunities in exercise psychology settings also exist for those individuals interested in corporate fitness, wellness, and cardiac-rehabilitation.

The specific research interests of Curt Lox are exercise and special populations (e. g. AIDS, African Americans, and the elderly), motivational and affective factors, and mental health. Darren Treasure is examing the social-cognitive antecedents and consequences of motivation in sport, exercise, and physical education (e. g. achievements goals, motivational cllimate).

UNIVERSITY OF SOUTHERN QUEENSLAND

Faculty of Sciences, Department of Psychology
University of Southern Queensland
Toowoomba, Queensland 4350, Australia

Program Rating:

3/4*	2	3	4	5	6	7**

Applied Orientation   Equal Emphasis   Research Orientation

*M.Psych.: 3/4   **M.Phil./Ph.D.: 7

CONTACT PERSONS: Gershon Tenenbaum or Steven Christensen
PHONE NUMBER: 76–311703
FAX NUMBER: 76–312721
E-MAIL ADDRESS: tenenbau@usq.edu.au
WEB SITE: http://www.usq.edu.au/faculty/science/depts/psych/psych.htm

FACULTY AND AREA OF INTEREST

Steven Christensen	Applied issues, decision making, expertise
Gerry Fogarty	Intelligence, applied sport psychology
Grace Pretty	Personal well-being, interpersonal skills, group dynamics related to performance
Jeff Summers	Motor control, skill learning, expertise
Gershon Tenenbaum	Psychometrics, cognitive constructs, motivation-performance linkage, expertise

PROGRAM INFORMATION

Degrees offered
- Master of Psychology (sport)
- Master of Psychology (community & health)
- M.Phil. (by research)
- Ph.D.

Approximate number of students in program
- 20 (10—sport; 10—community and health)

Approximate number of students in each degree program offered
- 70% master's/30% Ph.D.

Approximate number of students who apply/are accepted annually by program
- 27 apply/10 accepted

Admissions requirements
- 3 years plus honours for Australian students
- B.A./B.S. for foreign students
- GPA
- References

Assitantships
- 0% Fellowships
- 0% Research Assistantships
- 0% Teaching Assistantships
- 0% Tuition Waivers
- 0% Other Forms of Financial Aid

165

UNIVERSITY OF SOUTHERN QUEENSLAND ...

PROGRAM INFORMATION ...

Internship possibility
- Yes

Internship required for degree completion
- Yes

Number of hours required for internship
- 1000+

Description of typical internship experience
- Sport psychology practica provide applied sport and personal development services to talented and elite athletes within regional/state institute/national institute programs. Exercise and health psychology practica provide applied health and behaviour change services within community health clinics and corporate health and exercise settings.

SPALDING UNIVERSITY

Department of Psychology
Spalding University
851 S. Fourth
Louisville, KY 40203

Program Rating:

1	2	3	4	5	6	7
Applied Orientation			Equal Emphasis			Research Orientation

CONTACT PERSON: Thomas Titus (Chairman)
PHONE NUMBER: (502) 585–9911
FAX NUMBER: (502) 585–7159
PROGRAM WEB SITE: http://www.spalding.edu/

FACULTY AND AREA OF INTEREST

Thomas Bergandi	Sport psychology
John James	Systems theory
John Kalafat	Crisis intervention, consultation
David Morgan	Learning
Thomas Titus	Learning, addictions
Barbara Williams	Supervision issues

PROGRAM INFORMATION

Degrees offered
- M.A.
- Psy.D.

Approx. number of students in program
- 120

Approx. number of students in each degree program offered
- 20% M.A./80% Psy.D.

Approx. number of students who apply/are accepted annually by program
- 30 M.A. apply/5 M.A. accepted; 400 Psy.D. apply/25 Psy.D. accepted

Admissions requirements
- GRE—minimum for three tests: 1500 (M.A.), 1600 (Psy.D.)
- Three letters of recommendation
- Autobiography
- Professional/academic writing sample
- Personal interview for Psy.D. program

The program has available for qualified students
- Research Assistantships
- Other Forms of Financial Aid

Assistantships
- 0%   Fellowships
- 28%   Research Assistantships
- 0%   Teaching Assistantships
- 5%   Tuition Waivers (scholarships)
- 100%   Other Forms of Financial Aid (student loans)

SPALDING UNIVERSITY ...

PROGRAM INFORMATION ...

Internship possibility
- Yes (may not be in applied sport psychology per se)

Internship required for degree completion
- Yes

Number of hours required for internship
- M.A.—650 hours/Psy.D.—2000 hours

Description of typical internship experience
- Numerous experiences are available for clinical training—i.e., hospitals, outpatient agencies, drug and alcohol agencies, correctional facilities, community mental health centers, etc.

COMMENTS

The M.A. and Psy.D. programs are designed to train clinical psychology practitioners. At present one faculty member (Thomas Bergandi) has a strong research interest in sport psychology and directs the Spalding University Sport Psychology Laboratory. The program is ideally suited for the student who wants to be trained as a clinical psychologist with a side or part-time interest in the field of sport psychology.

SPRINGFIELD COLLEGE

School of Graduate Studies
Springfield College
Springfield, MA 01109

Program Rating:

1	2	3	**4**	5	6	7
Applied Orientation			Equal Emphasis			Research Orientation

CONTACT PERSON: Betty L. Mann
PHONE NUMBER: (413) 748–3125
FAX NUMBER: (413) 748–3745
PROGRAM WEB SITE: http://www.springfieldcollege.edu/

FACULTY AND AREA OF INTEREST

Barbara Jensen	Measurement, statistics, research
Betty L. Mann	Research advisement
Mimi Murray	Sport psychology

PROGRAM INFORMATION

Degrees offered
- M.S.
- D.P.E., specialization in sport psychology

Approx. number of students in program
- 8 M.S.
- 2–3 D.P.E. in sport psychology (expected)

Approx. number of students in each degree program offered
- 80% M.S./20% D.P.E.

Approx. number of students who apply/are accepted annually by program
- M.S. 15–20 apply/8–10 accepted
- D.P.E. 2–3 expected to be accepted into new program

Admissions requirements
- M.S.: GPA, references, applicant's statement of objectives
- D.P.E.: GPA, GRE, references, applicant's statement of objectives

The program has available for qualified students
- Associateships (Fellowships)
- Graduate Assistantships
- Other Forms of Financial Aid

Assistantships
- 20% Fellowships (include all forms of research/teaching assistantships and tuition waivers)
- 0% Research Assistantships
- 0% Teaching Assistantships
- 0% Tuition Waivers
- 0% Other Forms of Financial Aid

Internship possibility
- Sport psychology consulting internship opportunities are available for students in the doctoral program

SPRINGFIELD COLLEGE ...

COMMENTS ...

The sport psychology concentration at the master's level is designed for students who have a scholarly interest in sport psychology and wish to pursue this interest further in doctoral programs of study. The intent of the program is to provide theoretical understanding of sport from a philosophical, sociological, psychological, and physiological perspective, particularly as this knowledge may be practically applied to helping athletes maximize sport performance. A thesis is required for the M.S. degree.

The doctoral concentration in sport psychology has been designed to allow students, upon completion of the degree, to meet the requirements to apply for certification by AAASP. In addition, to theory-based and applied sport psychology course work, a series of seminars are offered that relate to current issues and research trends in the field, including topics such as youth sport, model building, behavioral observation, cohesion/collective efficacy, and motivation. Students will also complete course work in athletic counseling, health psychology, and psychopathology, as well as in related areas of physical education, including motor learning/control and development, exercise physiology, and sociology.

Students in the department are working on a variety of research topics. Some of the current research includes: the relationship of goal orientation to motivation among women golfers; coaching staff cohesion and success of intercollegiate field hockey teams; athletic injury: mood disturbances and hardiness of intercollegiate athletes; A model to examine perception of momentum, desire for control, and performance in sport; life events and depression of injured and noninjured college football players; and depression and life satisfaction level changes pre- and postretirement of collegiate athletes as compared to nonathletes.

SPRINGFIELD COLLEGE

Psychology Department
Springfield College
Springfield, MA 01109

Program Rating:

1	2	3	4 *	5	6	7

Applied Orientation   Equal Emphasis   Research Orientation

*Program offers opportunities to pursue an applied orientation OR a research orientation (as opposed to an equal emphasis on both).

CONTACT PERSON: Al Petitpas
PHONE NUMBER: (413) 748–3325
FAX NUMBER: (413) 748–3854
PROGRAM WEB SITE: http://www.spfldcol.edu/

FACULTY AND AREA OF INTEREST

Britton W. Brewer	Pain and injury in sport and exercise
Delight Champagne	Career development of athletes
Burt Giges	Intervention skills, self-awareness
Al Petitpas	Personal and career development of athletes
Judy L. Van Raalte	Social psychology of sport and exercise (attributions, self-talk)

PROGRAM INFORMATION

Degrees offered
- M.Ed.
- M.S.
- C.A.S.

Approx. number of students in program
- 24

Approx. number of students in each degree program offered
- 75% M.S./25% M.Ed.

Approx. number of students who apply/are accepted annually by program
- 45 apply/12 accepted

Admissions requirements
- Psychology or physical education majors preferred
- Applied experience helpful
- Completed application
- Five letters of support
- Personal statement required

The program has available for qualified students
- Fellowships
- Research Assistantships
- Teaching Assistantships
- Other Forms of Financial Aid

Assistantships
- 8% Fellowships
- 36% Research Assistantships
- 16% Teaching Assistantships

SPRINGFIELD COLLEGE ...

PROGRAM INFORMATION ...

8%   Tuition Waivers

0%   Other Forms of Financial Aid

Internship possibility

- Yes

Internship required for degree completion

- Yes, for all degrees

Number of hours required for internship

- Minimum of 300 hours required

Description of typical internship experience

- Academic/athletic counseling at colleges and universities; sports counseling in sport medicine clinics; career and personal development with athletes in sport agencies; work with college athletic teams.

COMMENTS

The athletic counseling program offers course work in psychology, physical education, and counseling. The primary job market for graduates has been academic athletic counseling positions at major universities. Approximately 25% of graduates go directly into counseling psychology doctoral programs to gain credentials necessary to develop independent practices in counseling with an emphasis in sport psychology.

STAFFORDSHIRE UNIVERSITY

Division of Sport, Health, and Exercise
Staffordshire University
Leek Road
Stoke-on-Trent ST4 2DF, United Kingdom

Program Rating:

1	2	3	4	5 *	6	7
Applied Orientation			Equal Emphasis			Research Orientation

*Program offers opportunities to pursue an applied orientation OR a research orientation (as opposed to an equal emphasis on both).

CONTACT PERSON: Bruce Hale
PHONE NUMBER: (44) 1782–412515
FAX NUMBER: (44) 1782–747167
E-MAIL ADDRESS: SCTBDH@CR41.STAFFS.AC.UK
PROGRAM WEB SITE: http://www.staffs.ac.uk/sands/scis/sport

FACULTY AND AREA OF INTEREST

Basil Ashford	Sport psychology
Kim Buxton	Exercise psychology
Jo Doyle	Sport psychology
John Erskine	Motor learning/control
Nigel Gleeson	Exercise physiology
Bruce Hale	Exercise adherence and addiction, imagery and performance, anxiety and performance, psychophysiology, individual differences
Tom Mercer	Exercise physiology
Jayne Mitchell	Exercise epidemiology, exercise psychology

PROGRAM INFORMATION

Degrees offered
- M.Phil., Ph.D.
- M.S. (Sport Science)

Approx. number of students in program
- 10–20

Approx. number of students in each degree program offered
- 3–4 M.Phil./6–10 M.S./2–3 Ph.D.

Approx. number of students who apply/are accepted annually by program
- 12 accepted

Admissions requirements
- Undergraduate degree
- Marks/grades
- References

The program has available for qualified students
- Research Assistantships
- Teaching Assistantships

Assistantships
0%   Fellowships
25%   Research Assistantships

STAFFORDSHIRE UNIVERSITY ...

PROGRAM INFORMATION ...

0%   Teaching Assistantships
0%   Tuition Waivers
0%   Other Forms of Financial Aid

Internship possibility
- Yes

Internship required for degree completion
- No

Description of typical internship experience
- Work with teams; work in leisure/fitness centers; work in performance center; work with individuals.

COMMENTS

Ph.D. and M.Phil. are research-based, independent courses with no taught courses. Students work on a research dissertation with their advisor, engage in detailed reading and writing, and may be involved in some teaching.

M.S. is a new, multidisciplinary taught course program with coursework in core areas and optional subjects. A research dissertation will be completed by all students. This program will commence for 1996–97.

UNIVERSITY OF STELLENBOSCH

Department of Human Movement Studies
University of Stellenbosch
Private Bag X1
Matieland, Stellenbosch 7602
Republic of South Africa

Program Rating:

1	2	3	4	5	**6**	7

Applied Orientation   Equal Emphasis   Research Orientation

CONTACT PERSON: Justus R. Potgieter
PHONE NUMBER: (27) 21–8084915
FAX NUMBER: (27) 21–8084817
E-MAIL ADDRESS: JRP@MATIES.SUN.AC.ZA

FACULTY AND AREA OF INTEREST

Liz Bressan   Motor learning
Justus R. Potgieter   Performance enhancement, exercise psychology

PROGRAM INFORMATION

Degrees offered
- M. in human movement studies
- Ph.D.

Approx. number of students in program
- 15 part-time

Approx. number of students in each degree program offered
- 66% M.H.S./34% Ph.D.

Approx. number of students who apply/are accepted annually by program
- 10 apply/9 accepted

Admissions requirements
- Recognized honour's degree for master's degree
- Recognized master's degree for Ph.D.

The program has available for qualified students
- Teaching Assistantships (limited)

Assistantships
- 0% Fellowships
- 0% Research Assistantships
- 25% Teaching Assistantships
- 0% Tuition Waivers
- 0% Other Forms of Financial Aid

Internship possibility
- No

COMMENTS

Each student develops his/her own program of study. Emphasis is placed on the research dissertation.

TEMPLE UNIVERSITY

Department of Kinesiology*-(048–00)
Temple University
Philadelphia, PA 19122

Program Rating:

1	2	3	4	**5**	6	7
Applied Orientation			Equal Emphasis			Research Orientation

CONTACT PERSON: Carole A. Oglesby   Michael L. Sachs
PHONE NUMBER: (215) 204–1948   (215) 204–8718
FAX NUMBER: (215) 204–8705   (215) 204–8705
E-MAIL ADDRESS: REDS@ASTRO.TEMPLE.EDU   MSACHS@VM.TEMPLE.EDU
PROGRAM WEB SITE: http://www.temple.edu/HPERD/phys.html

FACULTY AND AREA OF INTEREST

Carole A. Oglesby	Family systems theory, gender and sexuality, psychological skills training
Marcella Ridenour	Perceptual motor, motor development
Michael L. Sachs	Exercise psychology, psychology of running, exercise addiction/dependence, professional and ethical issues
Marianne Torbert	Psychosocial interactions in play

PROGRAM INFORMATION

Degrees offered
- M.S.*
- Ph.D.

*The department expects to change its name from physical education to kinesiology and the master's degree from an M.Ed. to an M.S. during the 1997–98 academic year.

Approx. number of students in program
- 40 (majority are part-time)

Approx. number of students in each degree program offered
- 30% M.S./70% Ph.D.

Approx. number of students who apply/are accepted annually by program
- 25 apply/7 accepted

Admissions requirements
- Undergraduate GPA (2.80 or 3.00 last two years) and MAT or GRE for master's program (GRE for doctoral) required, but specific score not required for standarized tests
- Portfolio approach emphasized, where totality of student's academic, work, life, exercise/sport experiences are considered
- Telephone or personal interview required

The program has available for qualified students
- Fellowships (Universitywide competition)
- Graduate Assistantships
- Research Assistantships

TEMPLE UNIVERSITY ...

PROGRAM INFORMATION ...

Assistantships:
- 0% Fellowships
- 0% Research Assistantships
- 16% Teaching Assistantships (includes tuition waivers)
- 0% Tuition Waivers
- 0% Other Forms of Financial Aid

Internship possibility
- Yes

Internship required for degree completion
- Yes, for the doctoral degree; optional for the master's degree

Number of hours required for internship
- At least 3 credit hours, usually 6 credit hours

Description of typical internship experience
- Quite varied and typically developed by the student—can range from work with individuals or teams, from youth to Olympic-level competitors, in exercise/wellness and sport psychology settings.

COMMENTS

Each student develops a personal program of study to the extent possible. There are some specific course requirements (especially at the doctoral level, where a core set of courses is required). The internship is "required" for each student's program of study at the doctoral level, and often is taken by students at the master's level as well. Each student assists in selecting/obtaining an internship site. Students have worked, for example, at the Velodrome in Allentown, PA; with two gymnastics schools in PA and NJ; at a local tennis center; with national-level triathletes and swimmers; and with varsity teams at area colleges and Temple's fencing, field hockey, football, lacrosse, basketball, softball, volleyball, and tennis teams. There is also a research/discussion group—the Exercise and Sport Psychology (ESP) Laboratory. The group meets occasionally and has put on programs to advance public information about sport psychology (such as work at the Penn Relays) as well as critique members' research efforts through help in preparing for upcoming conference presentations and providing a sounding board for research ideas. The graduate program attempts to offer students as much flexibility as possible in meeting their goals for graduate study.

The graduate students are diverse in age, racial/cultural background, experience (athletic training, social work, counseling psychology, coaching, etc.), providing an enriching experience for students and faculty. The program has had an international flavor over the years, with students (some currently in program) from Australia, England, India, Indonesia, Israel, Greece, and several Caribbean nations. Temple University and Philadelphia provide an exciting experience for those who choose the Temple challenge!

UNIVERSITY OF TENNESSEE, KNOXVILLE

Cultural Studies Unit
1914 Andy Holt Avenue
University of Tennessee
Knoxville, TN 37996–2700

Program Rating:

1	2	3	**4**	5	6	7
Applied Orientation			Equal Emphasis			Research Orientation

CONTACT PERSON: Craig A. Wrisberg
PHONE NUMBER: (423) 974–1283
FAX NUMBER: (423) 974–8981
E-MAIL ADDRESS: wrisberg@utkux.utcc.utk.edu
PROGRAM WEB SITE: http://www.coe.utk.edu/units/cultural.html

FACULTY AND AREA OF INTEREST

Patricia A. Beitel — Performance enhancement through motivation, goal setting, cognitive intervention, practice conditions, and augmented feedback; social-psychological considerations of cohesion, leader behavior, gender, and multiculturalism

Joy DeSensi — Sociocultural aspects of gender, race, ethnicity, and multiculturalism in sport; leadership and ethics in sport management

Craig Wrisberg — Performance enhancement, learning strategies, effects of augmented information, sources of stress, quality of life of athletes

PROGRAM INFORMATION

Degrees offered
- M.S.
- Ph.D.

Approx. number of students in program
- 12–15

Approx. number of students in each degree program offered
- 60% M.S./40% Ph.D.

Approx. number of students who apply/are accepted annually by program
- 40–50 apply/20–25 accepted (all accepted do not receive financial support and, therefore, some do not enroll)

Admissions requirements
- M.S.: minimum 3.00 undergraduate GPA
- Ph.D.: minimum 3.00 undergraduate and graduate GPA
- Minimum 1000 GRE (sum of two highest areas)
- Both graduate degree levels require writing sample and a specified number of recommendations from professionals

The program has available for qualified students
- Graduate Assistantships in sport psychology (doctoral students only)
- Research Assistantships (only when faculty have grant money)
- Teaching Assistantships

UNIVERSITY OF TENNESSEE, KNOXVILLE ...

PROGRAM INFORMATION ...

Assistantships

- 0%   Fellowships
- 0%   Research Assistantships
- 25%   Teaching Assistantships
- 33%   Tuition Waivers
- 15%   Other Forms of Financial Aid

Internship possibility

- Yes

Internship required for degree completion

- Sometimes. The student's committee determines the specific requirements based on the student's past and present experiences and on the student's outcome objectives.

Number of hours required for internship

- 15 credit hours are possible, plus additional independent work and/or research

Description of typical internship experience

- Working with teams and/or individual athletes.

COMMENTS

Degree programs are individually tailored as much as possible to the career goals of students. Support for the program is also provided by faculty from programs in clinical and counseling psychology, and from personnel associated with the Department of Intercollegiate Athletics. While the primary emphasis is on performance enhancement, a strong interest in and commitment to research and scholarly activity is an expectation of all students. As part of a cultural studies unit, faculty and students in sport psychology are also concerned about the impact of factors such as gender, race, sexual orientation, class, and power on sport participants.

Students are exposed to both quantitative and qualitative research methods and are encouraged to participate in projects using each form of analysis. The focus of faculty research in recent years has included the following topics: the relationship of life stress and recovery processes to the performance of athletes; the quality of life of intercollegiate athletes; the effect of performance reminders on subsequent sport performance; and athletes' perceptions of and preferences for different coach communication styles.

THE UNIVERSITY OF TEXAS, AUSTIN

Department of Kinesiology and Health Education
Bellmont Hall 222
The University of Texas
Austin, TX 78712

Program Rating:

1	2	3	4	5	**6**	7
Applied Orientation			Equal Emphasis		Research Orientation	

CONTACT PERSON: John B. Bartholomew
PHONE NUMBER: (512) 471–4407
FAX NUMBER: (512) 471–0946
E-MAIL ADDRESS: john.bart@mail.utexas.edu

FACULTY AND AREA OF INTEREST

John B. Bartholomew   Exercise and health psychology, stress reactivity, mood effects of aerobic and resistance exercise

PROGRAM INFORMATION

Degree Offered
- M.A.
- M.Ed.

Approximate number of students in program; approximate number of students who apply/are accepted annually by program
- The specialization in psychology was only recently approved at the time of publication, so no normative data are available on enrollment.

Admissions requirements
- Minimum undergraduate GPA of 3.0 (last two years)
- GRE of 1000

Assistantships:
0% Fellowships
0% Research Assistantships
0% Teaching Assistantships
0% Tuition Waivers
0% Other Forms of Financial Aid
- The specialization in psychology was only recently approved at the time of publication, so no normative data are available on enrollment.

Internship possibility
- Yes, but there is no formal placement program

Internship required for degree completion
- No

THE UNIVERSITY OF TEXAS, AUSTIN ...

COMMENTS

The University of Texas at Austin offers an M.A. and an M.Ed. in kinesiology with an area specialization in sport and exercise psychology. The program is primarily focused on research, and the student is strongly encouraged to seek out collaborative experiences both within the department (e.g., exercise physiology, health behavior, physical development and aging) as well as outside the department (e.g., psychology and educational psychology). As a result, students develop their own program from a psychophysiological, developmental, social-psychological, or health behavior perspective as it best fits their research interests.

TEXAS CHRISTIAN UNIVERSITY

Department of Kinesiology and Physical Education
TCU Box 297730
Texas Christian University
Fort Worth, TX 76129

Program Rating:

1	2	3	**4**	5	6	7
Applied Orientation			Equal Emphasis			Research Orientation

CONTACT PERSON: Gloria B. Solomon
PHONE NUMBER: (817) 921-7665 (ext. 6871)
FAX NUMBER: (817) 921-7702
E-MAIL ADDRESS: G.SOLOMON@TCU.EDU
PROGRAM WEB SITE: http://www.tcu.edu/

FACULTY AND AREA OF INTEREST

Gloria B. Solomon   Sociomoral development, coaching education, youth sport

PROGRAM INFORMATION

Degree Offered
- M.S.

Approximate number of students in program
- 5

Admissions requirements
- Undergraduate GPA of 2.80
- GRE
- Two Letters of recommendation
- Purpose/goal statement

Assistantships
- 0% Fellowships
- 20% Research Assistantships
- 20% Teaching Assistantships
- 100% Tuition Waivers (all assistantships come with tuition waivers)
- 60% Other Forms of Financial Aid (graduate coaching assistantships)

Internship possibility
- Yes

Internship required for degree completion
- No

Number of hours required for internship
- 3 credit hours

Description of typical internship experience
- An internship might consist of serving as a consultant with campus athletic teams with supervision and specialized training. Other internship opportunities include teaching elementary physical education in a lab school focusing on sociomoral skill development.

TEXAS CHRISTIAN UNIVERSITY ...

COMMENTS

This is a new program which offers a master's degree in kinesiology and physical education. It includes broad-based course work in kinesiology with an emphasis in sport psychology. Opportunities for internships are being created and will be available for second-year master's-level students.

The program of study for each student is personalized to meet professional interests and build on academic limitations. If coming from an exercise science background, students are offered more course work in psychology. If coming from a psychology background, more courses in the exercise sciences are included. There is a new sport psychology lab which offers opportunities to engage in ongoing research projects. The graduate students are diverse in age and background. Approximately 50% are planning to pursue doctoral-level work.

TEXAS CHRISTIAN UNIVERSITY

Department of Psychology
Texas Christian University
TCU Station
Fort Worth, TX 76129

CONTACT PERSON: Richard Fenker
PHONE NUMBER: (817) 921–7410
E-MAIL ADDRESS: rp131ps@tcuamus.bitnet

FACULTY AND AREA OF INTEREST

Richard Fenker   Peak performance, States of consciousness

PROGRAM INFORMATION

Degree offered
- Ph.D.

Approx. number of students in program
- 34 (in experimental psychology Ph.D. program)

Approx. number of students in each degree program offered
- 100% Ph.D.

Approx. number of students who apply/are accepted annually by program
- 28 apply/12 accepted

Admissions requirements
- B.S., B.A., or M.S. in psychology or related area

The program has available for qualified students
- Fellowships
- Research Assistantships
- Teaching Assistantships

Internship possibility
- Yes

Internship required for degree completion
- Yes

Number of hours required for internship
- 100 hours experience requirement

Description of typical internship experience
- Applied work or research with high school or college teams under supervision of Dr. Fenker.

COMMENTS

The Ph.D. program in experimental psychology offers sport psychology as a subject area for concentrated study and research. All students interested in the sport psychology program must be enrolled in one of the department's major areas and complete all the degree requirements of the major area and the department. The internship encompasses 100 hours of supervised experience conducting research or research applications in a sport environment (with athletes, a team, coaches, etc.). Students are expected to meet the academic requirements for AAASP certification with their course work in psychology or physical education.

TEXAS TECH UNIVERSITY

Health, Physical Education, and Recreation
P.O. Box 43011
Texas Tech University
Lubbock, TX 79409–3011

Program Rating:

1	2	3	4	5	**6**	7
Applied Orientation			Equal Emphasis			Research Orientation

CONTACT PERSON: Carl Hayashi
PHONE NUMBER: (806) 742–3371
FAX NUMBER: (806) 742–1688
E-MAIL ADDRESS: UNHAY@TTACS.TTU.EDU
PROGRAM WEB SITE: http://www.ttu.edu/~hper/

FACULTY AND AREA OF INTEREST

Carl Hayashi   Social psychology of sport and exercise

PROGRAM INFORMATION

Degrees offered
  - M.S.
  - Ed.D. (interdisciplinary through the College of Education)

Approx. number of students in program
  - 10

Approx. number of students in each degree program offered
  - 100% M.S.

Admissions requirements
  - Must take GRE; sliding scale is applied using GRE score and last 60 hours GPA

The program has available for qualified students
  - Research Assistantships
  - Teaching Assistantships
  - Other Forms of Financial Aid

Assistantships
   0% Fellowships
  10% Research Assistantships
  50% Teaching Assistantships
  50% Tuition Waivers
  50% Other Forms of Financial Aid

Internship possibility
  - Yes

Internship required for degree completion
  - No

Number of hours required for internship
  - Three-hour course requiring 120 hours of contact on site

Description of typical internship experience
  - Athletes from various teams within the university routinely receive training in psychological skills. Internship possibilities are available with these athletes.

TEXAS TECH UNIVERSITY ...

COMMENTS

An interdisciplinary area of emphasis in applied sport psychology is available within the M.S. program and within the Ed.D. degree through the College of Education. It is designed on an individual basis according to the student's background and career goals. Courses in physical education, psychology, educational and counseling psychology may typically be included in the area of emphasis.

UTAH STATE UNIVERSITY

**Department of Health,
Physical Education, and Recreation
Utah State University
Logan, UT 84322–7000**

Program Rating:

1	2	**3**	4	5	6	7

Applied Orientation   Equal Emphasis   Research Orientation

CONTACT PERSON: Richard Gordin
PHONE NUMBER: (435) 797–1506
FAX NUMBER: (435) 797–3759
E-MAIL ADDRESS: gordin@cc.usu.edu

FACULTY AND AREA OF INTEREST

Richard Gordin   Intervention/performance enhancement

PROGRAM INFORMATION

Degree offered
- M.S.

Approx. number of students in program
- 2–5

Approx. number of students in each degree program offered
- 100% M.S.

Approx. number of students who apply/are accepted annually by program
- 2–5 apply/2 accepted

Admissions requirements
- 3.00 GPA (undergraduate)
- 43 MAT or minimum of 40% percentile on GRE
- Three strong letters of recommendation

The program has available for qualified students
- Research Assistantships
- Teaching Assistantships

Assistantships
- 0% Fellowships
- 50% Research Assistantships
- 50% Teaching Assistantships
- 0% Tuition Waivers
- 0% Other Forms of Financial Aid

Internship possibility
- Yes

Internship required for degree completion
- No

UTAH STATE UNIVERSITY ...

PROGRAM INFORMATION ...

Number of hours required for internship
* Depends on opportunity, however we will attempt to amass the 400 hours required for AAASP certification

Description of typical internship experience
* The student will usually interact with an athlete or team either in a consulting relationship under the guidance of a certified consultant or will interact with the teams while collecting data for the thesis. The area of emphasis in research is usually intervention/performance enhancement. This is an applied program.

UNIVERSITY OF UTAH

Exercise and Sport Science Department
University of Utah
Salt Lake City, UT 84112

CONTACT PERSON: Evelyn Hall
PHONE NUMBER: (801) 581–7646
FAX NUMBER: (801) 581–5580
E-MAIL ADDRESS: EHall@deans.health.utah.edu

FACULTY AND AREA OF INTEREST

Evelyn Hall   Performance enhancement
Keith Henschen   Performance enhancement
Barry Shultz   Motor learning

PROGRAM INFORMATION

Degrees offered
- M.S.
- Ph.D.

Approx. number of students in program
- 20

Approx. number of students in each degree program offered
- 50% M.S./50% Ph.D.

Approx. number of students who apply/are accepted annually by program
- 30 apply/10 accepted

Admissions requirements
- M.S.: 3.00 GPA
- Two letters of reference
- Ph.D.: 3.30 GPA
- 51 on MAT or 1000 GRE
- Three letters of recommendation

The program has available for qualified students
- Fellowships
- Teaching Assistantships

Internship possibility
- Yes

Internship required for degree completion
- Yes, for the Ph.D. degree

Number of hours required for internship
- 10 quarter hours

VICTORIA UNIVERSITY OF TECHNOLOGY

Department of Human Movement, Recreation, and Performance
Flinders Street Campus
P.O. Box 14428
Melbourne Mail Centre, Melbourne
Victoria 8001, Australia

Program Rating: This program offers the opportunity to pursue an applied orientation OR a research orientation (as opposed to an equal emphasis on both). The M.A.P is an applied program and the M.A.S and Ph.D. are research oriented.

CONTACT PERSON:	Vance Tammen (M.A.P.)	Mark Andersen (Ph.D./M.A.S.)
PHONE NUMBER:	61 3 9248 1131	61 3 9248 1132
FAX NUMBER:	61 3 9248 1124	61 3 9248 1124
E-MAIL ADDRESS:	vancet@dingo.vut.edu.au	marka@dingo.vut.edu.au
PROGRAM WEB SITE:	http://www.vut.edu.au/	

FACULTY AND AREA OF INTEREST

Mark Andersen	Counselling, PST, injuries, supervision and training
Vanda Fortunato	Career transitions, counselling, sexuality
Daryl Marchant	Anxiety, PST, counselling
Tony Morris	PST, transitions, motivation, counselling
Terry Seedsman	Development, gerontology, exercise benefits
Jeffery Simons	PST (Director of Sport Psychology Services)
Vance Tammen	Achievement motivation, PST, children, crises

PROGRAM INFORMATION

Degrees offered
- M.A.P. (master of applied psychology) by course work
- M.A.S. (master of applied science) by research
- Ph.D. by research

Approx. number of students in program
- 12 M.A.P./30 M.A.S./Ph.D.

Approx. number of students in each degree program offered
- 28.5% M.A.P./71.5% M.A.S./Ph.D.

Approx. number of students who apply/are accepted annually by program
- 25 apply/12 accepted

Admissions requirements
- M.A.P.: 4 years of A.P.S. Accredited Psychology (Australian Psychological Society-national equivalents should be accepted, e.g., APA, BPS)
- M.A.S.: Undergraduate degree in any relevant area (M.A.S. candidates can transfer to Ph.D. subject to satisfactory progress—usually first study successfully completed)
- Ph.D.: Undergraduate degree and honours year or equivalent

The program has available for qualified students*
- Research Assistantships
- Teaching Assistantships
- Other Forms of Financial Aid

VICTORIA UNIVERSITY OF TECHNOLOGY ...

PROGRAM INFORMATION ...

Assistantships

- 20%   Fellowships/Scholarships
- 0%   Research Assistantships
- 10%   Teaching Assistantships
- 25–40%   Tuition Waivers (Approximately 25% of M.A.S students and 40% of Ph.D. students receive tuition waivers)
- 0%   Other Forms of Financial Aid

Internship possibility

- Yes

Internship required for degree completion

- Yes, for M.A.P. only; not required for M.A.S. or Ph.D.

Number of hours required for internship

- Approximately 1000 hours total, spread over several practica/internships

Description of typical internship experience

- Students are required to complete one general practicum not in sport psychology. These are very varied (potentially, at least), and one or *more* practica in sport psychology. The latter are also potentially varied, including work in our own clinic; work with private practitioners; work at the Australian Institute of Sport; the Victorian Institute of Sport; and other state institutions; work in sports clubs or with teams; work in exercise settings such as rehabilitation centres and sports medicine clinics.

*Only available for Ph.D. and M.A.S. Research students, and are rather limited, but plans for further opportunities are in development

COMMENTS

Master of Applied Psychology

This is a program offered in conjunction with the Department of Psychology (by Physical Education) to assure accreditation within the new Australian system for accrediting sport psychology professional training courses. It is one of only four such programs in Australia. The program consists of a core of professional skills in psychology, taught with specialists in other areas and including assessment, ethical issues, research methods, counselling practice, health and organisational psychology. Four specialist subjects in sport psychology cover theory, applications, practice issues, and practice organisation. In addition, there is the practicum and a substantial thesis on an applied topic. The thesis topic is largely up to the student to select, provided it has an applied focus. Students are also free to negotiate their own practicum placements, but help is available if needed.

Doctoral/Master's Research Program

The only required course work for research students in Australia, at V.U.T. at least, is

COMMENTS ...

a research design course (exception if equivalent can be demonstrated). Students may choose or be advised to sit subjects relevant to their research/career aims if not experienced in those areas. Students work closely with a principal supervisor, backed up by the sport psych team and a range of other specialists. They select and develop their own research areas under guidance. The department has a vast network of local and national connections in all aspects of sport to offer opportunities for field experiences and research. A sport psychology research group offers opportunities to communicate research plans, results, and conclusions in a friendly atmosphere, and to hear and discuss the ideas of staff and other research students for projects and on each other's work. This also offers good practice for conference presentations. There are also area-specific research groups on such issues as imagery, career transitions, motivation, and sports injuries, where sufficient staff and student research interest is focused.

UNIVERSITY OF VIRGINIA

Department of Human Services—Health and Physical Education
201 Memorial Gymnasium
University of Virginia
Charlottesville, VA 22903

Program Rating:

1	2	3	4	5	**6**	7
Applied Orientation			Equal Emphasis			Research Orientation

CONTACT PERSON: Maureen Weiss
PHONE NUMBER: (804) 924–7860
FAX NUMBER: (804) 924–1389
E-MAIL ADDRESS: mrw5d@curry.edschool.virginia.edu
PROGRAM WEB SITE: http://www.curry.edschool.virginia.edu/

FACULTY AND AREA OF INTEREST

Linda K. Bunker	Motor learning, youth sport, women in sport
Bruce Gansneder	Research design/statistics
Maureen R. Weiss	Developmental issues, self-perceptions, motivation, modeling, moral development

PROGRAM INFORMATION

Degrees offered
- M.Ed.
- Ed.D.
- Ph.D.

Approx. number of students in program
- 12

Approx. number of students in each degree program offered
- 75% M.Ed./25% Ed.D./Ph.D.

Approx. number of students who apply/are accepted annually by program
- 30 M.Ed. apply/5 M.Ed. accepted
- 20 Ed.D./Ph.D. apply/2 Ed.D./Ph.D. accepted

Admissions requirements
- Minimum 1500 on 3 GRE scores, 1000 on 2 GRE scores
- 3.00 GPA
- Two letters of recommendation
- Admissions decisions made by April 1 for fall
- Fall admissions only

The program has available for qualified students
- Fellowships
- Research Assistantships
- Teaching Assistantships
- Other Forms of Financial Aid

Internship possibility
- Yes

UNIVERSITY OF VIRGINIA ...

PROGRAM INFORMATION ...

Internship required for degree completion
- No

Number of hours required for internship
- Three to nine credit hours

Description of typical internship experience
- University of Virginia Athletic Department; other state colleges and universities; high schools or youth organizations; other sites possible.

COMMENTS

The area of sport and exercise psychology addresses the social influences and individual factors related to participation and performance. Two major categories of questions comprise the focus of this field: (a) How does participation in sport and exercise contribute to the personal development of participants? and (b) How do psychological factors influence participation and performance in sport and exercise? The first category includes topics such as self-esteem, character development, intrinsic motivation, and ability to cope with anxiety and stress. Topics under the second category include social support, motivation, self-confidence, and methods such as goal setting, arousal control, and mental imagery.

The research program will specialize in "developmental sport and exercise psychology," an area that that investigates age-related patterns in social and psychological factors related to participation in physical activity across the lifespan. Central topics will include determinants of self-esteem (i.e., perceptions of competence, social factors), motivational factors related to participation and performance (i.e., contextual and individual factors), and social influences on participation and performance (i.e., parents, peers, coaches). The applied aspect of the program entails opportunities for translating theory and practice to a variety of practical settings such as athletics, exercise and fitness management, sport management, and youth organizations.

The sport and exercise psychology program is committed to providing graduate students with the knowledge, skills, and experiences that will prepare them with the theoretical and practical background to be marketable for desired careers in athletics, health, or fitness, or for continued graduate training. Students who pursue a terminal master's degree will be prepared for positions as teachers, coaches, or professionals in fitness or athletic clubs. Students will also be well prepared to go on to Ph.D. programs to pursue research and teaching careers in higher education. Students in the doctoral program will be excellently prepared for careers in academe through their study of the breadth and depth of the field, as well as through ample opportunities to engage in research, teaching, mentoring students, collaborating in grant writing, and professional service activities.

VIRGINIA COMMONWEALTH UNIVERSITY

Department of Psychology
Box 2018
Virginia Commonwealth University
Richmond, VA 23284

Program Rating:

1	2	3	4	**5**	6	7
Applied Orientation			Equal Emphasis			Research Orientation

CONTACT PERSON: Steven J. Danish
PHONE NUMBER: (804) 828–4384
FAX NUMBER: (804) 828–0239
E-MAIL: sdanish@saturn.vcu.edu

FACULTY AND AREA OF INTEREST

Steven J. Danish   Life skills, youth sports, performance enhancement

PROGRAM INFORMATION

Degree offered
- Ph.D.

Approx. number of students in program
- 4 sport psychology (total of 150 graduate students in psychology, with 35 graduate students in counseling psychology)

Approx. number of students in each degree program offered
- 100% Ph.D.

Approx. number of students who apply/are accepted annually by program
- 240 apply/8 accepted (counseling psychology program)

Admissions requirements
- There are no minimum GRE or GPA scores
- Interested applicants are sent profiles of typical students accepted
- Because admissions is so competitive, GRE scores, GPA scores, human services and research experiences, the number of psychology courses taken, and references rank as important criteria

The program has available for qualified students
- Fellowships
- Research Assistantships
- Teaching Assistantships
- Other Forms of Financial Aid

Assistantships (during the first three years)
- 10%   Fellowships
- 30%   Research Assistantships
- 60%   Teaching Assistantships
- 0%   Tuition Waivers
- 0%   Other Forms of Financial Aid

VIRGINIA COMMONWEALTH UNIVERSITY ...

PROGRAM INFORMATION ...

Internship possibility (paid)
- Yes

Internship required for degree completion
- Yes

Number of hours required for internship
- 2000 hours required (APA-approved program)

Description of typical internship experience
- Internships in psychology are not done on campus and are a competitive process in themselves. They have nothing to do with sport psychology. Assistantships may have opportunities associated with one of the life skills and youth sport programs doing research/training.

COMMENTS

There are no formal courses in sport psychology within the department or the counseling program. The focus of the training and research opportunities is with children and adolescents through the Life Skills Center directed by Dr. Danish. Some of the center programs use sport as a metaphor for teaching life skills; other programs use sport as a vehicle to teach life skills. Sport psychology within the program is defined very broadly—it involves the use of sport to enhance competence and promote human development throughout the life span. Given this definition, sport psychologists are as concerned about life development as they are about athletic development.

VIRGINIA TECH UNIVERSITY

Department of Teaching and Learning
War Memorial Gymnasium
Virginia Polytechnic Institute and State University
Blacksburg, VA 24061–0313

Program Rating:

1	2	3	4	**5**	6	7
Applied Orientation			Equal Emphasis			Research Orientation

CONTACT PERSON: Richard Stratton (Department Head)
PHONE NUMBER: (540) 231–5617
FAX NUMBER: (540) 231–9075
E-MAIL ADDRESS: rstratto@VT.EDU
PROGRAM WEB SITE: http://www.chre.vt.edu/coe/COE_admin/programs/hpe/hpe_p.html

FACULTY AND AREA OF INTEREST

Richard Stratton   Motivation/stress in youth sports

PROGRAM INFORMATION

Degree offered
- M.S.

Approx. number of students in program
- 2

Approx. number of students in each degree program offered
- 100% M.S.

Admissions requirements
- Undergraduate degree
- 2.75 minimum GPA

The program has available for qualified students
- Fellowships
- Teaching Assistantships
- Other Forms of Financial Aid (tuition waivers)

Assistantships
- 0%   Fellowships
- 0%   Research Assistantships
- 0%   Teaching Assistantships
- 0%   Tuition Waivers
- 0%   Other Forms of Financial Aid

Internship possibility
- Yes

Internship required for degree completion
- No

Number of hours required for internship
- Varies for each student

Description of typical internship experience
- Varies; most students elect not to do internships

197

VIRGINIA TECH UNIVERSITY ...

COMMENTS

No new students are currently being admitted to our program. Status will be reviewed in late 1997–98 to determine whether to reopen the program. Please check with Dr. Stratton for further information.

UNIVERSITY OF WASHINGTON

Department of Psychology
Box 351525
University of Washington
Seattle, WA 98195–1525

Program Rating:

1	2	3	4	**5**	6	7
Applied Orientation			Equal Emphasis			Research Orientation

CONTACT PERSON: Graduate Program Assistant, Graduate Studies Office
PHONE NUMBER: (206) 543–8687
FAX NUMBER: (206) 685–3157
E-MAIL: dormont@u.washington.edu
PROGRAM WEB SITE: http://weber.u.washington.edu/~psychol/

FACULTY AND AREA OF INTEREST

David Coppel	Clinical sport psychology
Beth Kerr	Motor learning
Ronald E. Smith	Stress and coping, psychological skills training, coaching behaviors
Frank L. Smoll	Coaching behaviors, coach/parent interventions

PROGRAM INFORMATION

Degree offered
- Ph.D.

Approx. number of students in program
- 3

Approx. number of students in each degree program offered
- 100% Ph.D.

Approx. number of students who apply/are accepted annually by program
- 10 (500 to clinical) apply/1 (6–8 clinical) accepted

Admissions requirements
- Realistically, GRE (verbal + quantitative) of 1250 needed
- 3.50 GPA
- Research interest and experience highly desirable, given the scientist-practitioner emphasis of the program
- Master's-level training in sport sciences also desirable

The program has available for qualified students
- Fellowships
- Research Assistantships
- Teaching Assistantships
- All students admitted receive financial support

Assistantships
- 0% Fellowships
- 50% Research Assistantships
- 50% Teaching Assistantships
- 100% Tuition Waivers
- 0% Other Forms of Financial Aid

UNIVERSITY OF WASHINGTON ...

PROGRAM INFORMATION ...

Internship possibility
- Yes

Internship required for degree completion
- No

Number of hours required for internship
- Undetermined

Description of typical internship experience
- Paid assistantships and practicum experiences available in Athletic Department, working with University of Washington athletes. Other experiences can be arranged, depending on student's interests. Clinical/counseling experiences available at the Psychology Clinic and other local sites.

COMMENTS

Sport psychology examines the application of psychological theory, research methods, and intervention techniques in the realms of sport and physical activity. It includes the study of cognitive, emotional, and social factors influencing individual and group performance. Sport psychology is a minor area of study within the doctoral program in clinical psychology, and is usually pursued in conjunction with a major in clinical psychology. However, students in other programs (e.g., social, personality, developmental, cognitive) may elect to minor in sport psychology. Dr. Smith is a member of both the clinical and social-personality faculties and accepts students into both areas.

The clinical sport psychology program is based on a strong scientist-practitioner training model, with an emphasis on producing individuals who will make substantial contributions to the field. The program is unusual in its degree of flexibility and its explicit reliance on a competency-based mode of training and evaluation. This permits students to specialize and focus their competency development a great deal. Provisions for research and intervention activities in sport-related areas are included. Among the advantages of this model of training are the balance of academic, research, and clinical training, and the preparation of graduates for psychology licensure.

Drs. Smith and Smoll are core faculty members in sport psychology. Beth Kerr also teaches courses that are part of the curriculum. An adjunct faculty member is Dr. David Coppel, who works as a clinical sport psychologist in the private sector and consults to several professional sport teams.

UNIVERSITY OF WATERLOO

Department of Kinesiology
University of Waterloo
Waterloo, Ontario,
Canada N2L 3GI

Program Rating:

1	2	3	**4**	5	6	7
Applied Orientation			Equal Emphasis			Research Orientation

CONTACT PERSON:	L. R. Brawley
PHONE NUMBER:	(519) 885–1211 ext. 3153
FAX NUMBER:	(519) 746–6776
E-MAIL ADDRESS:	lrbrawle@healthy.uwaterloo.ca
PROGRAM WEB SITE:	http://www.ahs.uwaterloo.ca/kin/kinhome.html

FACULTY AND AREA OF INTEREST

F. Allard	Cognitive factors in movement performance, expert/novice differences
L.R. Brawley	Applied social psychology, sport psychology, group cohesion, collective efficacy, self-efficacy, attitude change, health and exercise in normal and diseased populations.
K. DuCharme*	Motivation, goal setting, self-efficacy, adherence in exercise, health, and sport
W. Neil Widmeyer*	Group cohesion, group dynamics, collective efficacy, aggression in sport, team building in groups

*Adjunct Faculty

PROGRAM INFORMATION

Degrees offered
- M.Sc.
- Ph.D.

Approx. number of students currently in program
- 14 full- and part-time in psychomotor behavior/social psychology
- Five of these students are supervised by faculty listed above

Approx. number of students in each degree program offered
- 45% M.Sc./55% Ph.D.

Approx. number of students who apply/are accepted annually by program
- M. Sc.: 36 apply/10 accepted
- Ph.D.: 16 apply/7 accepted

Admissions requirements
- Minimum B+ average in undergraduate (for M.S.) or graduate (Ph.D.) work
- Three letters of reference
- Copy of recent term paper (M.S.) or master's thesis (Ph.D.)
- Letter explaining interest in graduate program
- GRE scores (verbal, quantitative, analytical)

The program has available for qualified students
- Research Assistantships
- Teaching Assistantships

UNIVERSITY OF WATERLOO ....

PROGRAM INFORMATION ....

- Other Forms of Financial Aid

Assistantships

- 50% Fellowships (from major granting agencies only)
- 100% Research Assistantships
- 100% Teaching Assistantships
- N/A Tuition Waivers
- 75% Other Forms of Financial Aid

Note: These percentages apply only to full-time students studying social and sport psychology.

Internship possibility

- Yes, for Ph.D. only

Internship required for degree completion

- No

Number of hours required for internship

- Dependent on internship available

Description of typical internship experience

- Specific to Ph.D. program developed and is appropriate to needs of Ph.D. student.

COMMENTS

Sport psychology interests can be satisfied through the area in kinesiology called psychomotor behavior. Sport psychology is offered at the M.Sc. and Ph.D. levels in psychomotor behavior, which divides into three areas: (1) psychological and social psychological approaches to examining motor behavior, health, exercise, and rehabilitation, (2) motor control, and (3) motor learning and skill acquisition. Applicants with sport psychology interests apply in the first area in Psychomotor Behavior. Students can undertake problems incorporating interventions, but these must be examined in a research framework. For example, a problem must include a treatment and control group to examine intervention effects. International authorities in psychology at Waterloo include Donald Meichenbaum (adjunct faculty in clinical psychology) and Mark Zanna (attitudes).

The kinesiology program emphasizes a range of basic and applied research problems of human movement, including topics in sport, health, exercise, ergonomics, rehabilitation, and leisure. The student whose sport psychology interests are health related will find close ties between the Department of Kinesiology and Department of Health Studies and Gerontology. Dr. Brawley is a cross-appointed professor to both departments, which the faculty of applied health science as their home.

Dr. Brawley is a past president of AAASP, and on the editorial boards of the *Journal of Sport and Exercise Psychology* and the *Journal of Applied Sport Psychology*. He is currently the associate chair of graduate studies for the Department of Kinesiology.

All Ph.D. graduates of the program in the last five years have been placed in faculty positions in universities in Canada and the U.S.A.

WAYNE STATE UNIVERSITY

Division of Health, Physical Education, and Recreation
Matthaei Building
Wayne State University
Detroit, MI 48202

Program Rating:

1	2	3	4	5	6	**7**
Applied Orientation			Equal Emphasis			Research Orientation

CONTACT PERSON: Jeff Martin
PHONE NUMBER: (313) 577–1381
FAX NUMBER: (313) 577–5999
E-MAIL ADDRESS: jeff_martin@mts.cc.wayne.edu

FACULTY AND AREA OF INTEREST

Jeffrey J. Martin — Exercise and sport psychology, motivation, self-efficacy, disability sport

PROGRAM INFORMATION

Degree offered
- M.Ed.

Approx. number of students in program
- < 10 (almost all part-time)

Approx. number of students in each degree program offered
- 100% M.Ed.

Approx. number of students who apply/are accepted annually by program
- This is a new program

Admissions requirements
- Regular admisssion—3.00 GPA
- Degree in related area
- GRE
- Qualified admission-write for details

The program has available for qualified students (all on a competitive basis)
- Fellowships
- Research Assistantships
- Teaching Assistantships
- Other Forms of Financial Aid

Assistantships
- 0% Fellowships
- 5–10% Research Assistantships
- 5-10% Teaching Assistantships
- 0% Tuition Waivers
- 0% Other Forms of Financial Aid

Internship possibility
- Yes

WAYNE STATE UNIVERSITY ...

PROGRAM INFORMATION ...

Internship required for degree completion
- No

Number of hours required for internship
- 3 credits

Description of typical internship experience
- New program.

COMMENTS

We focus on "academic" sport psychology rather than on "applied" sport psychology.

UNIVERSITY OF WESTERN AUSTRALIA

Sport Psychology Laboratory
Department of Human Movement
The University of Western Australia
Nedlands, Western Australia
Australia 6907

Program Rating:

1	2	3	**4**	5	6	7
Applied Orientation			Equal Emphasis			Research Orientation

CONTACT PERSON:	J. Robert Grove	Sandy Gordon
PHONE NUMBER:	(61–8) 9380–2361	(61–8) 9380–2361
FAX NUMBER:	(61–8) 9380–1039	(61–8) 9380–1039
E-MAIL ADDRESS:	Bob.Grove@uwa.edu.au	sgordon@cyllene.uwa.edu.au
PROGRAM WEB SITE:	http://www.general.uwa.edu.au/~hmweb/	

FACULTY AND AREA OF INTEREST

Sandy Gordon   Social psychology of sport, performance enhancement
J. Robert Grove   Social psychology of sport, exercise psychology
A third appointment in sport psychology is anticipated in 1998.

PROGRAM INFORMATION

Degrees offered
- M.Sc.
- Ph.D.

Approx. number of students in program
- 15

Approx. number of students in each degree program offered
- 67% master's/33% Ph.D.

Approx. number of students who apply/are accepted annually by program
- 12–15 apply/4–5 accepted

Admissions requirements
- Master's: background in sport science and psychology at the undergraduate level
- Ph.D.: completion of research thesis at honours or master's level

The program has available for qualified students
- Fellowships
- Research Assistantships
- The financial aid is University-wide rather than specific to the Department. It is competitive and based on a ranking of all candidates being considered.

Assistantships
- 0%   Fellowships
- 20%   Research Assistantships
- 10%   Teaching Assistantships
- 0%   Tuition Waivers
- 10%   Other Forms of Financial Aid

Internship possibility
- Yes

UNIVERSITY OF WESTERN AUSTRALIA ...

PROGRAM INFORMATION ...

Internship required for degree completion
- Recommended but not required for Ph.D.
- Available as elective for M.Sc.

Number of hours required for internship
- 1000 hours (consistent with Australian Psychological Society guidelines for approved degree programs)

Description of typical internship experience
- Course credit is available for hands-on work with sport teams and/or with individual athletes. Experiences vary but usually include working with teams and/or players for a 6–9-month period under the supervision of a faculty member. Activities undertaken include needs assessment, intervention, and evaluation of treatment effects.

COMMENTS

The M.Sc. degree includes course work in social psychology of sport, applied sport psychology, and exercise psychology. Supervised internships can be taken as electives within the M.Sc. degree program.

The Ph.D. degree is research based, with course work required only if the student's background is considered deficient in relevant areas. Ph.D. candidates are expected to spend 2–4 years conducting and publishing research in a specific area within exercise and sport psychology. We recommend, but do not require, that doctoral students take part in both a teaching internship and a field internship. Ph.D. candidates are also encouraged to pursue external grants to support their research.

WESTERN ILLINOIS UNIVERSITY

Department of Physical Education
Brophy Hall
Western Illinois University
Macomb, IL 61455

Program Rating: Program offers opportunities to pursue an applied orientation OR a research orientation (as opposed to an equal emphasis on both)

CONTACT PERSON: Laura Finch
PHONE NUMBER: (309) 298–2350 (Office)   (309) 298–1981 (Department)
FAX NUMBER: (309) 298–2981
E-MAIL ADDRESS: LM-Finch@wiu.edu
PROGRAM WEB SITE: http://www.wiu.edu/users/mipe/

FACULTY AND AREA OF INTEREST

Laura Finch	Applied sport psychology, sport sociology, coping strategies, performance enhancement, youth sport
Letty Foutch	Coaching pedagogy
Donna Phillips	Coaching pedagogy

PROGRAM INFORMATION

Degrees offered
- M.S. in Physical Education
- M.S. in Physical Education/Sport Management

Approx. number of students in program
- 60 full-time in the department; about 5–6 per year in sport psychology program

Approx. number of students in each degree program offered
- 50% M.S. in P.E./50% M.S. in P.E./Sport Management

Approx. number of students who apply/are accepted annually by program
- 100 apply/50 accepted in department; about 12–16 apply, 8–12 accepted in sport psychology program

Admissions requirements
- 3.00 undergraduate GPA (cumulative), lower GPAs admitted on probation
- 3.20 GPA in last two years
- No GRE scores required

The program has available for qualified students
- Fellowships (university based)
- Research Assistantships
- Teaching Assistantships
- Other Forms of Financial Aid (university based, e.g., athletics, University Union, campus recreation)

Assistantships
- 0% Fellowships
- 33% Research Assistantships
- 33% Teaching Assistantships
- 100% Tuition Waivers (all students with assistantships receive tuition waivers)
- 33% Other Forms of Financial Aid

WESTERN ILLINOIS UNIVERSITY ...

PROGRAM INFORMATION ...

Internship possibility
- Yes

Internship required for degree completion
- Recommended for sport psychology specialization
- Recommended for coaching/teaching specialization
- Required for sport management specialization

Number of hours required for internship
- 4–6 semester hours

Description of typical internship experience
- Individual and team experiences ranging from youth to college- and master,s-level athletes in competitive sport environments as well as exercise and wellness settings. The internship is designed to enrich the student's academic and career goals, so the internship experience varies depending on the student.

COMMENTS

The program at Western Illinois is new and looking for motivated students. The public university enrolls about 12,000 students and is located in a rural community in west central Illinois. Most students begin the program in the fall, but January enrollment is possible. The goal of the graduate specialization in sport and exercise psychology is twofold: (1) to prepare future professionals in the field of sport and exercise psychology (i.e., doctoral study) and (2) to provide teachers, coaches, and sport, exercise, and fitness professionals with specialized study in sport and exercise psychology to complement their existing knowledge base and careers.

The emphasis at WIU is on flexibility so that the student's goals are met. Students design their own program around a departmental core. Course work options in sport psychology are available, including traditional classes, seminars and workshops, as well as independent studies and research projects. Some summer school is also available. Supporting departmental course work is available in coaching, pedagogy, sport sociology, fitness and wellness, exercise science, adapted physical education, and sport management.

The sport psychology program recognizes the contributions of both research and application to sport psychology; the flexibility of the program allows students to pursue either option after the core course work has been successfully completed. Supervised internship/practica opportunities can be arranged with faculty (AAASP certified consultant) for additional experiences in sport psychology. Both thesis and nonthesis degree options are available. The program takes 1–2 years to complete, depending on course work choices, thesis option selected, and summer school. Strong ties exist with the psychology department; thus possibilities for interdisciplinary work are high. The program is small enough to allow for one-on-one contact with faculty yet large enough to allow students to learn from each other in a team approach as well. Students can gain practical experience through teaching opportunities, joint research projects with faculty, and supervised consulting and workshop experiences.

UNIVERSITY OF WESTERN ONTARIO

School of Kinesiology
Faculty of Health Sciences
University of Western Ontario
London, Ontario
Canada N6A 3K7

Program Rating:

1	2	3	4	5	**6**	7

Applied Orientation   Equal Emphasis   Research Orientation

CONTACT PERSON: Craig R. Hall
PHONE NUMBER: (519) 679–2111 (Ext. 8388)
FAX NUMBER: (519) 661–2008
E-MAIL ADDRESS: CHALL@JULIAN.UWO.CA
PROGRAM WEB SITE: http://www.uwo.ca/kinesiology/

FACULTY AND AREA OF INTEREST

Albert V. Carron   Group dynamics, home advantage
Craig R. Hall   Imagery, psychological intervention

PROGRAM INFORMATION

Degrees offered
- M.A.
- Ph.D.

Approx. number of students in program
- 50

Approx. number of students in each degree program offered
- 60% M.A./40% Ph.D.

Approx. number of students who apply/are accepted annually by program
- 100 apply/15–20 accepted

Admissions requirements
- Master's: Honors B.A. or equivalent in kinesiology
  Mid B average
- Ph.D.: M.A./M.S. in kinesiology

The program has available for qualified students
- Research Assistantships
- Teaching Assistantships
- Other Forms of Financial Aid

Assistantships
- 30% Fellowships
- 10% Research Assistantships
- 50% Teaching Assistantships
- 0% Tuition Waivers
- 5% Other Forms of Financial Aid

Internship possibility
- Yes

Description of typical internship experience
- Developing psychological intervention programs for elite young athletes
  (e.g., figure skaters, tennis players).

CHICHESTER INSTITUTE OF HIGHER EDUCATION

School of Sports Studies
Chichester Institute of Higher Education
College Lane, Chichester
West Sussex, PO19 4PE, England

CONTACT PERSON: Jan Graydon
PHONE NUMBER: 01243 816320
FAX NUMBER: 01243 816080
E-MAIL ADDRESS: 100443.2067@compuserve.com

FACULTY AND AREA OF INTEREST

Jan Graydon   Gender issues, motor skills
Ian Maynard   Stress management
Terry McMorris   Cognitive processes and fatigue

PROGRAM INFORMATION

Degrees offered
- M.Phil.
- M.S.
- Ph.D.

Approx. number of students in program
- 6

Approx. number of students in each degree program offered
- Different system

Approx. number of students who apply/are accepted annually by program
- 6 apply/1–2 accepted

Admissions requirements
- Good standing undergraduate degree in sport science or related area
  or psychology

Internship possibility
- Consultancy experience available

Description of typical internship experience
- Funding is difficult. There is sometimes the possibility of laboratory work or
  governing body-funded consultancy work.

COMMENTS

At present the master's and doctoral programs are not taught per se. Higher degree
qualification is by research.

WEST VIRGINIA UNIVERSITY

School of Physical Education—Sport Behavior Program
268 Coliseum
West Virginia University
Morgantown, WV 26506–6116

Program Rating:

1	2	3	4	**5**	6	7

Applied Orientation   Equal Emphasis   Research Orientation

CONTACT PERSON:	Andrew Ostrow
PHONE NUMBER:	(304) 293–3295, ext. 268
FAX NUMBER:	(304) 293–4641
E-MAIL:	aostrow2@wvu.edu
PROGRAM WEB SITE:	http://www.wvu.edu/~physed/sportbeh.htm

FACULTY AND AREA OF INTEREST

Dana Brooks	Leadership, cohesion
Edward Etzel	Counseling college student-athletes, ethical issues, sport injury
Andrew Ostrow	Sport psychometrics, older adult populations
Frank Perna	Health/exercise psychology, career transitions, injury, performance enhancement

PROGRAM INFORMATION

Degrees offered
- M.S.
- Ed.D.

Approx. number of students in program
- 15

Approx. number of students in each degree program offered
- 30% M.S./70% Ed.D.

Approx. number of students who apply/are accepted annually by program
- 50–60 apply/3–5 accepted

Admissions requirements
- M.S.: 3.00 undergraduate GPA
  - 1000 GRE or 50 MAT (minimum)
- Ed.D.: 3.00 undergraduate GPA
  - 3.50 graduate GPA
  - 1050 GRE or 55 MAT (minimum)
- M.S. and Ed.D.: Three letters of reference
  - Personal interview (where possible)
  - Writing sample

The program has available for qualified students
- Fellowships
- Teaching Assistantships
- Other Forms of Financial Aid

Assistantships
0%   Fellowships

WEST VIRGINIA UNIVERSITY ...

PROGRAM INFORMATION ...

0% Research Assistantships
50% Teaching Assistantships
10% Tuition Waivers
40% Other Forms of Financial Aid

Internship possibility
- Yes

Internship required for degree completion
- No

Number of hours required for internship
- 6–15 semester credit hours

Description of typical internship experiences
- Experiences include (1) CHAMPS/LifeSkills program for WVU student athletes, (2) working in wellness or physical rehabilitation site in applied sport psychology area, (3) teaching practicum in undergraduate sport behavior program, and (4) performance enhancement with college athletes.

COMMENTS

The graduate program in sport behavior has positioned itself as one of the leading programs in applied sport psychology in the country. The program, while housed in the School of Physical Education, employs four full-time faculty members, two of whom are licensed psychologists with expertise in counseling athletes, performance enhancement interventions, and exercise/ health psychology. These two psychologists supervise all student practicum and internship experiences. In fact, one licensed psychologist is a former Olympic gold medalist in shooting and is also the psychologist for the WVU Department of Intercollegiate Athletics. The Sport Behavior Graduate Student Club promotes close professional and personal relationships among students enrolled in the program. The graduate program in sport behavior has very close ties with the Department of Counseling, Counseling Psychology, and Rehabilitation Psychology, with several faculty holding adjunct appointments between departments. There is a strong commitment to interdisciplinary graduate education. Further, a number of graduate students have pursued rewarding internal or external internships in applied sport and exercise psychology. The program prides itself on having an excellent balance between research training and opportunities for developing applied skills.

WESTERN WASHINGTON UNIVERSITY

Physical Education, Health, and Recreation
Mail Stop 9067
Western Washington University
Bellingham, WA 98225

Program Rating:

1	2	3	**4**	**5**	6	7
Applied Orientation			Equal Emphasis			Research Orientation

CONTACT PERSON: Ralph A. Vernacchia
PHONE NUMBER: (360) 650–3514
FAX NUMBER: (360) 650–7447
E-MAIL ADDRESS: anthony@cc.wwu.edu

FACULTY AND AREA OF INTEREST

Ralph A. Vernacchia   Psychology of coaching, mental skills training, mental imagery/practice

PROGRAM INFORMATION

Degree offered
- M.S.

Approx. number of students in program
- 5–10

Approx. number of students in each degree program offered
- 100% M.S.

Approx. number of students who apply/are accepted annually by program
- 10 apply/5 accepted

Admissions requirements
- 3.00 GPA in last 90 quarter or 60 semester hours
- Three letters of recommendation
- GRE scores
- Undergraduate degree appropriate to individual field of study

The program has available for qualified students
- Teaching Assistantships
- Other Forms of Financial Aid

Assistantships
- 0% Fellowships
- 50% Research Assistantships
- 0% Teaching Assistantships
- 0% Tuition Waivers
- 25% Other Forms of Financial Aid

Internship possibility
- Yes

Internship required for degree completion
- Yes

WESTERN WASHINGTON UNIVERSITY ...

PROGRAM INFORMATION ...

Number of hours required for internship
- 6 quarter credits under advisement

Description of typical internship experience
- Internships available with Western Washington University athletic teams, the Adult Fitness Program, and Western Washington University Athletic Training Program.

COMMENTS

Program emphasis is on the educational, behavioral, and applied orientations of psychology to sport/athletic/exercise settings

UNIVERSITY OF WISCONSIN, MILWAUKEE

Department of Human Kinetics
Enderis Hall, P.O. Box 413
University of Wisconsin, Milwaukee
Milwaukee, WI 53201

Program Rating:

1	2	3	4	5*	6	7
Applied Orientation			Equal Emphasis		Research Orientation	

*Program offers opportunities to pursue an applied orientation OR a research orientation (as opposed to an equal emphasis on both).

CONTACT PERSON:	Barbara B. Meyer
PHONE NUMBER:	(414) 229-6080
FAX NUMBER:	(414) 229-5100
E-MAIL ADDRESS:	bbmeyer@csd.uwm.edu
PROGRAM WEB SITE:	http://www.uwm.edu/SAHP/gp/hk/ghkmenu.htm

FACULTY AND AREA OF INTEREST

Margaret Duncan	Qualitative methodology, spectator sport, women and sport
Cynthia A. Hasbrook	Sociology of physical activity
Barbara B. Meyer	Adventure education (ropes and challenge courses), performance enhancement, social psychology

PROGRAM INFORMATION

Degree offered
- M.S.

Approx. number of students in program
- 25

Approx. number of students in each degree program offered
- 100% M.S.

Approx. number of students who apply/are accepted annually by program
- 15 apply   accepted

Admissions requirements
- Undergraduate GPA of 2.75 or better
- GRE total score (verbal + quantitative) = 1000

The program has available for qualified students
- Research Assistantships (dependent upon extramural funding)
- Teaching Assistantships
- Other Forms of Financial Aid (including fellowships & nonresident tuition remission)

Assistantships
- 5%   Fellowships
- 15%   Research Assistantships
- 25%   Teaching Assistantships
- 0%   Tuition Waivers
- 0%   Other Forms of Financial Aid

Approximately 40% of students are employed full time in related fields and, therefore, do not seek financial aid of any sort.

UNIVERSITY OF WISCONSIN, MILWAUKEE ...

PROGRAM INFORMATION ...

Internship possibility
- Yes, interdisciplinary internships may be arranged in conjunction with other campus disciplines such as psychology or counseling psychology

Internship required for degree completion
- No

Description of typical internship experience
- Dependent upon student interest and faculty availability.

COMMENTS

The objective of the master of science degree program in human kinetics is to provide students with the scientific background necessary for service delivery and/or future study. The focus of the curriculum is the integration of the body of knowledge fundamental to the science of human movement through study in two of the five subdiscipline areas of (1) psychology of physical activity, (2) sociology of physical activity, (3) motor control/learning, (4) exercise physiology, and (5) biomechanics. The integrative nature of the human kinetics degree provides an excellent background for continued education in the movement sciences. This is particularly true in sport and exercise psychology, as course work in related disciplines is currently being discussed as a requirement for consultant certification. The psychology of physical activity emphasis at UW-Milwaukee utilizes a broad-based perspective to focus on psychological issues related to physical activity in general, including but not limited to organized sport, fitness and wellness, cardiac rehabilitation, physical therapy, and athletic training.

UNIVERSITY OF WOLLONGONG

Department of Psychology
University of Wollongong
Wollongong, New South Wales
2522 Australia

Program Rating:

1	2	3	**4**	5	6	7

Applied Orientation   Equal Emphasis   Research Orientation

CONTACT PERSON: Postgraduate Coordinator
PHONE NUMBER: (61) 42-213742 (Department)   (61) 42-213732 (Mark Anshel)
FAX NUMBER: (61) 42-214163
E-MAIL ADDRESS: Mark_Anshel@UOW.EDU.AU

FACULTY AND AREA OF INTEREST

Mark H. Anshel (Wollongong)   Coping with stress, cognitive strategies
Patsy Tremayne (Western Sydney)   Children and exercise, psychophysiology

PROGRAM INFORMATION

Degrees offered
- M.S.
- M. Psych. in Sport Psychology in conjunction with the University of Western Sydney
- Ph.D. (3 years)

Approx. number of students in program
- 8

Approx. number of students in each degree program offered
- 80% M.S./20% Ph.D.

Approx. number of students who apply/are accepted annually by program
- 10–12 apply/6 accepted

Admissions requirements
- M.S.: Completion of undergraduate degree in psychology
- Ph.D.: Completion of master's program with a master's thesis research in psychology
- Minimum of B (U.S.) or Credit (Australian) average required

The program has available for qualified students
- Tutor Assistantships (teaching class tutorials, marking)
- Foreign Student Scholarship
- Other Forms of Financial Aid
- Write: International Student Office, University of Wollongong, for scholarship, financial aid, and admission forms

Assistantships
0% Fellowships
0% Graduate Assistantships
20% Teaching Assistantships

UNIVERSITY OF WOLLONGONG ...

PROGRAM INFORMATION ...

0%   Tuition Waivers
0%   Other Forms of Financial Aid

Internship possibility
  • Yes, called "practicum"

Internship required for degree completion
  • Yes

Number of hours required for internship
  • 6 credit hours

Description of typical internship experience
  • Opportunities exist to work directly with elite athletes at the Australian Institute of Sport and with high school and college teams and coaches. There is an excellent relationship and history of interaction between sport psychology and local sports teams. Three practica are required, at least 50% of which is in sport. Other options include exercise rehabilitation, and medical facilities.

COMMENTS

Australian doctoral study allows for flexibility in completing all requirements. Selection of graduate courses (subjects) is jointly decided by student and advisor. Emphasis is on a three-year doctoral thesis consisting of multiple studies.

The master of psychology in sport psychology degree is a professional two-year program offered jointly by the Universities of Wollongong (Dr. Mark Anshel, coordinator) and Western Sydney (Dr. Patsy Tremayne, Department of Sport Studies, University of Western Sydney-Macarthur, P.O. Box 555, Campbelltown, NSW 2560 Australia; phone: 02-9772-9568; e-mail: p.tremayne@uws.edu.au; fax: 02-9772-1017). Students may apply and be admitted in either university, completing courses offered by faculty in both schools. Students are required to complete five core sport and exercise psychology courses (called "subjects" in Australian parlance); additional required subjects are from each university's psychology department, including supervised field placements. The one objective of the program is for students to become eligible for membership in the Australian Psychological Society and *toward* requirements for registration with the New South Wales Board of Psychologists. The program includes an applied research thesis. For further information about the program, please contact Dr. Steve Roodenrys, Postgraduate Coordinator, University of Wollongong, Wollongong, New South Wales 2522 Australia.

Foreign students are encouraged to write to the International Student Office for information about scholarships. Australia's semester dates are the last week of February until the first week of June (Session 1) and mid-July to early November (Session 2).The application deadline for study during the following school year is October 31. Decisions for acceptance are early to mid-January. Wollongong is approximately one hour from Sydney along the South Pacific Ocean.

UNIVERSITY OF WYOMING

School of Physical and Health Education
University of Wyoming
Laramie, WY 82071

Program Rating:

1	2	3	4	**5**	6	7

Applied Orientation   Equal Emphasis   Research Orientation

CONTACT PERSON: Bonnie G. Berger
PHONE NUMBER: (307) 766-2494
FAX NUMBER: (307) 766-6608
E-MAIL ADDRESS: BBERGER@UWYO.EDU
PROGRAM WEB SITE: http://www.uwyo.edu/

FACULTY AND AREA OF INTEREST

Bonnie Berger	Exercise and health psychology; psychological benefits of exercise; mood benefits as related to exercise intensity, high and low risk activities, and life-span considerations
Larry Fahlberg	Health and exercise psychology; exercise and wellness; meaning of physical activity; risk sport
Kathy Parker	Performance enhancement; goal setting; athletic counseling

PROGRAM INFORMATION

Degree offered
- M.S.

Approx. number of students in program
- 30 (nearly all full-time)

Approx. number of students in each degree program offered
- 100% M.S.
  - 10% Sport Psychology
  - 40% Exercise Physiology
  - 20% Pedagogy
  - 30% Health

Approx. number of students who apply/are accepted annually by program
- 25 apply/15 accepted

Admissions requirements
- 900 GRE
- 3.00 GPA

The program has available for qualified students
- Research Assistantships
- Teaching Assistantships

Assistantships
0%   Fellowships
0%   Research Assistantships
80%   Teaching Assistantships/Tuition Waivers
10%   Other Forms of Financial Aid

UNIVERSITY OF WYOMING ...

PROGRAM INFORMATION ...

Internship possibility
- Yes, close ties to the Department of Athletics

Internship required for degree completion
- No

Number of hours required for internship
- Depends on the number of academic credit hours taken

Description of typical internship experience
- Experience is quite varied. Internships range from working with university teams, summer sport camps on campus, local high school teams, health clubs, and cardiac rehabilitation settings for health and exercise psychology experiences.

XAVIER UNIVERSITY

Department of Psychology
Xavier University
3800 Victory Parkway
Cincinnati, OH 45207

CONTACT PERSON: W. Michael Nelson III
PHONE NUMBER: (513) 745-3533
FAX NUMBER: (513) 745-3327
E-MAIL: xupsych@xavier.xu.edu
PROGRAM WEB SITE: http://www.xu.edu/

FACULTY AND AREA OF INTEREST

W. Michael Nelson   General

PROGRAM INFORMATION

Degree offered
- Psy.D.

Approx. number of students in program
- 16 each year

Approx. number of students in each degree program offered
- 100% Psy.D.

Approx. number of students who apply/are accepted annually by program
- 150 apply/16 accepted

Admissions requirements
- Must possess a Bachelor's degree or its equivalent from a regionally accredited institution
- 18 semester hours of undergraduate courses in psychology that must include general psychology, introductory statistics, experimental psychology, mental measurements, and 6 semester hours of other upper-division, undergraduate courses.
- Minimum undergraduate GPA of 2.70 (on a 4.00 scale)
- GRE aptitude portions and psychology subject area
- Three letters of reference
- A written statement of purpose

Assistantships
- 0% Fellowships
- 0% Research Assistantships
- 0% Teaching Assistantships
- 0% Tuition Waivers
- 0% Other Forms of Financial Aid

Internship possibility
- No

Description of typical internship experience
- None in sport psychology—all practicum are in specific areas of interest.

XAVIER UNIVERSITY ...

PROGRAM INFORMATION ...

Xavier University's doctor of psychology (Psy.D.) program builds upon the university's strong commitment to the Jesuit tradition of service in the context of scholarship. Accordingly, the program provides students with the knowledge and range of skills necessary to provide psychological services in today's changing professional climate. Our professional-scientist orientation emphases the importance of the scientific foundation in psychology. Although the Psy.D. program is designed to prepare students for the general practice of clinical psychology, it also addresses service to three important groups of underserved people in today's society—children, the elderly, and the severely mentally disabled. All students must be in one of these three Areas of Interest. A separate track is available in sport psychology in which the student would take a course in sport psychology and do research in this area.

YORK UNIVERSITY

Graduate Programme in Exercise and Health Science
York University
344 Bethune College
4700 Keele Street
North York, Ontario
Canada   M3J 1P3

Program Rating:

1	2	3	4	5	6	**7**

Applied Orientation   Equal Emphasis   Research Orientation

CONTACT PERSON: Barry Fowler, Director, Graduate Programme
PHONE NUMBER: (416) 736-5728
FAX NUMBER: (416) 736-5892
E-MAIL ADDRESS: EAHS@YORKU.CA
PROGRAM WEB SITE: http://www.yorku.ca/academics/bfowier/

FACULTY AND AREA OF INTEREST

Health Psychology

B. Cheung	Mechanism of spatial disorientation
M. Cowles	Individual differences, psychophysiology
C. Davis	Personality, health, and exercise psychology
L. Fillion	Stress, health behaviours, psychoneuroimmunology
B. Fowler	Stressors and performance, electrophysiological indices of stress and performance
K. Helmers	Personality, stress, and cardiovascular disease
S.H. Kennedy*	Psychobiology of mood, anxiety, and wellness

Exercise Physiology

F. Buick*	Aerospace physiology
E. Cafarelli	Neuromuscular physiology/muscle sensory processes
N. Gledhill	Cardiovascular/respiratory physiology and fitness
L.S. Goodman*	Cardiovascular physiology
D. Hood	Biochemistry and molecular biology of skeletal muscle adaptations and cardiac hypertrophy
J.C. McDermott	Regulation of muscle gene expression/skeletal muscle regeneration
T.M. McLellan*	Heat strain of protective clothing: influence of heat acclimation, hydration, and fitness
M.P. Olmsted*	Eating disorders

*adjunct

PROGRAM INFORMATION

Degrees offered
- M.S. in exercise physiology
- M.A. in health psychology

Approx. number of students in program
- 24

Approx. number of students in each degree program offered
- 50% M.S./50% M.A.

YORK UNIVERSITY ...

PROGRAM INFORMATION ...

Approx. number of students who apply/are accepted annually by program
- 43 apply / 12 accepted

The program has available for qualified students
- Research Assistantships
- Teaching Assistantships
- Other Forms of Financial Aid
- All students accepted in the program are funded to a minimal level of $10,000 per year for two years

Assistantships
- 0%   Fellowships
- 100%   Research Assistantships
- 100%   Teaching Assistantships
- 0%   Tuition Waivers
- 10%   Other Forms of Financial Aid

Internship possibility
- Yes

Internship required for degree completion
- No

Number of hours required for internship
- Two courses (see below)

Description of typical internship experience
- There are two practicum courses involving laboratory work under the students supervisors (10 hours per week minimum)

COMMENTS

The programme takes two years and is experimentally oriented. The standard for the thesis is that it should be of publishable quality in a refereed journal.

APPENDIXES

GUIDE TO APPENDIXES

There are 13 appendixes in this directory. The appendixes are designed to facilitate your use of the information in the directory, as well as provide other resources to use to your advantage in learning more about applied sport psychology and considering the various programs. A brief description of each appendix follows.

Appendix A: Additions, Deletions, and Changes to Directory Entries

Appendix A indicates the programs that have been added to this fourth edition of the directory, those that have been deleted from the third edition, and changes in program entries (i.e., movement from one department to another). These listings may be particularly useful for those familiar with earlier editions of the directory.

Appendix B: Other Programs

Appendix B provides information on searching for other programs with information about applied sport psychology, in addition to (or instead of) those available in this *Directory*.

Appendix C: A Word about Internships

Appendix C provides information about internships. Many students are interested in finding internships and/or learning more about them.

Appendix D: Doctoral Programs in Clinical/Counseling Psychology

Appendix D provides information about doctoral programs in clinical/counseling psychology that are not listed in this directory but may still be of interest to the student with a passion for applied sport psychology.

Appendix E: Graduate Training and Career Possibilities

Appendix E provides a copy of the graduate training and career possibilities brochure published jointly by Division 47 (Exercise and Sport Psychology), of APA (American Psychological Association), AAASP (Association for the Advancement of Applied Sport Psychology), and NASPSPA (North American Society for the Psychology of Sport and Physical Activity). This brochure is very valuable background reading for students interested in applied sport psychology.

Appendix F: Texts in Applied Sport Psychology

Appendix F provides a listing of texts in applied sport psychology that readers may wish to consider for valuable background reading in the field.

Appendix G: References in Applied Sport Psychology: Professional & Ethical Issues

Appendix G provides a listing of references in applied sport psychology, focusing on professional and ethical issues, that readers may wish to consider for valuable background reading in the field.

Appendix H: Reading List in Applied Sport Psychology: Psychological Skills Training, by Michael Sachs and Alan Kornspan

Appendix H provides a listing of books in applied sport psychology, focusing particularly on psychological skills training, that readers may wish to consider for valuable background reading in the field.

Appendix I: Geographical Listing of Graduate Programs

Appendix I provides a geographical listing, by country, of programs in the *Directory*.

Appendix J: Contact Persons

Appendix J provides a listing of contact persons, alphabetically, for programs in the Directory.

Appendix K: Telephone Number Listing of Contact Persons

Appendix K provides a listing of telephone numbers for contact persons, numerically by area code within each country, for programs in the *Directory*.

Appendix L: Electronic-Mail Address Listing of Contact Persons

Appendix L provides a listing of electronic-mail addresses for contact persons, alphabetically by program and by individual, for programs in the *Directory*.

Appendix M: Location of Graduate Programs: Physical Education and Psychology, Master's and Doctoral Level

Appendix M provides a listing of programs divided into master's and doctoral degrees, for physical education and psychology departments.

Appendix N: Quick Chart of Program Information: Degrees Offered, Financial Aid, and Internship Possibility

Appendix N provides a 'quick chart' listing programs and degrees offered, financial aid available, and the possibility of an internship.

Additions, Deletions, and Changes to Directory Entries

Seven programs have been deleted from those listed in the fourth edition of the directory, primarily due to programmatic changes, faculty moving on to other universities, and/or retirements. Six programs have been added to this fourth edition of the directory. One program has changed departments (other than name changes, such as Physical Education to Kinesiology), and one university had a name change. The specific changes are as follows.

Deleted:
University of California, Davis
East Stroudsburg University
University of Oklahoma
University of Oregon
Pacific Lutheran University
South Dakota State University
University of Windsor

Added:
University of Memphis (Physical Education)
Southeastern Louisiana University
Southern Illinois University, Edwardsville
University of Southern Queensland
University of Texas, Austin
Texas Christian University (Physical Education)

Changes:
University of California, Berkeley (from Department of Physical Education to Division of Social Science)
Chichester Institute of Higher Education (name changed from West Sussex Institute of Higher Education)
University of Exeter (from School of Education to School of Health Sciences)
University of Kansas (from Health, Physical Education, and Recreation to Health, Sport, and Exercise Sciences)
University of Minnesota (from Physical Education to School of Kinesiology and Leisure Studies)
University of Missouri, Columbia (from Health and Exercise Science to Department of Educational and Counseling Psychology)
University of New Hampshire (from Physical Education to Department of Kinesiology)
University of Western Ontario (from Physical Education to School of Kinesiology)

Other Programs

A number of universities and other sites have selected courses, certificate programs, interest groups, or other links with applied sport psychology. Readers are encouraged to check with area colleges and universities for courses, workshops, etc., that may be available, even if a "program" per se is not offered. One example is the following:

University of California, Irvine
Extension/Health Services,
P.O. Box 6050
Irvine, CA 92616-6050

Contact person: Mickie Shapiro
Telephone number: (714) 751-1792
Fax number: (714) 725-2090
e-mail: ironmickie@aol.com

A certificate program in fitness instruction upon completion of 18 units is available for nurses and health fitness specialists. The courses include exercise physiology, exercise psychology, nutrition, anatomy, athletic injuries, and teaching of fitness programs. The 10-week, 30-hour quarter course taught by Mickie Shapiro, "The Psychology of Exercise," includes the following areas: adherence, personality and choice of fitness activity; gender/cultural/aging/youth sport issues; addiction, motivation; psychological implications of injury/decrease in performance; anxiety/competition; healthy lifestyle; cognitive therapy; and procrastination/burnout. The course is a general overview introducing students to the research and clinical issues of sport psychology.

Late Breaking Programs

Brock University (M.Ed.)
Contact Person: Jean Cote
                      Dept. of Physical Education
                      Brock University
                      St. Catharines, Ontario
                      Canada L2S 3A1
                      Phone: (905) 688-5550, ext. 4360
                      e-mail: jeancote@arnie.pec.brocku.ca

The Optimal Performance Institute (M.A., Ph.D.)
Contact Person: Mitchell Flaum
                      The Optimal Performance Institute
                      520 S. Murphy Ave., Suite #256
                      Sunnyvale, CA 94086
                      Phone: (212) 352-9532 — NOT in service
                      Fax: (212) 352-9516
                      web site: http://www.chelseapiers.com
Note: This is a new program that is by correspondence.

A Word About Internships

Michael L. Sachs, Lois A. Butcher, and Shelley A. Wiechman
Temple University and University of Washington

Supervised field experiences are an important component in sport psychology training. A number of programs in this directory list internships as part of their sport psychology programs. It is imperative for students to look at these internship opportunities as vehicles toward practical application of course work and as part of the process for qualification as a certified consultant. Please remember, though, the differences (qualitative and quantitative) between practicum experiences and internships noted in the introduction to this directory and make sure you are informed about what is being asked of you and what experiences you may receive.

There are some cautions for the prospective student and, once again, as a consumer of the goods and services provided by the institution of choice, you need to make sure you get what you have bargained for. The expectations of a master's student may be quite different from those of a doctoral student or postdoctoral individual who needs supervised hours to become a certified consultant. Commitment of time is critical! You need to decide if you are able to work independently. You need to decide if you have enough financial support to get through the entire endeavor. Flexibility is essential. Your ideas about interning may not match the reality of the opportunities offered. For example, if you desire to work with elite athletes only, or to deal with one specific high level team, you may not get what you want. It is important to be open to experiences at clubs, schools, YMCAs, etc.

You also need to be aware that if an institution states that it provides internships for its graduate students, only a small number of students in the program may be able to get them. Supervision is another issue. It may be nonexistent, minimal, or not what was expected. Check Appendix H for a listing of references which include some dealing with supervision issues.

Some programs have internships already identified for students and simply place students in those "slots." Other programs provide networking opportunities and encourage students to find internships on their own. This has a "real world" advantage in requiring students to make connections, develop relationships, and secure their own opportunities, as many will have to do after completing their degree work. Clearly, you need to ask questions of faculty and current students, investigate options, and gather additional information to assist you in your choice of school and avoid potential problems and disappointments in your program.

Many of the institutions in this directory list internship opportunities for their students. There are many internship opportunities that are not listed within the program information. The United States Olympic Committee internship opportunity is one such option. The Sport Science and Technology Division of the United States Olympic Committee, which includes a sport psychology department, has one clinical research assistant position open every year. The position is open to students with a master's degree, and is two calendar years in length. The position includes consultation with athletes, opportunities to present educational sport psychology information to athletes and coaches, and the chance to participate in applied sport psychology research projects. For further information contact Dr. Sean McCann, Mental Training and Counseling Program, United States Olympic Committee, 1 Olympic Plaza, Colorado Springs, CO 80909.

Internships in exercise and sport psychology as well as APA-approved pre-doctoral internships may not be clearly identified within the program listings—a listing of those known to the authors by July 1, 1997 follows. Complete information on one of these (Washington State University) is provided as well. Another internship opportunity that is not connected with a program listed in this directory is that at the Lewis-Gale Clinic, in Roanoke, VA. Information concerning the program follows at the end of this appendix.

It is important to remember, though, the individual nature of each internship experience, and the facilities provided by or connected to each school. It is critical for the prospective student to dig for information, especially if one's interests and goals require some practical background experiences. Whether you are in an applied or research area, you need to know certain things about what to do and what to expect with regard to your time, your energy, and your resources. A few questions may help in your search:

1. Is the internship a requirement for degree completion?
2. If your interests are research oriented, are you able to gain practical lab/research experience?
3. If you are a "hands-on" applied person, will you be able to work with the populations in which you are interested (i.e., young children, eating disordered individuals), or will you be required to work only with the teams/athletes at your school?
4. Are the internships made available to you through your department or advisor? If internships are made available, how many are there for someone with your particular interest/focus? (It helps to know if you must compete for the spot)
5. Is it up to you to create your own internship or seek out an experience? Are contact lists provided to aid in the search?
6. Are you able to work independently, or do you need to work in tandem with your supervisor and/or another (perhaps more advanced) student/intern as an "assistant"?
7. If you do work independently, how much supervision will you get? Is it available or required for the internship? Who will be your supervisor?
8. Will you receive course credit for your internship work?
9. Are paid internships a possibility, or is the internship a volunteer one? If it is volunteer, will you have the financial capability to support yourself during the internship period?
10. How much time are you willing/able to commit to your internship? Don't forget all the details that go into the work of a sport psychologist: notes must be recorded, records must be kept, meetings with coaches, athletes, and your supervisor need to be arranged, etc. Keeping this information is also important if you decide to apply for certified consultant status (which currently requires 400 hours of supervised experience—keep good records!).

To gain especially valuable information on internships, talk to students who have done them. They will be able to tell you what to expect in terms of time and effort, the effects on your personal life, impact on your other school/course work, what the supervisors are like, etc. Another good source may be the student representative for Division 47 (Exercise and Sport Psychology) of the American Psychological Association. The current representative is Kevin Antshel, of the University of Kentucky (Athletics Association, Memorial Coliseum, University of Kentucky, Lexington, KY 40506-0019), and internships are an important focus of his work with Division 47. Kevin's e-mail address is kmants00@ukcc.uky.edu

Remember, internships are critical to honing your skills in sport psychology. An internship experience with appropriate supervision will give you important feedback which will allow you to refine your good points, improve your weak areas, and form a solid base for future reference with clients when you've left the cocoon of school and entered the real world.

Sport Psychology Internships

Exercise and Sport Sciences

Many programs provide applied experiences for their own graduate students. These programs are listed in the directory. The following programs provide internships for students separate from their graduate programs:

United States Olympic Committee—two year clinical research
  assistantship, (719) 578-4810
The Pennsylvania State University—Department of
  Intercollegiate Athletics (contact Dr. David Yukelson—see PSU entry).

APA-approved Pre-Doctoral Internships

The following are APA-approved internships through university counseling centers. They either offer a rotation through the athletic department or are willing to work with the intern in providing experiences with athletes. We recommend that you call the internship director at each site to get more details. The telephone numbers listed below for the contact person at each internship site were correct as of July 1, 1997 (ask for the contact person for the internship—we have not provided a given person's name because that may change from year to year):

Arizona State University, (602) 965-6147

UCLA, (310) 794-7950

University of Delaware, (302) 831-8107

George Washington University, (202) 994-6550

Indiana University, (812) 855-5711

Iowa State University, (515) 294-5056

Lewis-Gale Clinic (Salem, VA—not a counseling center), (703) 982-2463, ext. 2930

Kansas State University, (913) 532-6927

University of Memphis, (901) 678-2067

University of Missouri, Columbia, (314) 882-6601

University of Nebraska, Lincoln, (402) 472-6208

University of New Hampshire, (603) 862-2090
Notre Dame University, (219) 631-7336

Ohio State University (also offers a postdoctoral
  fellowship), (614) 293-2440

University of Oregon, (503) 346-3227

The Pennsylvania State University, (814) 863-0395

University of Tennessee, (615) 974-2196

Virginia Commonwealth University, (804) 828-3964

Virginia Polytechnic Institute and State University
  (Virginia Tech—not yet APA approved), (540) 231-6557

Washington State University, (509) 335-3792

West Virginia University, (304) 293-4431

LEWIS-GALE CLINIC

Psychological Medicine Department
Lewis-Gale Clinic
4910 Valley View Boulevard
Roanoke, VA 24012

CONTACT PERSON: John Heil
PHONE NUMBER: (703) 265-1605   (703) 772-3485
FAX NUMBER: (703) 366-7353

FACULTY AND AREA OF INTEREST
Lola Byrd, Ph.D.
John Heil, D.A.
Rob Lanahan, Psy.D.
Samuel Rogers, Ph.D.
Bruce Sellars, Psy.D.

COMMENTS

Lewis-Gale clinic provides elective training rotations as part of a Veteran's Administration Medical Center APA-approved predoctoral psychology internship. The clinic is a multispecialty physician group practice with approximately 130 physicians representing a wide range of medical specialties. The Psychological Medicine Department has 16 staff members. The department offers a broad range of assessment and treatment approaches to a variety of inpatient and outpatient populations. All interns can elect to serve up to 8 hours per week at the Lewis-Gale Clinic for the training year. Different training experiences are available according to the intern's interests. Supervision for the sport psychology experience is provided by Dr. John Heil.

Sport Psychology. The sport psychology rotation has 2 distinct foci: enhancing performance and psychological well-being in athletes (and others who perform in highly demanding environments); and the use of sport, exercise, and performance enhancement techniques in the treatment of medical problems.

Training in the use of sport, exercise, and performance enhancement methods with general medical populations is centered in the Lewis-Gale Hospital Pain Center. Applications include consultation with rehabilitation staff in the design and monitoring of aerobic and therapeutic exercise programs focusing on goal setting, pacing, motivation, and compliance; resumption of lost recreational activities; use of performance anxiety treatment protocols; and use of activity-based muscular biofeedback.

Work with athletes and other performers may include participation in educational programs for coaches and parents, consultation with sports teams, sport organizations, and health professionals, and individual consultation and therapy with athletes. Direct work with athletes is contingent on prior training and sport experience. Interns undergo personal mental training for application in performance settings (e.g., sport, music, public speaking).

WASHINGTON STATE UNIVERSITY

Department of Intercollegiate Athletics
Washington State University
Pullman, WA 99164-1610

Contact Person:	Jim Bauman, Ph.D.
	Sport Psychology and Performance Enhancement Services
Phone Number:	(509) 335-0245
FAX Number:	(509) 335-0328
E-mail Address:	jimb@wsu.edu

PROGRAM INFORMATION

Pre-Doctoral Psychology Internship (July 1–June 30)
- Fully approved American Psychological Association Internship Center
- Rotation in Sport Psychology
- 3–5 hours/week—Athletics, approximately 35 hours/week—Counseling Center
- Stipend and benefits provided by WSU Counseling Center
- intern position, one year internship

Application timeframe/requirements
- Application deadline: typically the first week in December
- Counseling/clinical Ph.D. and Psy.D. candidates only
- Applications submitted to WSU Counseling and Testing Services
- Application procedures pursuant to Internship and Postdoctoral Programs in Professional Psychology (Association of Psychology Postdoctoral and Internship Centers)

Predoctoral/master's sport psychology/consultant internship
- 9-month practicum/internship (August–May)
- 15–18 hours/week
- Small stipend available (Sport Psychology Funding)

Application Procedure
- Predoctoral or Master's degrees in psychology, kinesiology, physical education, motor development, biomechanics, exercise physiology, athletic medicine, etc.
- Previous experience as an athlete or in athletics preferred
- Submit cover letter, vita/resume, and names/telephone numbers of references to Dr. Jim Bauman at the address noted above. Submit application material no later than March 1.

COMMENTS

In 1986, WSU's Athletic Department and Counseling Center collaborated in creating a sport psychology position to provide counseling and other sport-related services to student-athletes. This position has since developed into a full-time position providing sport psychology and performance enhancement services to individual athletes, teams, coaches, and departmental support staff. Requests for sport psychology services have increased in youth, recreational, collegiate, Olympic, and professional levels of competition. As the demand for services has increased, it has also become necessary to increase the opportunities for new professionals to gain quality supervised experience in providing sport psychology services. In response to this need and with the same futuristic insight of eleven years ago, Washington State University has created two internship opportunities.

Doctoral Programs in Clinical/Counseling Psychology

Now that you've examined the offerings of the 109 graduate programs in applied sport psychology listed in this directory, you may be feeling a bit overwhelmed. The programs outlined in the directory display a range of interests, applications, and orientations which demonstrate the breadth of the field of applied sport psychology. An additional aspect of your graduate program search to consider is programs in clinical and counseling psychology. While only a few of these programs have a specialization in sport psychology per se, others offer specialties which are directly related to athletes and exercise/sport/physical activity.

Decisions regarding graduate programs require one vitally important consideration: What do you want at the end of it all? Do you want to work with people? Are your skills strongest in research? Do you enjoy working from a particular theoretical perspective? Are your talents going to be put to the best possible use through the program you have chosen? Often the best possible match of a program to a person's goals and talents may be in a clinical/counseling program with sport psychology as a component, rather than a primary focus. With this in mind, you need to think about where you want to fit in as a professional, and where you will best be able to do "your thing" once you have left the cocoon of graduate school. Be sure to read the section earlier in the directory "Taking the Next Step: What to Ask as You Review the Directory," by Patricia Latham Bach.

It is critical to understand several important points about clinical/counseling programs:

1. The programs listed in the specialty categories table *are not* applied sport psychology programs. They are clinical/counseling psychology programs. Please do not contact these programs for information about their sport psychology specializations—they do not have one! Rather, ask them about their clinical/counseling psychology program and follow up with questions about work in exercise and sport. Be sure to talk with the person(s) on the faculty interested in exercise and sport, if there are one or more such individuals.

2. If the institution you choose offers sport psychology courses, you may be able to take them as electives within your clinical/counseling program of study. As before, be sure to talk with faculty who have an interest in sport and exercise.

3. A number of schools have both a clinical/counseling program and a doctoral program in physical education (or kinesiology, exercise and sport sciences, or a related name). In these cases you might get the best of both worlds. If the two programs have good relations, collaborative work may be more likely than at a school where both programs are not available. It takes some effort to check out institutions with both programs, but the end result may be exactly what you want or need!

A resource which will prove to be an important tool in your decision-making process is the *Insider's Guide to Graduate Programs in Clinical and Counseling Psychology* (1996/1997 edition, published 1996) by John C. Norcross, Michael A. Sayette, and Tracy J. Mayne, published by The Guilford Press (72 Spring Street, New York, New York 10012, but also available in bookstores).

he *Insider's Guide* provides the prospective student with a wealth of information, from choosing programs which might make a good match, to working through the application and interview process. The guide gives a visual means of determining the research to application orientations of each program, and lists the basic entrance requirements and program prerequisites, specialty areas of each program, and research/grant funding for those areas.

Sport psychology specialties can be found at the following institutions:

Georgia State University
Illinois Institute of Technology 312-567-3000 3009
University of Manitoba
Memphis State University
University of Washington

Note that three of these programs (University of Manitoba, University of Memphis, and University of Washington) are listed in this directory.

The following institutions are listed as having faculty interested in sport psychology as a research area:

Hofstra University
Illinois Institute of Technology
University of Manitoba
University of Memphis
University of Missouri, Kansas City
University of North Texas
Oklahoma State University
University of South Carolina
Spalding University
University of Washington
West Virginia University

Note that seven of these programs (University of Manitoba, University of Memphis, University of Missouri, Kansas City, University of North Texas, Spalding University, University of Washington, and West Virginia University) are listed in this directory.

Additional program areas listed in the directory related to sport and exercise include: Behavioral medicine; biofeedback/relaxation; eating disorders; gender roles/sex differences; health psychology; hypnosis; minority/cross cultural psychology; pain; substance abuse/addictive behaviors.

Other resources which may help your decision-making process are available through the American Psychological Association (APA). They have published a helpful booklet on "Graduate Training and Career Possibilities in Exercise and Sport Psychology" (see Appendix E). They also publish an additional important source of information, the *Graduate Study in Psychology* volume, which is regularly updated. Contacting the Division 47 (Exercise and Sport Psychology) student representative is another good idea. The current student representative is Kevin Antshel (Athletics Association, Memorial Coliseum, University of Kentucky, Lexington, KY 40506-0019). Kevin's e-mail address is kmants00@ukcc.uky.edu

Graduate Training &
Career Possibilities
In Exercise
& Sport Psychology

Sponsored by:

American Psychological Association
Division of Exercise and Sport
Psychology (APA Division 47)

Association for the Advancement of
Applied Sport Psychology (AAASP)

North American Society for the
Psychology of Sport and Physical
Activity (NASPSPA)

Table Of Contents

Graduate Training and Career Possibilities In Exercise and Sport Psychology

As interest has grown in exercise and sport psychology, requests from students and prospective students for information about graduate training and career possibilities have increased. This booklet addresses some of the commonly asked questions about careers and academic preparation in the field of exercise and sport psychology. The answers reflect the current state of the field, not necessarily the ideal state.

CONSIDERATIONS IN SELECTING EXERCISE AND SPORT PSYCHOLOGY CAREERS

What roles do exercise and sport psychologists perform?

Exercise and sport psychologists typically perform three primary roles: 1) teaching, 2) research, and 3) practice. Career opportunities in exercise and sport psychology may emphasize various aspects or combinations of these roles. Careful selection of a career track will guide you in determining the type of graduate training needed to qualify for career opportunities available in the field of exercise and sport psychology, hereafter referred to as sport psychology.

What sort of education do I need to become involved in sport psychology?

Sport psychology has traditionally been an interdisciplinary field and, therefore, academic training can come from departments of physical education, psychology, or counseling. Many departments of physical education have changed their emphases and now call themselves Exercise and Sport Sciences, Kinesiology, Movement Sciences, Human Performance, or some similar variation (hereafter referred to as sport sciences). The career track that you select will determine the type of academic preparation needed, and will ultimately influence the career opportunities for which you optimally qualify.

Whatever degree you choose to obtain (masters or doctorate), and whether the degree comes from a department of sport sciences or psychology, you should take supplemental course work from the allied discipline

1

not represented by your home department. For instance, both the U. S. Olympic Committee (USOC) Sport Psychology Registry and the Association for the Advancement of Applied Sport Psychology (AAASP) "Certification Criteria" recommend that psychology majors take sport psychology classes and supplemental course work in sport sciences (e.g., biomechanics, exercise physiology, motor development/learning/ control, and sport sociology). Likewise, sport sciences graduate students specializing in sport psychology should take undergraduate and graduate courses in departments of psychology or counseling psychology (e.g., abnormal psychology, principles of counseling, psychopathology, personality, and social psychology). Further information about the specific coursework requirements for becoming an AAASP certified consultant is available from AAASP.

A well-integrated graduate program would combine traditional psychology, sport sciences, and sport psychology; however, few such formal programs exist. Often students must seek courses as well as research and applied mentoring from professionals in different disciplines/departments.

How much training will I need?

Most of the professional employment opportunities in sport psychology require doctoral degrees from accredited colleges and universities. In addition, students in counseling or clinical psychology doctoral programs usually complete post-graduate internships (normally not in sport psychology) as part of their education. Even if students with a masters degree complete sport psychology internships, these graduates compete at a distinct disadvantage for the limited number of full-time positions available in sport psychology.

Because of the limited number of full-time positions, many individuals work in the sport psychology field on a part-time basis. Whether you want a part- or full-time position in the field is a salient consideration in selecting a graduate program. Depending upon the area you wish to pursue within the field (i.e., teaching, research, and/or practice), there are four possible career tracks that are discussed below. Three of the career tracks (academic sport sciences, academic psychology, clinical/ counseling sport psychology) require doctoral degrees while one rather diverse track (e.g., academic athletic counseling, health promotion, or coaching) requires at least a masters degree.

2

TRACK I

TEACHING/RESEARCH IN SPORT SCIENCES AND WORK WITH ATHLETES ON PERFORMANCE ENHANCEMENT

Educational Requirements for Track I

• Doctoral Degree in Sport Sciences with a Specialization in Sport Psychology and a Significant Proportion of Course Work in Psychology or Counseling.

Primary Employment for Track I

• Academic Position in College/University

• Researcher in Research Institute or Medical Research Laboratory

• Coaching Educator for College/University or Sport Organization

Opportunities with the above may include part-time consulting with amateur and professional athletes and teams and on *rare* occasions, full-time consulting

If you decide that you want a job that primarily involves teaching and research in sport psychology as well as the possibility of providing performance enhancement techniques to athletes (e.g., relaxation, imagery, goal setting), a doctoral degree from a graduate program in sport sciences is the safest possibility because, with very few exceptions, the academic positions (mostly tenure track) in sport psychology exist in sport sciences departments. (College or university positions are often tenure-track. A person who receives tenure is assured some job security. Job termination cannot occur without "just cause" [e.g., demonstrated incompetence, substantial neglect of assigned duties, or substantial physical or mental incapacity]).

Individuals trained in sport psychology through sport sciences departments also can provide performance enhancement skills to athletes, but training in recognizing psychopathology is crucial. When athletes experience emotional difficulties such as depression, substance abuse, or eating disorders, individuals consulting with teams/athletes should have the competence to recognize these disorders and refer athletes to licensed clinical/ counseling psychologists.

3

Because sport sciences departments monopolize the academic job market in sport psychology, applicants for these positions usually need formal academic course work in sport science core areas such as exercise physiology, biomechanics, motor development, motor learning/control, and sport sociology, in addition to specialized training in sport psychology.

Obtaining a job usually depends more on the applicants' research and teaching records in sport psychology than their ability to provide athletes with performance enhancement and consultation. Having a license to provide counseling or clinical services to athletes is not a prerequisite and may even be a liability if it prevents the applicant from developing competence in the research and teaching aspects of the field. Thus, if you want to stress teaching and research in a relatively secure academic environment, a doctoral degree in sport sciences is the most logical route to obtain academic or research positions that deal exclusively with exercise and sport.

On rare occasions (see the last paragraph of Track III), individuals with the preceding training may work full-time primarily consulting with athletes. We cannot emphasize strongly enough, however, how rarely these opportunities occur. When these full-time sport psychology consulting positions do occur, they normally go to individuals with extensive post-doctoral experience working with athletes.

TRACK II

TEACHING/RESEARCH IN PSYCHOLOGY AND ALSO INTERESTED IN WORKING WITH ATHLETES

Educational Requirements for Track II

• Doctoral Degree in Psychological Field with a Significant Proportion of Course Work in Exercise and Sport Science.

Primary Employment for Track II

• Academic Psychology Position in College/University
• Researcher in Research Institute or Medical Research Laboratory

Opportunities with the above may include part-time consulting with amateur and professional athletes and teams and on *rare* occasions, full-time consulting.

This is an appropriate track if your interest lies more in a career in which you teach and conduct psychological research on a variety of topics (including sport psychology) and consult with athletes. Some positions exist each year in research institutes, medical research laboratories, and college or university departments of psychology, counseling psychology, or educational psychology. Applicants usually are hired for their teaching and research competence in traditional subject matter areas of psychology (e.g., counseling psychology, group procedures, learning and motivation, psychotherapy, social psychology) rather than experience in sport psychology. Sometimes, these faculty may offer a sport psychology course, consult with athletes/athletic teams, or conduct research in this area.

To prepare for an academic or research position in psychology, you should attempt to enter a doctoral program in psychology, counseling, or educational psychology. Since these departments typically do not offer training in sport psychology, look for a psychology program that at least permits students to take graduate classes in sport psychology and courses in other relevant areas from a sport sciences department.

4

5

TRACK III

PROVIDE CLINICAL/COUNSELING SERVICES TO VARIOUS POPULATIONS, INCLUDING ATHLETES

Educational Requirements for Track III

• Doctoral Degree in an American Psychological
Association (APA) Accredited Clinical/Counseling
Psychology Program with a Significant
Proportion of Course Work in Sport Psychology
and Related Sport Sciences.

Primary Employment for Track III

• Private Psychology Practice
• Clinical/Counseling Psychologist in University
Counseling Center
• University Health Education Psychologist
• Sports Medicine Clinic Psychological Consultant
• University Substance Abuse Specialist
• Career Specialist

Many of the above may include part-time consulting
with amateur and professional athletes and teams and
on *rare* occasions, full-time consulting.

If you would like a career in which you work with athletes
as well as non-athletes (e.g., business people, college
students, hospital patients, or the general population)
there are several reasons for pursuing a doctoral degree
in an APA accredited clinical or counseling psychology
program.

First, various career opportunities working with clinical
problems *require* a doctoral degree in clinical or counseling psychology from an APA accredited program that
includes a 1-year APA approved internship. There are
laws that govern the practice of psychology such that, in
most states, these positions typically require applicants to
have a state license or certificate to practice (see AAASP
certified consultant criteria for guidance regarding
recommended training for working with athletes).
People receiving traditional graduate training from sport
sciences departments that are not APA accredited will
rarely qualify for these positions. Thus, if you want to
provide psychological services for people in general (of
whom a percentage may be athletes), this track has the
distinct advantage of providing the greatest variety of
career opportunities as well as the best chance for you to
obtain employment upon completion of a doctoral
degree and internship.

6

Second, very few sport psychologists earn most of their
income working full-time with competitive athletes.
Those professionals who consult with athletes on a part-
time basis usually have other employment, such as
academic positions, or more traditional clinical or
counseling practices in which they earn most of their
income. Over the past 3-5 years, only one or two *full-
time* positions occurred each year for people to work with
collegiate, Olympic, or professional athletes, or athletes
attending private sport academies.

Typically, these positions are filled by people with
extensive post-doctoral experience working with athletes.
Not only are these positions few in number with no
dramatic increase in sight, but they generally offer less
job security than other positions. At present, staking
your hopes on full-time work with elite athletes appears a
risky venture.

7

TRACK IV

HEALTH PROMOTION AND WORKING WITH ATHLETES BUT NOT NECESSARILY DIRECTLY IN SPORT PSYCHOLOGY

Educational Requirements for Track IV

• Masters Degree in Clinical/Counseling Psychology Program with a Significant Proportion of Course Work in Exercise and Sport Science or Masters Degree in Sport Sciences Department with a Significant Proportion of Course Work in Psychology (some colleges, universities, and health centers look for doctoral degrees)

Primary Employment for Track IV

• College or University Academic Athletic Advisor
• Health Promotion Worker
• Coach

If you would like to provide general support services to and work closely with athletes and/or exercisers, you may decide to pursue a career in academic athletic counseling or coaching. Sport psychology programs that have considerable emphasis in the area of exercise/health psychology may provide opportunities for their graduates to seek careers in health promotion and rehabilitation.

In terms of academic athletic counseling, the vast majority of positions are at Division I colleges and universities. Academic athletic counselors often organize academic tutoring services, monitor academic progress, assist in academic scheduling, and provide other support services for college student-athletes. In larger universities, academic athletic counselors may be assigned to work with a specific team on academic, personal, or sport performance issues, and/or may provide specialized services, such as career development, new student orientation, substance abuse prevention, learning disabilities assessment, or life skills development. In selecting graduate programs that might best prepare you for an academic athletic counseling position, it is imperative to find programs that can offer you fieldwork placements working directly with college student-athletes. Specific course work in counseling, college student development, career development, and sport psychology are particularly relevant. Job opportunities in academic athletic counseling have continued to grow at a slow but steady pace over the last decade.

8

Health care settings may offer opportunities for people interested in working in health promotion and rehabilitation settings such as employee wellness programs, HMOs, rehabilitation programs, and sports medicine clinics. Although a recent study found that only 2.8% of sports medicine clinics currently have counselors working with injured athletes on psychological factors associated with injury and rehabilitation, it seems likely that employment opportunities in this and other health promotion areas will increase. To maximize your chances in these areas, it is imperative to find a program that permits internships in health promotion. You also may want to seek certification by the American College of Sports Medicine when appropriate to do so.

For individuals interested in coaching, a degree in sport psychology may make you an outstanding candidate for positions at the college or university level. Your degree work should be complemented by coaching experience and knowledge of NCAA guidelines. Certification by the American Coaching Effectiveness Program (ACEP) may increase your marketability if you are considering youth sport jobs.

9

ADDITIONAL SUGGESTIONS

How can I obtain information about graduate programs in sport psychology?

The Association for the Advancement of Applied Sport Psychology (AAASP) publishes the *Directory of Graduate Programs in Applied Sport Psychology.* The *Directory* describes each graduate program and lists a contact person. The North American Society for the Psychology of Sport and Physical Activity (NASPSPA) publishes a list of graduate programs in sport psychology in its newsletter. The American Psychological Association (APA) also publishes some information about sport psychology graduate programs in its *Graduate Study in Psychology,* but has a focus on programs in psychology departments.

Once you have an idea of what colleges or universities interest you, you can ask them to send you a description of their programs, degrees, and faculty. The types of degrees and specific requirements for a particular degree differ from school to school. Degrees may be available in counseling psychology, clinical psychology, or sport psychology. Departments of education, counseling, psychology, and sports sciences may offer M.A., M.S., M.Ed., Ph.D., Ed.D., or Psy.D. degrees. The Psy.D. is a relatively new degree which is comparable to the Ph.D., and is designed for people who are primarily interested in applied psychology practice with less emphasis on research.

What else should I ask?

Make sure the program offers the career track and degree you desire. Investigate the reputation of the faculty and program in terms of the opportunities and emphasis in sport psychology, the average time taken by students to complete the program, the funding for graduate students, and the success of graduates in obtaining the kind of sport psychology positions you desire.

Next, check to see if appropriate interdisciplinary course work exists and is an accepted part of the program of study. Opportunities for sport psychology research and graduate sport psychology internship/practica experiences also vary across programs. Give careful consideration to the research and/or clinical/practice focus of the program to ensure that the faculty conducts research on topics of interest to you and is qualified to supervise internship/practica experiences.

For the most thorough information, you should talk to both faculty and students at the programs you have selected. Consideration of the preceding factors can lead to better quality training, which ultimately should make you more competitive for part- or full-time sport psychology positions.

SUGGESTED REFERENCES

For further information on graduate training and career possibilities, and the field of sport psychology in general, the following references may be helpful:

Association for the Advancement of Applied Sport Psychology (1990). Certification criteria. *AAASP Newsletter, 5,* (Winter).

Clark, K. S. (1984). The U.S.O.C. sport psychology registry: A clarification. *Journal of Sport Psychology, 6,* 365-366.

Dishman, R. K. (1983). Identity crisis in North American sport psychology: Academics in professional issues. *Journal of Sport Psychology, 5,* 123-134.

Heyman, S. R. (1984). The development of models for sport psychology: Examining the U.S.O.C. guidelines. *Journal of Sport Psychology, 6,* 125-132.

Sachs, M. L. (1991). Reading list in applied sport psychology: Psychological skills training. *The Sport Psychologist, 5,* 88-91.

Sachs, M. L., Burke, K. L., Salitsky, P. B. (1992). *Directory of graduate programs in applied sport psychology* (3rd ed.). Boise, ID: Association for the Advancement of Applied Sport Psychology.

Taylor, J. (1991). Career direction, development, and opportunities in applied sport psychology. *The Sport Psychologist, 5,* 266-280.

Revised June 1994 by:

Judy L. Van Raalte, Ph.D. &
Jean M. Williams, Ph.D.

12

Ethical Principles and Standards of the Association
for the Advancement of Applied Sport Psychology

Considering Ethics

<u>AAASP Ethics Committee</u>

In 1987 AAASP established an ethics committee. After considerable deliberation, this committee recommended that the association temporarily adopt the American Psychological Association's (APA) 1981 Ethics Standards for Psychologists. One reason for this recommendation was the APA tradition for maintaining high standards for practice, research, and teaching. Another reason was that this code addressed many issues that AAASP members appeared to face.

After certification passed, however, the idea of an ethics code for the AAASP membership. In 1990 the chairman of the Ethics Committee, Al Petitpas, addressed this issue with a study of AAASP members' experiences and attitudes about various ethical problems. The results of this survey revealed the advantages and disadvantages of the continued reliance on the APA Ethics code. These results were published in the *Journal of Applied Sport Psychology* in 1994.

With these results in hand, the 1993 Ethics Committee co-chairs, Andy Meyers and Dan Gould, were asked to develop a new code of ethics written specifically for the association. This charge was completed in two steps. The first was the development of a set of ethics principles, or statements of ethical aspirations that should guide members' decision making. These principles were discussed and adopted by the association at the 1994 convention. The second step was to articulate a set of specific ethics guidelines that could be use as rules for specific professional situations. After being approved by the AAASP board, these guidelines were discussed and adopted by the AAASP during the 1996 convention.

INTRODUCTION

AAASP is dedicated to the development and professionalization of the field of sport psychology. As we establish ourselves as a profession, we must attend to both the privileges and responsibilities of a profession. Privileges derive from society's agreement to accept our designation as a group of trained individuals possessing specialized knowledge and, therefore, the power implicit in this knowledge. Our responsibilities, in turn, result from the society's trust that the profession will regulate itself to do no harm, and to govern itself to ensure the dignity and welfare of individuals we serve and the public. To maintain this status, professional organizations must develop and enforce guidelines that regulate their members' professional conduct. A code of ethical principles and standards is one such set of self-regulatory guidelines. This code guides professionals to act responsibly as they employ the privileges granted by society. A profession's inability to regulate itself violates the public's trust and undermines the profession's potential to be of service to society.

Ethical codes of conduct that professions adopt are based in the values of the society. Consequently, these values include the balance between the rights and privacy of the individual and the general welfare of society. Each profession must determine its values and social function. The profession must then develop and adopt an ethics code which guides professional conduct. While no set of guidelines can anticipate all situations, a useful code should provide guidance when problems or dilemmas arise. This code should also proactively direct the actions of its members in work-related settings. If this is accomplished, the code will ensure society's trust in the profession.

The Association for the Advancement of Applied Sport Psychology's (AAASP) Ethical Principles and Standards (hereinafter referred to as the Ethics Code) is presented here and consists of this Introduction, a Preamble, six general Principles, and 25 Standards. The Introduction discusses the intent and organizational considerations of the Ethics Code. The Preamble and General Principles are intended to guide AAASP members toward the highest ideals of the profession. The Standards more precisely specify the boundaries of ethical conduct. Although the Preamble and the General Principles are not themselves enforceable rules, they should be considered by AAASP members in arriving at an ethical course of action. Ethical Standards are enforceable rules that mandate behavioral choices.

Membership in the AAASP commits members to adhere to the AAASP Ethics Code. AAASP members should be aware that, in many situations, additional ethical and legal codes may be applied to them by other professional organizations or public bodies. In the process of making decisions regarding their professional behavior, AAASP members must consider this Ethics Code, in addition to other ethical guidelines or legal codes. If the Ethics Code suggests a higher standard of conduct than is required by legal codes or other ethical guidelines, AAASP members should meet the higher ethical standard. If the Ethics Code standard appears to conflict with the requirements of law, then AAASP members must make known their commitment to the Ethics Code and take steps to resolve the conflict in a responsible manner. If neither law nor the Ethics Code resolves an issue, AAASP members should consider other professional materials (e.g., guidelines and standards that have been adopted or endorsed by other professional physical education, sport science, and social science organizations), the dictates of their own conscience, and consultation with others within the field when this is practical.[1]

PREAMBLE

AAASP members may fulfill many roles based on their professional training and competence. In these roles they may work to develop a valid and reliable body of scientific knowledge based on research; they may apply that knowledge to human behavior in a variety of sport, exercise, physical activity, and health contexts. Their goals are to broaden knowledge of this behavior and, where appropriate, to apply it pragmatically to improve the condition of both the individual and society. AAASP members respect the central importance of freedom of inquiry and expression in research, teaching, and consulting. They also strive to help the public to develop informed judgments and choices concerning sport, exercise, physical activity, and health behavior. This Ethics Code provides a common set of values upon which AAASP members build their professional and scientific work.

This Code is intended to provide the general principles and specific ethical standards for

---

1. This Ethics Code is based in large part on the American Psychological Association's Ethical Principles of Psychologists and Code of Conduct (*American Psychologist*, 1992, *V.47*, #12, pp. 1597–1611.). Over 50 other organizational ethics codes, including the code of the American College of Sports Medicine, were also examined and many influenced this document. We wish to thank all of these organizations.

managing many situations encountered by AAASP members. It has as its primary goal the welfare and protection of the individuals and groups with whom AAASP members work. It is the individual responsibility of each AAASP member to aspire to the highest possible standards of conduct. AAASP members respect and protect human and civil rights, and do not knowingly participate in or condone unfair discriminatory practices.

The development of a dynamic ethical code for an AAASP member's work-related conduct requires a personal commitment to a lifelong effort to act ethically; to encourage ethical behavior by students, supervisees, employees, and colleagues, as appropriate; and to consult with others, as needed, concerning ethical problems, Each AAASP member supplements, but does not violate, the Ethics Code's values, on the basis of guidance drawn from personal values, culture, and experience.

GENERAL PRINCIPLES

Principle A: Competence

AAASP members maintain the highest standards of competence in their work. They recognize the boundaries of their professional competencies and the limitations of their expertise. They maintain knowledge related to the services they render, and they recognize the need for ongoing education. AAASP members make appropriate use of scientific, professional, technical, and administrative resources. They provide only those services and use only those techniques for which they are qualified by education, training, or experience. AAASP members are cognizant of the fact that the competencies required in serving, teaching, and/or studying groups of people vary with the distinctive characteristics of those groups. In those areas in which recognized professional standards do not yet exist. AAASP members exercise careful judgment and take appropriate precautions to protect the welfare of those with whom they work.

Principle B: Integrity

AAASP members promote integrity in the science, teaching, and practice of their profession. In these activities AAASP members are honest and fair. When describing or reporting their qualifications, services, products, fees, research, or teaching, they do not make statements that are false, misleading, or deceptive. They clarify for relevant parties the roles they are performing and the obligations they adopt. They function appropriately in accordance with those roles and obligations. AAASP members avoid improper and potentially harmful dual relationships.

Principle C: Professional and Scientific Responsibility

AAASP members are responsible for safeguarding the public and AAASP from members who are deficient in ethical conduct. They uphold professional standards of conduct and accept appropriate responsibility for their behavior. AAASP members consult with, refer to, or cooperate with other professionals and institutions to the extent needed to serve the best interests of the recipients of their services. AAASP members' moral standards and conduct are personal matters to the same degree as is true for any other person, except as their conduct may compromise their professional responsibilities or reduce the public's trust in the profession and the organization. AAASP members are concerned about the ethical compliance of their colleagues' scientific and professional conduct. When appropriate, they consult with colleagues in order to prevent, avoid, or terminate unethical conduct.

Principle D: Respect for People's Rights and Dignity

AAASP members accord appropriate respect to the fundamental rights, dignity, and worth of all people. They respect the rights of individuals to privacy, confidentiality, self-determination, and autonomy, mindful that legal and other obligations may lead to inconsistency and conflict with the exercise of these rights. AAASP members are aware of cultural, individual, and role differences, including those due to age, gender, race, ethnicity, national origin, religion, sexual orientation, disability, language, and socioeconomic status. AAASP members try to eliminate the effect on their work of biases based on those factors, and they do not knowingly participate in or condone unfair discriminatory practices.

Principle E: Concern for Others' Welfare

AAASP members seek to contribute to the welfare of those with whom they interact professionally. When conflicts occur among AAASP members' obligations or concerns, they attempt to resolve those conflicts and to perform those roles in a responsible fashion that avoids or minimizes harm. AAASP members are sensitive to real and ascribed differences in power between themselves and others. They do not exploit or mislead other people during or after professional relationships.

Principle F: Social Responsibility

AAASP members are aware of their professional and scientific responsibilities to the community and the society in which they work and live. They apply and make public their knowledge in order to contribute to human welfare. When undertaking research, AAASP members strive to advance human welfare and their profession while always protecting the rights of the participants. AAASP members try to avoid misuse of their work, and they comply with the law.

GENERAL ETHICAL STANDARDS

These General Standards are applicable to AAASP members across all their professional roles and in all their professional interactions and communications.

1. Professional and Scientific Relationship

AAASP members provide diagnostic, therapeutic, teaching, research, educational, supervisory, or other consultative services only in the context of a defined professional or scientific relationship or role.

2. Boundaries of Competence

(a) AAASP members represent diverse academic and professional backgrounds. These different training histories provide different competencies. Those trained in clinical and counseling psychology must be aware of potential limitations in their sport science competencies. AAASP members trained in the sport sciences must be aware of their limitations in clinical and counseling psychology. Individuals from different training backgrounds must deliver services, teach, and conduct research only within the boundaries of their competence.

(b) AAASP members provide services, teach, or conduct research in new areas only after taking the necessary actions to guarantee a high level of competence in those areas.

(c) AAASP members who engage in assessment, therapy, teaching, research, organizational consulting, or other professional activities maintain a reasonable level of awareness of current scientific and professional information in their fields of activity, and undertake ongoing efforts to maintain competence in the skills they use.

(d) AAASP members are aware of the limitations of their scientific work and do not make claims or take actions that exceed these limitations.

3. Human Differences

(a) AAASP members recognize that differences of age, gender, race, ethnicity, national origin, religion, sexual orientation, disability, language, or socioeconomic status can significantly affect their work. AAASP members working with specific populations have the responsibility to develop the necessary skills to be competent with these populations, or they make appropriate referrals.

(b) AAASP members do not engage in unfair discrimination based on age, gender, race, ethnicity, national origin, religion, sexual orientation, disability, socioeconomic status, or any basis proscribed by law.

4. Exploitation and Harassment

(a) AAASP members do not exploit persons over whom they have supervisory, evaluative, or other authority, such as students, supervisees, employees, research participants, and clients or patients.

(b) AAASP members do not engage in behavior that is harassing or demeaning to persons with whom they interact in their work.

(c) AAASP members do not solicit testimonials from current psychotherapy clients or patients or other persons who because of their particular circumstances are vulnerable to undue influence.

5. Personal Problems and Conflicts

(a) AAASP members recognize that personal problems, including addictions, and personal conflicts may interfere with their effectiveness. Accordingly, they refrain from undertaking an activity when their personal problems may harm others to whom they may owe a professional or scientific obligation.

(b) AAASP members are aware that the extreme visibility and notoriety of some of the clients and organizations that they work with may compromise their professional objectivity and competence. In such situations, it is the AAASP member's responsibility to take corrective action, including consultation with other professionals and termination and referral if necessary.

(c) In their professional roles AAASP members may obtain privileged information about clients or client organizations. AAASP members do not use this information for personal gain.

6. Avoiding Harm

AAASP members take reasonable steps to avoid harming their patients or clients, research participants, students, and others with whom they work, and to minimize harm where it is foreseeable and unavoidable.

7. Misuse of AAASP Members' Influence

Because AAASP members' scientific and professional judgments and actions may affect the lives of others, they are alert to and guard against personal, financial, social, organizational, or political factors that might lead to misuse of their influence.

8. Misuse of AAASP Members' Work

AAASP members do not participate in activities in which it appears likely that their skills or products will be misused by others. If AAASP members learn of misuse or misrepresentation of their work, they take reasonable steps to correct or minimize the misuse or misrepresentation.

9. Multiple Relationships

(a) AAASP members must always be sensitive to the potential harmful if unintended effects of social or other nonprofessional contacts on their work and on those persons with whom they deal. Such multiple relationships might impair the AAASP member's objectivity or might harm or exploit the other party.

(b) An AAASP member refrains from taking on professional or scientific obligations when preexisting relationships would create a risk of such harm.

(c) AAASP members do not engage in sexual relationships with students, supervisees, and clients over whom the AAASP member has evaluative, direct, or indirect authority, because such relationships are so likely to impair judgment or be exploitative.

(d) AAASP members avoid personal, scientific, professional, financial, or other relationships with family members of minor clients because such relationships are so likely to impair judgment or be exploitative.

(e) If an AAASP member finds that, due to unforeseen factors, a potentially harmful multiple relationship has arisen, the AAASP member attempts to resolve it with due regard for the best interests of the affected person and maximal compliance with the Ethics Code.

10. Barter (with Patients or Clients)

AAASP members refrain from accepting goods, services, or other nonmonetary remuneration from patients, clients, students, supervisees, or research subjects in return for services, because such arrangements create inherent potential for conflicts, exploitation, and distortion of the professional relationship. In certain circumstances AAASP members may receive tokens of appreciation from clients or client organizations. In these situations it is the AAASP member's responsibility to determine that the gifts are appropriate for the setting, not exploitative, and that the gifts do not serve as payment for services.

11. Consultations and Referrals

(a) AAASP members arrange for appropriate consultations and referrals based principally on the best interests of their patients or clients, with appropriate consent and subject to other relevant considerations, including applicable law and contractual obligations.

(b) AAASP members cooperate with other professionals in order to serve their patients or clients effectively and appropriately.

12. Third-Party Requests for Services

(a) When an AAASP member agrees to provide services to a person or entity at the request of a third party, the AAASP member clarifies, at the outset of the service, the nature of the relationship with each party. This clarification includes the role of the AAASP member, the probable uses of the services provided or the information obtained, and the fact that there may be limits to confidentiality.

(b) If there is a foreseeable risk of the AAASP member's being called upon to perform conflicting roles because of the involvement of a third party, the AAASP member clarifies the nature and direction of his or her responsibilities, keeps all parties appropriately informed as matters develop, and resolves the situation in accordance with the Ethics Code.

13. Delegation to and Supervision of Subordinates

(a) AAASP members delegate to their employees, supervisees, and research assistants only those responsibilities that such persons can reasonably be expected to perform competently.

(b) AAASP members provide proper training and supervision to their employees or supervisees and take reasonable steps to see that such persons perform services responsibly, competently, and ethically.

14. Documentation of Professional and Scientific Work

AAASP members appropriately document their professional and scientific work in order to facilitate provision of services later by them or by other professionals, to ensure accountability, and to meet other requirements of institutions or the law.

15. Fees and Financial Arrangements

(a) As early as is feasible in a professional or scientific relationship, the AAASP member and the patient, client, or other appropriate recipient of services reach an agreement clearly specifying the compensation and the billing arrangements.

(b) AAASP members do not exploit recipients of services or payers with respect to fees.

(c) If limitations to services can be anticipated because of limitations in financing, this is discussed with the patient, client, or other appropriate recipient of services as early as is feasible.

(d) AAASP members do not deliver services for future remuneration based on the client's future achievements nor do they accept testimonials in place of fees for services.

16. Definition of Public Statements

AAASP members are responsible for the clarity and honesty of public statements about their work made to students, clients, colleagues, or the public, by themselves or others representing them. If AAASP members learn of deceptive statements about their work made by others, AAASP members make reasonable efforts to correct such statements.

17. Informed Consent to Practice

(a) AAASP members obtain appropriate informed consent to educational and counseling procedures, using language that is reasonably understandable to participants. The content of informed consent will vary depending on circumstances. However, informed consent generally implies that the person (1) has the capacity to consent, (2) has been informed of significant information concerning the procedure, (3) has freely and without undue influence expressed consent, and (4) consent has been appropriately documented.

(b) When persons are legally incapable of giving informed consent, AAASP members obtain informed permission from a legally authorized person, if such substitute consent is permitted by law.

(c) In addition, AAASP members (1) inform those persons who are legally incapable of giving informed consent about the proposed interventions in a manner commensurate with the persons' psychological capacities, (2) seek their assent to those interventions, and (3) consider such persons' preferences and best interests.

18. Maintaining Confidentiality

(a) AAASP members have a primary obligation to uphold and take reasonable precautions to respect the confidentiality rights of those with whom they work or consult, recognizing that confidentiality may be established by law, institutional rules, and/or professional or scientific relationships.

(b) AAASP members discuss with persons and organizations with whom they work (1) the relevant limitations on confidentiality, including limitations where applicable in group, marital, and family counseling or in organizational consulting, and (2) the foreseeable uses of the information generated through their services.

(c) AAASP members do not disclose in their writings, lectures, or other public media, confidential, personally identifiable information concerning their patients, individual or organizational clients, students, research participants, or other recipients of their services that they obtained during the course of their work, unless the person or organization has consented in writing or unless there is other ethical or legal authorization for doing so.

19. Informed Consent to Research

(a) Prior to conducting research (except research involving only anonymous surveys, naturalistic observations, or similar methods where the risk of harm is minimal), AAASP members enter into an agreement with participants that clarifies the nature of the research and the responsibilities of each party.

(b) AAASP members use language that is reasonably understandable to research participants in obtaining their appropriate informed consent. Such informed consent is appropriately documented.

(c) Using language that is reasonably understandable to participants, AAASP members inform participants of the nature of the research; they inform participants that they are free to participate or to decline to participate or to withdraw from the research; they explain the foreseeable consequences of declining or withdrawing; they inform participants of significant factors that may be expected to influence their willingness to participate (such as risks, discomfort, adverse effects, or limitations on confidentiality); and they explain other aspects about which the prospective participants inquire.

(d) When AAASP members conduct research with individuals such as students or subordinates, AAASP members take special care to protect the prospective participants from adverse consequences of declining or withdrawing from participation.

(e) When research participation is a course or team requirement or opportunity for extra course credit, the prospective participant is given the choice of equitable alternative activities.

(f) For persons who are legally incapable of giving informed consent, AAASP members nevertheless (1) provide an appropriate explanation, (2) where possible, obtain the participant's assent, and (3) obtain appropriate permission from a legally authorized person, if such substitute consent is permitted by law.

20. Conduct of Research

(a) AAASP members design, conduct, and report research in accordance with recognized standards of scientific competence and ethical research.

(b) AAASP members plan their research so as to minimize the possibility that results will be misleading.

(c) AAASP members take reasonable steps to implement appropriate protections for the rights and welfare of human participants, other persons affected by the research, and the welfare of animal subjects.

(d) AAASP members obtain from host institutions or organizations appropriate approval prior to conducting research, and they provide accurate information about their research proposals. They conduct the research in accordance with the approved research protocol.

(e) AAASP members do not offer excessive or inappropriate financial or other inducements to obtain research participants, particularly when it might tend to coerce participation.

21. Deception in Research

(a) AAASP members do not conduct a study involving deception unless they have determined that the use of deceptive techniques is justified by the study's prospective scientific, educational, or applied value, will not harm the participant, and that equally effective alternative procedures that do not use deception are not feasible.

(b) AAASP members never deceive research participants about significant aspects that would affect their willingness to participate, such as physical risks, discomfort, or unpleasant emotional experiences.

(c) Any other deception that is an integral feature of the design and conduct of an experiment must be explained to participants as early as is feasible, preferably at the conclusion of their participation, but no later than at the conclusion of the research. If scientific or humane values justify delaying or withholding this information, AAASP members take reasonable measures to reduce the risk of harm.

22. Minimizing Invasiveness

In conducting research, AAASP members interfere with the participants or milieu from which data are collected only in a manner that is warranted by an appropriate research design and that is consistent with AAASP members' roles as scientific investigators.

23. Honesty in Research

(a) AAASP members do not fabricate data or falsify results in their publications.

(b) If AAASP members discover errors in their published data, they take reasonable steps to correct such errors in a correction, retraction, erratum, or other appropriate publication means.

(c) AAASP members do not present substantial portions or elements of another's work or data as their own, even if the other work or data source is cited occasionally. AAASP members only accept publication and other credit for work that they have created or performed.

24. Conflicts between Ethics and Organizational Demands

If the demands of an organization with which AAASP members are affiliated conflict with the Ethics Code, members clarify the nature of the conflict, make known their commitment to the Ethics Code, and to the extent feasible, seek to resolve the conflict in a way that permits the fullest adherence to the Ethics Code.

25. Resolution of Ethical Conflicts

The successful implementation of an ethics code requires a personal commitment to act ethically, encourage ethical behavior by others, and consult with others concerning ethical problems. When applying the code of ethical conduct, AAASP members may encounter problems in identifying unethical conduct or in resolving ethical conflict. When faced with significant ethical concerns, one should consider the following courses of action.

- Before any action is taken, one may benefit from advice from uninvolved and objective advisors or peers familiar with ethical issues.
- When members believes that there may have been an ethical violation by another member, they may attempt to clarify and resolve the issue by bringing the matter to the attention of the other involved parties if such an informal resolution appears appropriate and the intervention does not violate any confidentiality rights that may be involved.
- Discuss ethical problems with your immediate supervisor except when it appears that the supervisor is involved in the ethical issue, in which case the problem should be presented to the next higher administrative level. If satisfactory resolution cannot be achieved when the problem is initially presented, the issue should be submitted to the next higher administrative level.
- Contact with levels above the immediate administrator should be initiated only with the administrator's knowledge, assuming that the administrator is not involved.
- If the ethical problem or conflict still exists after exhausting all levels of internal review, support from appropriate professional organizations should be obtained.

It is important for AAASP members to understand that unethical conduct is a serious matter. However, the primary aims of these ethical principles are to inform and motivate the highest standards of conduct among AAASP members as we serve our clients, our professions, and our community.

(Submitted by Dr. James Whelan, University of Memphis, on behalf of the AAASP Ethics Committee)

APPENDIX G

Texts in Applied Sport Psychology

There are numerous texts in applied sport psychology that you may find of interest. An excellent reference list in this area may be found in Mary Beth Allen's 1994 article in *The Sport Psychologist* (volume 8, pp. 94–99) entitled "Authorship in Sport Psychology: A Reference List." Some selected books that you may find particularly helpful include the following.

Texts in Sport Psychology

Anshel, Mark H. (1997). *Sport psychology: From theory to practice.* (3 ed.) Scottsdale, AZ: Gorsuch Scarisbrick, Publishers.

Cox, Richard H. (1994). *Sport psychology: Concepts and applications.* (3 ed.). Dubuque, IA: Wm. C. Brown, Publishers.

Gill, Diane L. (1986). *Psychological dynamics of sport.* Champaign, IL: Human Kinetics Publishers.

Horn, Thelma S. (Ed.). (1992). *Advances in sport psychology.* Champaign, IL: Human Kinetics Books.

Kremer, John M., & Scully, Deidre. (1994). *Psychology in sport.* Bristol, PA: Taylor & Francis, Inc.

LeUnes, Arnold D., & Nation, Jack R. (1995). *Sport psychology: An introduction.* (2nd ed.) Chicago: Nelson-Hall.

Morris, Tony, & Summers, J. (Eds.). *Sport psychology: Theory, applications and issues.* Brisbane, Australia: John Wiley & Sons.

Murphy, Shane M. (Ed.). (1995). *Sport psychology interventions.* Champaign, IL: Human Kinetics.

Rotella, Robert, Boyce, Ann B., Allyson, Billy, & Savis, Jacqueline. (1997). *Case studies in sport psychology.* Boston, MA: Jones and Bartlett Publishers.

Silva, John M., & Weinberg, Robert S. (1984). *Psychological foundations of sport.* Champaign, IL: Human Kinetics Publishers.

Weinberg, Robert S., & Gould, Daniel. (1995). *Foundations of sport and exercise psychology.* Champaign, IL: Human Kinetics.

Williams, Jean M. (Ed.). (1997). *Applied sport psychology: Personal growth to peak performance.* (3rd ed.) Mountain View, CA: Mayfield Publishing Company.

Wann, Daniel L. (1997). *Sport psychology.* Upper Saddle River, NJ: Prentice Hall.

Texts in Exercise Psychology

Berger, Bonnie G., & Pargman, David. (expected publication date: 1998). *Exercise psychology.* Morgantown, WV: Fitness Information Technology, Inc.

Willis, Joe D., & Campbell, Linda Frye. (1992). *Exercise psychology.* Champaign, IL: Human Kinetics Books.

General References

Salmela, John H. (1992). *The world sport psychology sourcebook.* (2nd ed.). Champaign, IL: Human Kinetics Books.

> Excellent publication with background information and a comprehensive
> Who's Who's in the world of sport psychology.

Singer, Robert N., Murphey, Milledge, & Tennant, L. Keith. (1993). *Handbook of research on sport psychology.* New York: Macmillan Publishing Company.

> The definitive reference work in sport psychology,
> with 44 chapters (984 pages in length).

Skinner, James S., Corbin, Charles B., Landers, Daniel M., Martin, Philip E., & Wells, Christine L. (Eds.). (1989). *Future directions in exercise and sport science research.* Champaign, IL: Human Kinetics Books.

> This volume contains numerous excellent chapters in the exercise and sport sciences in
> general, with sport psychology chapters written by Deborah Feltz, Daniel Landers,
> William Morgan, Glyn Roberts, Ronald Smith, and Richard Suinn.

Van Raalte, Judy L., & Brewer, Britton W. (Eds.). (1996). *Exploring sport and exercise psychology.* Washington, DC: American Psychological Association.

> An excellent resource with 21 chapters in sections on performance enhancement,
> promoting well-being, clinical issues, working with
> specific populations, and professional issues.

APPENDIX H

References in Applied Sport Psychology:
Professional and Ethical Issues

There are numerous references in applied sport psychology that deal with professional and ethical issues that you may find of interest. An excellent reference list in this area may be found in Vincent Granito and Betty Wenz's 1995 article in *The Sport Psychologist* (volume 9, pp. 96–103) entitled "Reading List for Professional Issues in Applied Sport Psychology." The following listing represents an updated version of the listing provided in the third edition of this directory. Readers may wish to review both this list and the Granito and Wenz list.

Allen, M. B. (1994). Authorship in sport psychology: A reference list. *The Sport Psychologist*, *8*, 94–99.

American Psychological Association. (1987). *Casebook on ethical principles of psychologists*. Washington, DC: American Psychological Association.

American Psychological Association. (1990). Ethical principles of psychologists (Amended June 2, 1989). *American Psychologist, 45*, 390–395.

Andersen, M. B. (1994). Ethical considerations in the supervision of applied sport psychology graduate students. *Journal of Applied Sport Psychology, 6*, 152–167.

Andersen, M. B., & Williams-Rice, B. T. (1996). Supervision in the education and training of sport psychology service providers. *Journal of Applied Sport Psychology, 10*, 278–290.

Andersen, M. B., Van Raalte, J. L., & Brewer, B. W. (1994). Assessing the skills of sport psychology supervisors. *The Sport Psychologist, 8*, 238–247.

Anshel, M. H. (1990). Perceptions of black intercollegiate football players: Implications for the sport psychology consultant. *The Sport Psychologist, 4*, 235–248.

Anshel, M. H. (1992). The case against the certification of sport psychologists: In search of the phantom expert. *The Sport Psychologist, 6*, 265–286.

Anshel, M. H. (1993). Against the certification of sport psychology consultants: A response to Zaichkowsky and Perna. *The Sport Psychologist, 7*, 344–353.

Barney, S. T., Andersen, M. B., & Riggs, C. A. (1996). Supervision in sport psychology: Some recommendations for practicum training. *Journal of Applied Sport Psychology, 8*, 200–217.

Brown, J. M. (1982). Are sport psychologists really psychologists? *Journal of Sport Psychology, 4*, 13–18.

Brustad, R. J., & Ritter-Taylor, M. (1997). Applying social psychological perspectives to the sport psychology consulting process. *The Sport Psychologist, 11*, 107–119.

Buceta, J. M. (1993). The sport psychologist/athletic coach dual role: Advantages, difficulties, and ethical considerations. *Journal of Applied Sport Psychology, 5*, 64–77.

Burke, K. L., & Johnson, J. J. (1992). The sport psychologist-coach dual role position: A rebuttal to Ellickson and Brown (1990). *Journal of Applied Sport Psychology, 4*, 51–55.

Butki, B. D., & Andersen, M. B. (1994). Mentoring in sport psychology: Students' perceptions of training in publications and presentation guidelines. *The Sport Psychologist, 8*, 143–148.

Carron, A. V. (1993). The Coleman Roberts Griffith address: Toward the integration of theory, research, and practice in sport psychology. *Journal of Applied Sport Psychology, 5,* 207–221.

Clarke, K. S. (1984). The USOC Sports Psychology Registry: A clarification. *Journal of Sport Psychology, 6,* 365–366.

DeFrancesco, C., & Cronin, J. J. (1988). Marketing the sport psychologist. *The Sport Psychologist, 2,* 28–38.

Danish, S. J., & Hale, B. D. (1981). Toward an understanding of the practice of sport psychology. *Journal of Sport Psychology, 3,* 90–99.

Danish, S. J., & Hale, B. D. (1982). Let the discussions continue: Further considerations on the practice of sport psychology. *Journal of Sport Psychology, 4,* 10–12.

Danish, S. J., Petitpas, A. J., & Hale, B. D. (1990). Sport as a context for developing competence. In T. Gullotta, G. Adams, & R. Monteymar (Eds.), *Developing social competency in adolescence* (volume 3, pp. 169–194). Newbury Park, CA: Sage.

Danish, S. J., Petitpas, A. J., & Hale, B. D. (in press). Life development intervention for athletes: Life skills through sports. *The Counseling Psychologist* (in special issue on sport psychology—expected date: summer 1993).

Danish, S. J., Petitpas, A. J., & Hale, B. D. (1992). A developmental-educational intervention model of sport psychology. *The Sport Psychologist, 6,* 403–415.

Dishman, R. K. (1983). Identity crises in North American sport psychology: Academics in professional issues. *Journal of Sport Psychology, 5,* 123–134.

Ellickson, K. A., & Brown, D. R. (1990). Ethical considerations in dual relationships: The sport psychologist-coach. *Journal of Applied Sport Psychology, 2,* 186–190.

Gardner, F. L. (1991). Professionalization of sport psychology: A reply to Silva. *The Sport Psychologist, 5,* 55–60.

Gill, D. L. (1994). A feminist perspective on sport psychology practice. *The Sport Psychologist, 8,* 411–426.

Gould, D. (1990). AAASP: A vision for the 1990's. *Journal of Applied Sport Psychology, 2,* 99–116.

Gould, D., Tammen, V., Murphy, S., & May, J. (1989). An examination of U. S. Olympic sport psychology consultants and the services they provide. *The Sport Psychologist, 3,* 300–312.

Granito, Jr., V. J., & Wenz, B. J. (1995). Reading list for professional issues in applied sport psychology. *The Sport Psychologist, 9,* 96–103.

Halliwell, W. (1989). Applied sport psychology in Canada. *Journal of Applied Sport Psychology, 1,* 35–44.

Hardy, C. J. (1994). Nurturing our future through effective mentoring: Developing roots as well as wings. AAASP 1993 Presidential Address. *Journal of Applied Sport Psychology, 6,* 196–204.

Harrison, R. P., & Feltz, D. L. (1979). The professionalization of sport psychology: Legal considerations. *Journal of Sport Psychology, 1,* 182–190.

Hays, K. F. (1995). Putting sport psychology into (your) practice. *Professional Psychology: Research and Practice, 26*, 33–40.

Heyman, S. R. (1982). A reaction to Danish and Hale: A minority report. *Journal of Sport Psychology, 4*, 7–9.

Heyman, S. R. (1984). The development of models for sport psychology: Examining the USOC guidelines. *Journal of Sport Psychology, 6*, 125–132.

Heyman, S. R. (1987). Counseling and psychotherapy with athletes: Special considerations. In J. R. May & M. J. Asken (Eds.), *Sport psychology: The psychological health of the athlete* (pp. 135–156). New York: PMA Publishing Corp.

Heyman, S. R. (1990). Ethical issues in performance enhancement approaches with amateur boxers. *The Sport Psychologist, 4*, 48–54.

Kirschenbaum, D. S., Parham, W. D., & Murphy, S. M. (1993). Provision of sport psychology services at Olympic events: The 1991 U.S. Olympic Festival and beyond. *The Sport Psychologist, 7*, 419–440.

Krane, V. (1994). A feminist perspective on contemporary sport psychology research. *The Sport Psychologist, 8*, 393–410.

Krane, V., Andersen, M. B., & Strean, W. B. (1997). Issues of qualitative research methods and presentation. *Journal of Sport & Exercise Psychology, 19*, 213–218.

Landers, D. M. (1983). Whatever happened to theory testing in sport psychology? *Journal of Sport Psychology, 5*, 135–151.

Mahoney, M. J., & Suinn, R. M. (1986). History and overview of modern sport psychology. *The Clinical Psychologist, 10*, 64–68.

Murphy, S. (Ed.). (1993). *Clinical sport psychology.* Champaign: Human Kinetics Publishers.

Nideffer, R. M. (1981). *The ethics and practice of applied sport psychology.* Ithaca, NY: Mouvement Publications.

Nideffer, R. M., Dufresne, P., Nesvig, D., & Selder, D. (1980). The future of applied sport psychology. *Journal of Sport Psychology, 2*, 170–174.

Nideffer, R. M., Feltz, D., & Salmela, J. (1982). A rebuttal to Danish and Hale: A committee report. *Journal of Sport Psychology, 4*, 3–6.

Ogilvie, B. C. (1979). The sport psychologist and his professional credibility. In P. Klavora & J. V. Daniel (Eds.), *Coach, athlete, and the sport psychologist* (pp. 44–55). Toronto, Ontario, Canada: University of Toronto.

Ogilvie, B. C. (1989). Applied sport psychology: Reflections on the future. *Journal of Applied Sport Psychology, 1*, 4–7.

Petitpas, A. J., Brewer, B. W., Rivera, P. M., & Van Raalte, J. L. (1994). Ethical beliefs and behaviors in applied sport psychology: The AAASP Ethics Survey. *Journal of Applied Sport Psychology, 6*, 135–151.

Petrie, T. A., & Diehl, N. S. (1995). Sport psychology in the profession of psychology. *Professional Psychology: Research and Practice, 26*, 288–291.

Petrie, T. A., & Watkins, Jr., C. E. (1994a). A survey of counseling psychology programs and exercise/sport science departments: Sport psychology issues and training. *The Sport Psychologist, 8*, 28–36.

Petrie, T. A., & Watkins, Jr., C. E. (1994b). Sport psychology training in counseling psychology programs: Is there room at the inn? *The Counseling Psychologist, 22*, 335–341.

Ravizza, K. (1988). Gaining entry with athletic personnel for season-long consulting. *The Sport Psychologist, 2*, 243–254.

Rejeski, W. J., & Brawley, L. R. (1988). Defining the boundaries of sport psychology. *The Sport Psychologist, 2*, 231–242.

Sachs, M. L. (1993). Professional ethics in sport psychology. In R. N. Singer, M. Murphey, & K. Tennant, (Eds.), *Handbook on research in sport psychology*. New York: Macmillan Publishing Company.

Sachs, M. L. (1991). Reading list in applied sport psychology: Psychological skills training. *The Sport Psychologist, 5*, 88–91.

Schell, B., Hunt, J., & Lloyd, C. (1984). An investigation of future market opportunities for sport psychologists. *Journal of Sport Psychology, 6*, 335–350.

Silva, III, J. M. (1989). The evolution of AAASP and JASP. *Journal of Applied Sport Psychology, 1*, 1–3.

Silva, III, J. M. (1989). Toward the professionalization of sport psychology. *The Sport Psychologist, 3*, 265–273.

Silva, III, J. M. (1992). On advancement: An editorial. *Journal of Applied Sport Psychology, 4*, 1–9.

Silva, III, J. M. (1996). 1995 Coleman Roberts Griffith address: Profiles of excellence. *Journal of Applied Sport Psychology, 8*, 119–130.

Simons, J. P., & Andersen, M. B. (1995). The development of consulting practice in applied sport psychology: Some personal perspectives. *The Sport Psychologist, 9*, 449–468.

Singer, R. N. (1989). Applied sport psychology in the United States. *Journal of Applied Sport Psychology, 1*, 61–80.

Singer, R. N. (1992). What in the world is happening in sport psychology. *Journal of Applied Sport Psychology, 4*, 63–76.

Smith, D. (1992). The coach as sport psychologist: An alternate view. *Journal of Applied Sport Psychology, 4*, 56–62.

Smith, R. E. (1989). Applied sport psychology in an age of accountability. *Journal of Applied Sport Psychology, 1*, 166–180.

Smith, Y. R. (1991). Issues and strategies for working with multicultural athletes. *Journal of Physical Education, Recreation, and Dance, 62(3)*, 39–44.

Straub, W. F., & Hinman, D. A. (1992). Profiles and professional perspectives of 10 leading sport psychologists. *The Sport Psychologist, 6*, 297–312.

Strean, W. B., & Roberts, G. C. (1992). Future directions in applied sport psychology reserach. *The Sport Psychologist, 6*, 55–65.

Taylor, J. (1991). Career direction, development, and opportunities in applied sport psychology. *The Sport Psychologist, 5*, 266–280.

Taylor, J. (1994). Examining the boundaries of sport science and psychology trained practitioners in applied sport psychology: Title usage and area of competence. *Journal of Applied Sport Psychology, 6*, 185–195.

Taylor, J. (1995). A conceptual model for integrating athletes' needs and sport demands in the development of competitive mental preparation strategies. *The Sport Psychologist, 9*, 339–357.

United States Olympic Committee. (1983). United States Olympic Committee establishes guidelines for sport psychology services. *Journal of Sport Psychology, 5*, 4–7.

Van Raalte, J. L., Brewer, D. D., Brewer, B. W., & Linder, D. E. (1993). Sport psychologists' perceptions of sport and mental health practitioners. *Journal of Applied Sport Psychology, 5*, 222–233.

Vealey, R. S. (1988). Future directions in psychological skills training. *The Sport Psychologist, 2*, 318–336.

Waite, B. T., & Pettit, M. E. (1993). Work experiences of graduates from doctoral programs in sport psychology. *Journal of Applied Sport Psychology, 5*, 234–250.

Weinberg, R. S. (1989). Applied sport psychology: Issues and challenges. *Journal of Applied Sport Psychology, 1*, 181–195.

Williams, J. M. (1995). Applied sport psychology: Goals, issues, and challenges. *Journal of Applied Sport Psychology, 7*, 81–91.

Zaichkowsky, L. D., & Perna, F. M. (1992). Certification of consultants in sport psychology: A rebuttal to Anshel. *The Sport Psychologist, 6*, 287–296.

Zeigler, E. F. (1987). Rationale and suggested dimensions for a code of ethics for sport psychologists. *The Sport Psychologist, 1*, 138–150.

READING LIST IN APPLIED SPORT PSYCHOLOGY: PSYCHOLOGICAL SKILLS TRAINING

Michael L. Sachs and Alan S. Kornspan
Temple University and University of Akron

Note: This reading list originally appeared in *The Sport Psychologist* as: Sachs, M. L. (1991). "Reading List in Applied Sport Psychology: Psychological Skills Training," *The Sport Psychologist*, 5, 88–91.

The reading list was updated in the third and fourth editions of the directory and has been updated further in this fifth edition to include books and reviews published since the fourth edition.

One of the questions that applied sport psychologists frequently get concerns finding information about psychological skills training (PST). In an effort to answer this question, the following reading list was developed to identify books in applied sport psychology that focus on PST. The information may carry a different label, such as mental training, but the focus is still upon a set of psychological skills that will help athletes enhance performance. These psychological skills encompass relaxation, concentration, visualization, goal setting, and so on.

The list was drawn from a review of library materials, from the appendix in Vealey's (1988) excellent article on future directions in PST, and an examination of the following journals: *The Sport Psychologist* (*TSP*), the *Journal of Applied Sport Psychology* (*JASP*), the *Journal of Sport & Exercise Psychology* (*JSEP*, formerly the *Journal of Sport Psychology*), and the *Journal of Physical Education, Recreation, and Dance* (*JOPERD*).

In some cases the books listed have been reviewed in one or more of the journals examined. These book reviews are noted, if available, following each book. The primary goal of this listing has not been to judge the quality of the books listed, although the book reviews may help in this regard. Indeed, the books available range from scientifically oriented texts designed for those more scholarly oriented to popular press paperbacks designed for the layperson. Similarly, the quality of the books ranges from comparatively poor to excellent.

The reader looking for a good place to get started in applied sport psychology, even considering the diversity of orientation in the books available, would be most likely to benefit from the following books from the list as being among the best available: Martens (1987), Orlick (1990), and Williams (1993). Progressing from these more general volumes to more specific ones, there are many books dealing with golf, tennis, and skiing, as well as ones focusing upon running, basketball, bodybuilding, and other sports.

A key question that arises concerns the efficacy of these books. Some are designed to be used in academically oriented settings, as parts of courses or workshops. Others have been written to stand alone, to presumably give the reader the basics in applied sport psychology and let him/her proceed from there. The number of books available (and the variety of sports covered) is increasing exponentially, with many authors seeking to get *their* psychological skills training book in press as soon as possible.

Studies are not yet available in the sport psychology literature concerning the efficacy of psychological skills training books. One meta-analysis of self-administered treatment programs found them to be effective in comparison with no treatment, and not significantly different from therapist-administered programs of psychotherapy (Scogin, Bynum, Stephens, & Calhoon, 1990). However, limitations of the work precluded the authors from indicating that self-administered treatments were as effective as programs administered by therapists.

Readers looking for a broader array of sensory stimulation modes will find that there are also many videotapes and audiotapes available in applied sport psychology. Many of these are listed, and some reviewed, in issues of *The Sport Psychologist*.

A noteworthy development since the earlier publication and update of this listing has been the considerable number of workbooks and related guides available for athletes and coaches. These assist athletes and coaches in direct work through the various areas within psychological skills training. Martens (1987) has had an excellent workbook available for coaches for quite some time, but more recently a number of authors, particularly Dalloway (1992, 1993a, b, c, 1994), Miner, Shelley, & Henschen (1995), and Taylor (1993, 1994a, b, c, d) have developed additional publications of note.

Recent developments have seen books focused towards psychological skills training and children as well. Orlick in particular (1992, 1993) has published a number of books that "translate these lessons [of elite performers and use of psychological skills] into practical guidelines for quality parenting and quality living" (1992, back cover).

Vealey (1988) indicated that the Hendricks and Carlson (1982) and Kappas (1984) books were out of print and not available at a number of libraries that she searched. Readers who have trouble obtaining such volumes should enlist the aid of their librarian in requesting materials through interlibrary loan. This is often the only way of obtaining some of the older and lesser known (not to mention out-of-print) titles. A final note should indicate that there are many excellent articles on applied sport psychology in the journals listed above, particularly *The Sport Psychologist* and the *Journal of Applied Sport Psychology*.

Albinson, John G., & Bull, S. J. (1988). *The mental game plan*. London, Ontario: Spodym. Book review: *TSP*, 1990, *4*, 76–77.

Alder, Harry, & Morris, Karl (1996). *Masterstroke: Use the power of your mind to improve your golf with NLP neurolinguistic programming*. London: Piatkus.

Allen, George. (1983). *The mental game: The inner game of bowling*. Deerfield, IL: Tech Ed Publishing Co.

Alexander, Don. (1994). *Think to win*. Cambridge, MA: R. Bentley. (auto racing).

American Sport Education Program. (1994). *SportParent*. Champaign, IL: Human Kinetics.

Anderson, Eric. (1994). *Training games: Coaching runners creatively*. Mountain View, CA: TAFNEWS Press.

Backley, Steve, & Stafford, Ian. (1996). *The winning mind: A guide to achieving success and overcoming failure*. London: Aurum Press.

Barden, R. Christopher, Jackson, Bruce, & Ford, Martin E. (1992). *Optimal performance in tennis: Mental skills for maximum achievement in athletics and life*. Plymouth, MN: Optimal Performance Systems Research. Book review: *TSP*, 1995, *9*, 112–113.

Barzdukas, Audrus. (1995). *Gold minds: Gold medal mental strategies for everyday life*. Indianapolis, IN: Masters Press.

Bell, Keith F. (1983). *Championship thinking: The athlete's guide to winning performance in all sports*. Englewood Cliffs, NJ: Prentice-Hall.

Bell, Keith F. (1983). *Target on gold: Goal setting for swimmers and other kinds of people*. Austin, TX: Keel Publications.

Bennett, James G., & Pravitz, James E. (1982). *The miracle of sports psychology*. Englewood Cliffs, NJ: Prentice-Hall. Book review: *JOPERD*, 1984, *55*(5), 98–99.

Bennett, James G., & Pravitz, James E. (1987). *Profile of a winner: Advanced mental training for athletes*. Ithaca, NY: Sport Science International. Book review: *TSP*, 1987, 1, 361–363.

Benzel, David. (1989). *Psyching for slalom: An illustrated guide to the mind and muscle of the complete skier*. Winter Park, FL: World Publications.

Braden, Vic, & Wool, R. (1993). *Vic Braden's mental tennis: How to psych yourself to a winning game*. Boston: Little, Brown and Company.

Brennan, Stephen J. (1990). *Competitive excellence: The psychology and strategy of successful team building*. Omaha, NE: Peak Performance Publishing. Book review: *TSP*, 1991, 5, 290–291.

Brennan, Stephen J. (1993). *The mental edge: Basketball's peak performance workbook*. (2nd ed.) Omaha, NE: Peak Performance Publishing. Book review: *TSP*, 1994, *8*, 321–323.

Brown, R. A. (1994). *The golfing mind: The psychological principles of good golf*. New York: Lyons & Burford.

Bull, Stephen J. (1991). *Sport psychology: A self-help guide*. Swindon: Crowood.

Bull, Stephen J., Albinson, J. G., & Shambrook, Christopher J. (1996). *The mental game plan: Getting psyched for sport*. Eastbourne: Sports Dynamics.

Bump, Linda. (1989). *Sport psychology study guide* (and accompanying workbook). Champaign, IL: Human Kinetics Publishers. Book review: *TSP*, 1990, 4, 72–73.

Burnett, Darrell J. (1993). *Youth sports & self-esteem: A guide for parents*. Indianapolis, IN: Masters Press.

Butler, Richard J. (1996). *Sports psychology in action*. Boston, MA: Butterworth Heinemann.

Cahill, Bernard R. & Pearl, Arthur J. (1993). *Intensive participation in children's sports*. Champaign, IL: Human Kinetics.

Clayton, Lawrence, & Smith, Betty S. (1992). *Coping with sport injuries*. New York: Rosen Publishing Group.

Cohn, Patrick J. (1994). *The mental game of golf: A guide to peak performance*. South Bend, IN: Diamond Communications. Book review: *TSP*, 1996, *10*, 213–216.

Cohn, Patrick J., & Winters, K. (1995). *The mental art of putting: Using your mind to putt your best*. South Bend, IN: Diamond Communications, Inc.

Colby, M. (1996). *Motor learning applied to sports*. (2nd ed.) Boston, MA: American Press.

Coop, Richard H., & Fields, Bill. (1993). *Mind over golf: Play your best by thinking smart*. New York: Macmillan Publishing Company.

Cratty, Bryant J. (1984). *Psychological preparation and athletic excellence*. Ithaca, NY:

Mouvement Publications. Book review: *JSP*, 1986, *8*, 252–254.

Cunningham, Les. (1981). *Hypnosport: How you can improve your sporting performances*. Glendale, CA: Westwood.

Curtis, John D. (1989). *The mindset for winning*. La Crosse, WI: Coulee Press. Book review: *JSEP*, 1990, *12*, 439–441.

Dalloway, Marie. (1992). *Visualization: The master skill in mental training*. Phoenix, AZ: Optimal Performance Institute Press. Book review: *TSP*, 1995, *9*, 109–111.

Dalloway, Marie. (1993a). *Concentration: Focus your mind, power your game*. Phoenix, AZ: Optimal Performance Institute Press. Book review: *TSP*, 1995, *9*, 109–111.

Dalloway, Marie. (1993b). *Drive and determination: Developing your inner motivation*. Phoenix, AZ: Optimal Performance Institute Press. Book review: *TSP*, 1995, *9*, 109–111.

Dalloway, Marie. (1993c). *Risk taking: Performing your best during critical times*. Phoenix, AZ: Optimal Performance Institute Press. Book review: *TSP*, 1995, *9*, 109–111.

Dalloway, Marie. (1994). *Reflections on the mental side of sports*. Phoenix, AZ: Optimal Performance Institute Press. Book review: *TSP*, 1996, *10*, 300–301.

Decoursey, Doug, & Linder, Darwyn, E. (1990). *Visual skiing: Essential mental and physical skills for the modern skier*. New York: Doubleday.

Devenzio, Dick. (1997). *Think like a champion: A guide to championship performance in all sports*. Charlotte, NC: Fool Court Press.

Domey, Richard L. (1989). *Mental training for shooting success.* (2nd ed.) Pullman, WA: College Hill Communications.

Dorfman, Harvey A., & Kuehl, Karl. (1995). *The mental game of baseball: A guide to peak performance.* (2nd ed.) South Bend, IN: Diamond Communications, Inc. Book review: *TSP*, 1991, *5*, 92–93.

Douillard, John. (1994). *Body, mind and sport: The mind-body guide to lifelong fitness and your personal best*. London: Bantam Inc.

Edgette, Janet Sasson. (1996). *Heads up! Practical sports psychology for riders, their trainers, and their families*. New York: Doubleday.

Elliot, Richard. (1991). *The competitive edge: Mental preparation for distance running*. Mountain View, CA: TAFNEWS Press.

Evans, Eric. (1990). *Mental toughness training for cross-country skiing*. New York: The Stephen Greene Press/Pelham Books.

Farley, Kara Leverte, & Curry, Sheila M. (1994). *Get motivated: Daily psych-ups*. New York: A Fireside book published by Simon & Schuster.

Figone, Al. (1991). *Teaching the mental aspects of baseball: A coach's handbook*. Madison, WI: Brown & Benchmark.

Fine, Aubrey H., & Sachs, Michael L. (1997). *The total sports experience for kids: A parent's guide to success in youth sports*. South Bend, IN: Diamond Communications, Inc.

Fortanasce, Vincent M. (1995). *Life lessons from Little League: A guide for parents and coaches*. New York: Image/Doubleday.

Fox, Allen. (1993). *Think to win: The strategic dimension of tennis.* New York: Harper.

Garfield, Charles A., & Bennett, Hal Z. (1984). *Peak performance: Mental training techniques of the world's greatest athletes.* Los Angeles: Jeremy P. Tarcher, Inc. Book review: *JOPERD*, 1985, *56*(9), 77–78.

Gauron, Eugene F. (1984). *Mental training for peak performance.* Lansing, NY: Sport Science Associates. Book review: *JSP*, 1987, *9*, 83–84.

Goldberg, Alan. (1988). *The sports mind: A workbook of mental skills for athletes.* Northampton, MA: Competitive Advantage.

Graham, David, & Yocum, Guy. (1990). *Mental toughness training for golf.* New York: Stephen Greene Press/Pelham Books.

Grant, Robert W. (1988). *The psychology of sport: Facing one's true opponent.* Jefferson, NC: McFarland.

Hackfort, Dieter. (1994). *Psycho-social issues and interventions in elite sport.* New York: P. Lang.

Hardy, Lew, Jones, J. Graham, & Gould, Daniel. (1996). *Understanding psychological preparation for sport: Theory and practice of elite performers.* New York: J. Wiley.

Harley, Ned R. (1994). *Let's go skiing with a psychiatrist: The mental game of sensational skiing.* Vail, CO: Vail Press.

Harris, Dorothy V., & Harris, Bette L. (1984). *The athlete's guide to sports psychology: Mental skills for physical people.* New York: Leisure Press.

Hassler, Jill K., & Jahiel, Jessica. (1993). *In search of your image: A practical guide to the mental and spiritual aspects of horsemanship.* Colora, MD: Goals Unlimited Press.

Henderson, Joe. (Ed.) (1972). *Practical running psychology.* Mountain View, CA: Runner's World Magazine.

Henderson, Joe. (1991). *Think fast: Mental toughness training for runners.* New York: Pengiun Books.

Hendricks, Gay, & Carlson, Jon. (1982). *The centered athlete: A conditioning program for your mind.* Englewood Cliffs, NJ: Prentice-Hall.

Hogg, John M. (1995a). *Mental skills for competitive swimmers.* Edmonton, Alberta, Canada: Sport Excel Publishing.

Hogg, John M. (1995b). *Mental skills for competitive swimmers: A workbook to improve mental performance.* Edmonton, Alberta, Canada: Sport Excel Publishing.

Hogg, John M. (1995c). *Mental skills for swim coaches: A coaching text on the psychological aspects of competitive swimming.* Edmonton, Alberta, Canada: Sport Excel Publishing.

Hogg, John M. (1997). *Mental skills for young athletes: A mental skills workbook for athletes 12 and under.* Edmonton, Alberta, Canada: Sport Excel Publishing.

Holzel, Petra, & Holzel, Wolfgang. (1996). *Learn to ride using sports psychology: A training aid for riders and instructors.* North Pomfret, VT: Trafalgar Square.

Huang, Chungliang Al, & Lynch, Jerry. (1992). *Thinking body, dancing mind: Taosports for extraordinary performance in athletics, business, and life.* New York: Bantam Books.

Jaeger, Alan J. (1994). *Getting focused, staying focused: A Far Eastern approach to sports and life*. Glendale, CA: Griffith Printing.

Janssen, Jefferey J., & Candrea, Mike. (1994). *Mental toughness training for softball: A guide and workbook for athletes and coaches*. Casa Grande, AZ: Southwest Camps Publications.

Jordan, Jacob H. (1995). *Total mindbody training: A guide to peak athletic performance*. Hartford: Turtle Press.

Kappas, John G. (1984). *Self-hypnosis: The key to athletic success*. Englewood Cliffs, NJ: Prentice-Hall.

Kauss, David R. (1980). *Peak performance: Mental game plans for maximizing your athletic potential*. Englewood Cliffs, NJ: Prentice-Hall. Book review: *JSP*, 1982, 4, 410–413.

Keogh, Barbara K., & Smith, Carol E. (1985). *Personal par: A psychological system of golf for women*. Champaign, IL: Human Kinetics Publishers. Book review: *JOPERD*, 1986, *57*(8), 83.

Keyes, Michael J. (1996). *Mental training for shotgun sports*. Auburn, CA: Shotgun Sports, Inc.

Kirschenbaum, Daniel S. (1997). *Mind matters: Seven sportpsych steps to maximize performance*. Carmel, IN: Cooper Publishing Group.

Kogler, Aladar. (1993). *Preparing the mind: Improving fencing performance through psychological preparation*. Lansdowne, PA: ConterParry Press.

Kubistant, Tom. (1986). *Performing your best: A guide to psychological skills for high achievers*. Champaign, IL: Human Kinetics Publishers.

Kubistant, Tom. (1988). *Mind pump: The psychology of bodybuilding*. Champaign, IL: Leisure Press.

Kubistant, Tom. (1994). *Mind links: The psychology of golf*. Reno, NV: Performance and Productivity Specialists.

Lilliefors, Jim. (1978). *The running mind*. Mountain View, CA: World Publications, Inc.

Loehr, James E. (1982). *Mental toughness training for sports: Achieving athletic excellence training*. Lexington, MA: Stephen Greene.

Loehr, James E. (1990). *The mental game*. New York: The Stephen Greene Press/Pelham Books.

Loehr, J. E. (1994). *The new toughness training for sports: Achieving athletic excellence*. New York: Dutton.

Loudis, L. A., Lobitz, W. C., & Singer, K. M. (1986). *Skiing out of your mind*. Champaign, IL: Leisure Press.

Lucas, Geoffrey. (1987). *Images for golf: Visualizing your way to a better game*. Calgary: Arizona Academic Sport Resources.

Lynberg, Michael. (1993). *Winning: Great coaches and athletes share their secrets of success*. New York: Doubleday.

Lynch, Jerry. (1987). *The total runner: A complete mind-body guide to optimal performance*. Englewood Cliffs, NJ: Prentice-Hall. Book review: *TSP*, 1987, *1*, 265–266.

Mackenzie, Marlin M., & Denlinger, Ken. (1990). *Golf: The mind game*. New York: Dell. Book review: *TSP*, 1992, *6*, 314.

Mackenzie, Marlin M., & Denlinger, Ken. (1991). *Skiing: The mind game*. New York: Dell.

Mackenzie, Marlin M., & Denlinger, Ken. (1991). *Tennis: The mind game*. New York: Dell.

Margenau, Eric. (1990). *Sports without pressure: A guide for parents & coaches of young athletes*. New York: Gardner Press.

Martens, Rainer. (1987). *Coaches guide to sport psychology*. Champaign, IL: Human Kinetics Publishers. Book review: *TSP*, 1990, *4*, 78.

Martin, Garry L., & Ingraham, Derek. (1993). *New mental skills for better golf: Test your self-talk*. Winnipeg, Manitoba, Canada.

May, Jerry R., & Asken, Michael J. (Eds.) (1987). *Sport psychology: The psychological health of the athlete*. New York: PMA Publishing Corp. Book review: *TSP*, 1989, *3*, 274–277.

Meyer, J. E., & Plodzien, C. A. (1988). *Excelling in sports through thinking straight*. Springfield, IL: Charles C. Thomas. Book review: *JSEP*, 1990, *12*, 437–438.

Micheli, Lyle J. (1990). *Sportswise: An essential guide for young athletes, parents, and coaches*. Boston: Houghton Mifflin Company.

Mikes, Jay. (1987). *Basketball fundamentals: A complete mental training guide*. Champaign, IL: Leisure Press. Book review: *JOPERD*, 1987, *58*(9), 141–142.

Mills, Brett D. (1994). *Mental training and performance enhancement: A guide for volleyball coaches and players*. Dubuque, IA: Eddie Bowers Publishing, Inc. Book review: *TSP*, 1996, *10*, 415–416.

Miner, M. Jane, Shelley, Greg A., & Henschen, Keith P. (1995). *Moving toward your potential: The athlete's guide to peak performance*. Farmington, UT: Performance Publications.

Missoum, Guy. (1991). *Guide du training mental*. Paris: RETZ. Book review: *TSP*, 1992, *6*, 315–316.

Moran, Aidan P. (1996). *The psychology of concentration in sport performers: A cognitive analysis*. Hove: Psychology Press.

Murphy, Shane. (1996). *The achievement zone: Eight skills for winning all the time from the playing field to the boardroom*. New York: G. P. Putnam's Sons.

Nakamura, Raymond M. (1996). *The power of positive coaching*. Sudbury, MA: Jones and Bartlett Publishers, Inc.

Nideffer, Robert M. (1981). *The ethics and practice of applied sport psychology*. Ithaca, NY: Mouvement Publications. Book review: *JOPERD*, 1982, *53*(4), 100.

Nideffer, Robert M. (1985). *Athletes' guide to mental training*. Champaign, IL: Human Kinetics Publishers.

Nideffer, Robert M. (1992). *Psyched to win*. Champaign, IL: Leisure Press: Book reviews: *JSEP*, 1993, *15*, 355–356. *TSP*, 1993, *7*, 204–206.

Nowicki, Dariusz. (1993). *Gold medal mental workout: A step-by-step program of mental exercises to make you a winner every time*. Island Pond, VT: Stadion Publishing Co., Inc.

Orlick, Terry. (1986). *Coaches training manual to psyching for sport*. Champaign, IL: Leisure Press. Book review: *TSP*, 1987, *1*, 82.

Orlick, Terry. (1986). *Psyching for sport: Mental training for athletes*. Champaign, IL: Leisure Press. Book review: *TSP*, 1987, *1*, 82.

Orlick, Terry. (1990). *In pursuit of excellence: How to win in sport and life through mental training*. (2nd ed.) Champaign, IL: Human Kinetics Publishers. Book review: *TSP*, 1992, *6*, 99–100.

Orlick, Terry. (1992) *Nice on my feelings*. Sacramento, CA: ITA Publications.

Orlick, Terry. (1993) *Free to feel great: Teaching children to excel at living*. Carp, Ontario, Canada: Creative Bound Inc.

Orlick, Terry. (1995). *Nice on my feelings: Nurturing the best in children and parents*. Carp, Ontario, Canada: Creative Bound.

Orlick, Terry, & Partington, John. (1986). *Psyched: Inner views of winning*. Ottawa, Canada: The Coaching Association of Canada. Book review: *TSP*, 1987, *1*, 166–167.

Owens, DeDe, & Kirschenbaum, Daniel. (1997). *Smart golf: How to simplify and score your mental game*. San Francisco: Jossey-Bass Publishers.

Pargman, David. (1986). *Stress and motor performance: Understanding and coping*. Ithaca, NY: Mouvement Publications. Book review: *TSP*, 1988, *2*, 266–267.

Pirozzolo, Francis J., & Pate, Russ. (1996). *The mental game pocket companion for golf*. New York: Harper Collins Publishers.

Pitcher, Bruce L. (1996). *The Mental Proficiency System: A proven, step-by-step guide to thinking and planning your way to lower golf scores*. Safety Harbor, FL: Pitcher Golf Group.

Porter, Clyde W. (1993). *Top golf: Peak performance through brain body integration*. Sparks, NV: Life Enhancement Services.

Porter, Kay, & Foster, Judy. (1986). *The mental athlete*. Dubuque, IA: Wm. C. Brown Co. Book review: *TSP*, 1988, *2*, 173–174.

Porter, Kay, & Foster, Judy. (1990). *Visual athletics*. Dubuque, IA: Wm. C. Brown Co.

Railo, Willi. (1986). *Willing to win*. West Yorkshire, England: Springfield Books Limited. Book review: *JSP*, 1987, *9*, 186–189.

Ravizza, Ken, & Hanson, Tom. (1995). *Heads-up baseball: Playing the game one pitch at a time*. Indianapolis: Masters Press.

Richard, Jim. (1991). *Not too high, not too low: Stress management strategies for professional baseball players and their fans*. Dubuque, IA: Kendall/Hunt.

Rodionow, A. W. (Ed.) (1982). *Psychology for training and competition*. German version translated by Professor Lothar Pickenhain. Berlin: Sportverlag Berlin. Book review: *TSP*, 1989, *3*, 278–280.

Rotella, Robert J., & Bunker, Linda K. (1981). *Mind mastery for winning golf*. Englewood Cliffs, NJ: Prentice-Hall.

Rotella, Robert J., & Bunker, Linda K. (1982). *Mind, set and match*. Charlottesville, VA: LINKS, Inc.

Rotella, Robert J., & Bunker, Linda K. (1987). *Parenting your superstar.* Chapaign, IL: Human Kinetics Publishers. Book review: *TSP*, 1989, *3*, 281–282.

Rotella, Robert, & Cullen, Bob. (1995). *Golf is not a game of perfect.* New York: Simon & Schuster.

Rotella, Robert, & Cullen, Bob. (1996). *Golf is a game of confidence.* New York: Simon & Schuster.

Rushall, Brent S. (1979). *Psyching in sports.* London: Pelham Books.

Rushall, Brent S. (1986). *The psychology of successful cross-country ski racing.* Ottawa, Ontario, Canada: Cross Country Canada.

Rushall, Brent S. (1991). *Imagery training in sports: A handbook for athletes, coaches, and sport psychologists.* Spring Valley, CA: Sport Science Associates.

Rushall, Brent S. (1992). *Mental skills training for sports: A manual for athletes, coaches, and sport psychologists.* Spring Valley, CA: Sport Science Associates.

Rushall, Brent S. (1995). *Think and act like a champion.* Spring Valley, CA: Sport Science Associates.

Rushall, Brent S., & Potgieter, Justus. (1987). *The psychology of successful competing in endurance events.* Pretoria: South African Association for Sport Sceince, Physical Education and Recreation.

Sailes, Gary A. (1995). *Mental training for tennis.* Dubuque, IA: Kendall/Hunt Publishers.

Savoie, Jane. (1992). *That winning feeling: A new approach to riding using psychocybernetics.* London: Allen.

Schultheis, R. (1996). *Bone games: Extreme sports, shamanism, zen and the search for transcendence.* New York: Breakaway Sports.

Scott, Michael D., & Pellicioni, Louis, Jr. (1982). *Don't choke: How athletes can become winners.* Englewood Cliffs, NJ: Prentice-Hall. Book review: *JOPERD*, 1984, *55*(2), 73.

Selleck, George A. (1995). *How to play the game of your life: A guide to success in sports and life.* South Bend, IN: Diamond Communications, Inc.

Shapiro, Alan. (1996). *Golf's mental hazards: Overcome them and put an end to the self-destructive round.* New York: Fireside/Simon and Schuster.

Sheikh, A. A., & Korn, E. R. (Eds.). (1994). *Imagery in sports and physical performance.* Amityville, NY: Baywood.

Simek, Thomas C., & O'Brien, Richard M. (1981). *Total golf: A behavioral approach to lowering your score and getting more out of your game.* New York: Doubleday & Company. Book review: *JOPERD*, 1982, *53*(4), 102, 104.

Singer, Robert N. (1986). *Peak performance ... and more.* Ithaca, NY: Mouvement Publications. Book review: *JOPERD*, 1987, *58*(9), 141.

Smith, Aynsley M. (1991). *Power play: Mental toughness for hockey and beyond.* Rochester, MN: Power Play.

Smith, Edward W. L. (1989). *Not just pumping iron: On the psychology of lifting weights.* Springfield, IL: Charles C Thomas.

Smith, Nathan J., Smith, Ronald E., & Smoll, Frank L. (1983). *Kidsports: A survival guide for parents*. Reading, MA: Addison-Wesley Publishing Company.

Smith, Ronald E., & Smoll, Frank L. (1996). *Way to go, coach: A scientifically proven approach to coaching effectiveness*. Portola Valley, CA: Warde.

Smoll, Frank L., & Smith, Ronald E. (1987). *Sport psychology for youth coaches: Personal growth to athlete excellence*. Washington, DC: National Federation for Catholic Youth Ministry. Book review: *TSP*, 1988, *2*, 175–177.

Smoll, Frank L., & Smith, Ronald E. (1995). *Children and youth in sport: A biopsychosocial perspective*. Dubuque, IA: Brown and Benchmark.

Strossen, Randall J. (1994). *IronMind: Stronger minds, stronger bodies*. Nevada City, CA: IronMind Enterprises, Inc.

Stein, M., & Hollowitz, J. (1994). *Psyche and sports: Baseball, hockey, martial arts, running, tennis, and others*. Wilmette, IL: Chiron.

Straub, William F., & Williams, Jean M. (Eds.). (1984). *Cognitive sport psychology*. Lansing, NH: Sport Science Associates.

Suinn, Richard M. (1986). *Seven steps to peak performance: The mental training manual for athletes*. Lewiston, NY: Hans Huber Publishers. Book reviews: *TSP*, 1987, *1*, 359–360. *JSEP*, 1989, *11*, 343–345.

Swindley, D. (1996). *Decide to win: A total approach to winning in sport and life*. London: Ward Lock.

Syer, J., & Connolly, C. (1984). *Sporting mind, sporting body: An athlete's guide to mental training*. New York: Cambridge University Press.

Taylor, Debbi. (1989). *Challenge yourself: Goal-setting workbook for athletes*. Coquitlam, British Columbia, Canada: Challenge Yourself Press.

Taylor, Jim. (1993). *The mental edge for competitive sports*. (3rd ed.) Aspen, CO: Alpine*Taylor Consulting. Book review: *TSP*, 1996, *10*, 298–299.

Taylor, Jim. (1994a). *The mental edge for alpine ski racing*. Aspen, CO: Alpine*Taylor Consulting.

Taylor, Jim. (1994b). *The mental edge for golf*. Aspen, CO: Alpine*Taylor Consulting.

Taylor, Jim. (1994c). *The mental edge for tennis*. Aspen, CO: Alpine*Taylor Consulting.

Taylor, Jim. (1994d). *The mental edge for skiing*. Aspen, CO: Alpine*Taylor Consulting.

Terry, Peter. (1989). *The winning mind*. Wellingborough, Northamptonshire, England: Thorsons Publishing Group. Book reviews: *JSEP*, 1990, *12*, 434–436. *TSP*, 1990, *4*, 437–439.

Thomas, Jerry R. (Ed.) (1977). *Youth sports guide for coaches and parents*. Washington, DC: AAHPER Publications.

Ungerleider, Steven. (1996). *Mental training for peak performance: Top athletes reveal the mind exercises they use to excel*. Emmaus, PA: Rodale Press, Inc.

Vardy, D. (1996). *The mental game of golf*. Thrumpton: Castle.

Vernacchia, Ralph A., McGuire, Richard T., & Cook, David L. (1992). *Coaching mental excellence: "It does matter whether you win or lose ..."* Dubuque, IA: Brown & Benchmark. Book review: *TSP*, 1993, *7*, 210–212.

Vicory, Jim. (1996). *Mind golf: It's brain over ball.* Aurora, IL: Kelmscott Press.

Waitley, Denis. (1994). *The new dynamics of winning: Gain the mind-set of a champion.* London: Brealey. (Originally published in 1993 by Nightingale-Conant.)

Wallach, Jeff. (1995). *Beyond the fairway: Zen lessons, insights, and inner attitudes of golf.* New York: Bantam Books.

Wanless, Mary. (1991). *Ride with your mind: An illustrated masterclass in right brain riding.* North Pomfrey, VT: Trafalgar Square Publishing.

Weinberg, Robert S. (1988). *The mental advantage: Developing your psychological skills in tennis.* Champaign, IL: Leisure Press. Book reviews: *TSP*, 1988, *2*, 357–358.*JSEP*, 1990, *12*, 98–99.

Whittam, Paula. (1995). *Tennis talk, psych yourself in to win!!! Affirmations for mental fitness in tennis.* Bahamas: Sapphire Publishing Corporation.

Williams, Jean M. (Ed.). (1993). *Applied sport psychology: Personal growth to peak performance.* (2nd ed.) Palo Alto, CA: Mayfield. Book review: *TSP*, 1994, *8*, 100–101.

Wilt, Fred, & Bosen, Ken. (1971). *Motivation and coaching psychology.* Los Altos, CA: TAFNEWS Press.

Winter, Brad. (1981). *Relax and win: Championship performance in whatever you do.* La Jolla, CA: A. S. Barnes and Company. Book reviews: *JOPERD*, 1982, *53*(7), 86. *JSP*, 1983, *5*, 466–467.

Winter, Graham. (1992). *The psychology of cricket: How to play the inner game of cricket.* Melbourne: Sun.

Winter, Graham, & Martin, Cathy. (1988). *A practical guide to sport psychology.* Underdale, Australia: SA Sports Institute.

Wiren, Gary, Coop, Richard, & Sheehan, Larry. (1985). *The new golf mind.* New York: Simon & Schuster.

Wolff, Rick. (1993). *Good sports.* New York: Dell.

Young, Bryce, & Bunker, Linda K. (1995). *The courtside coach.* Charlottesville, VA: LINKS, Inc.

Zaichkowsky, Leonard, D., & Sime, Wesley E. (Eds.). (1982). *Stress management for sport.* Reston, VA: American Association for Health, Physical Education, Recreation, and Dance.

Zinsser, Nate. (1991). *Dear Dr. Psych.* Little Brown: Boston.

Zulewski, Richard. (1994). *The parent's guide to coaching physically challenged children.* Cincinnati, OH: Betterway Books.

References

Scogin, F., Bynum, J., Stephens, G., & Calhoon, S. (1990). Efficacy of self-administered treatment programs: Meta-analytic review. *Professional Psychology: Research and Practice, 21*(1), 42–47.

Vealey, R. S. (1988). Future directions in psychological skills training. *The Sport Psychologist, 2*, 318–336.

Reference List of Mental Training/Sport Psychology Videos

Alan S. Kornspan, University of Akron

Christopher Lantz, Truman State University

Bart S. Lerner, The Citadel

Scott R. Johnson, West Virginia University

Author Notes: Alan S. Kornspan, Department of Physical and Health Education; Christopher Lantz, Department of Health and Exercise Science; Bart S. Lerner, Counseling Center; Scott R. Johnson, School of Physical Education. Correspondence concerning this article should be addressed to Alan S. Kornspan, 2774 Lochraven, Apt. G., Copley, OH 44321; telephone number: (330) 665-3396. Electronic mail may be sent via the Internet to au440@yfn.ysu.edu

Reprinted from A. S. Kornspan, C. Lantz, B. S. Lerner, and S. R. Johnson. (1998). "A Reference List of Mental Training/Sport Psychology Videos." In W. K. Simpson, A. LeUnes, & J. S. Picou (Eds.), *Applied Research in Coaching and Athletics Annual*. Boston: American Press.

Abstract

The continued growth of sport psychology has resulted in an influx of mental training techniques. These techniques are presented in a variety of books, journals, and audio/visual materials. While reference lists exist for sport psychology texts (Allen, 1994; Sachs & Kornspan, 1995) and journal articles (Granito & Wenz, 1995), there remained no such resource for locating and obtaining sport psychology videos. This article presents an extensive list of mental training and sport psychology videos that can be used by sport psychologists, coaches, and athletes. In addition, this list provides purchasing information such as addresses, telephone numbers, and price of the video.

Reference List of Mental Training/Sport Psychology Videos

As the field of sport psychology experiences increasing popularity, members of the athletic community are recognizing the benefits of psychological skills training. As a result, coaches and athletes are obtaining sport psychology information from books and videos. As technology continues to advance in the classroom and on the field, many coaches and sport psychologists are beginning to use videos to introduce athletes to psychological skills training.

Often, the coach or sport psychologist will introduce athletes to mental skills training through the use of videotapes. Murphy (1991) explains how he has used the video "Visualization: What You See Is What You Get" to lead into group discussions. For example, Murphy explained, "I might have one group identify ways visualization can be used in practice and may tell another group to watch for ways visualization can be used at competition" (p. 95). Gould (1987) suggests that videos introducing mental training can be useful, but the teacher, coach, or sport psychologist should provide guidance to athletes on the use of the video. Further, Weinberg (1990) suggests that some videos may be limited in that they do not give specific demonstrations of how to use the psychological techniques. However, Weinberg suggests that videos can be useful in introducing basic information for those who are unfamiliar with applied sport psychology.

Although sport psychology videos may be useful (Gould, 1987; Murphy, 1988; Weinberg, 1990), a problem exists in that only a very limited number of videos have been reviewed in the literature. Also, the phone numbers and prices that are listed in the video review are often outdated. Thus coaches and sport psychology consultants may have great difficulty in locating and purchasing sport psychology videos. While reference lists exist for sport psychology texts (Allen, 1994; Sachs & Kornspan, 1995) and journal articles (Granito & Wenz, 1995), there remained no such resource for locating and obtaining sport psychology videos.

An effort to provide the coaching community with information on sport psychology videos began with a comprehensive list generated via various computerized searches. After completing the list, addresses and telephone numbers of the distributors were obtained. Current prices (as of 1997), telephone numbers, and addresses for 39 videos were located. It should be noted that these videos address a wide range of sport psychology and coaching topics. It is not the purpose of this article to review the videos presented but to provide the information necessary to help individuals in locating videos of interest.

References

Allen, M. B. (1994). Authorship in sport psychology: A reference list. *The Sport Psychologist, 8*, 94–99.

Gould, D. (1987). Mental training for peak athletic performance [Review of the video program *Mental training for peak athletic performance*]. *The Sport Psychologist, 1*, 364–365.

Granito, V., & Wenz, B. (1995). Reading list for professional issues in applied sport psychology. *The Sport Psychologist, 9*, 96–103.

Murphy, S. M. (1991). Visualization: What you see is what you get [Review of the video program *Visualization: What you see is what you get*]. *The Sport Psychologist, 5*, 94–95.

Sachs, M. L., & Kornspan, A. (1995). Reading list in applied sport psychology: Psychological skills training. In M. Sachs, K. Burke, & L. Butcher (Eds.), *Directory of graduate programs in applied sport psychology* (4th ed.) (pp. 216–227). Morgantown, WV: Fitness Information Technology.

Weinberg, R. (1990). Sports psychology: The winning edge in sports [Review of the video program *Sports psychology: What winning edge in sports*]. *The Sport Psychologist, 4*, 192–194.

Video List

Bassham, L. (1989). *Mental management seminar, part 1. The principles of mental management* [Videotape]. (Available from Mental Management Systems, P.O. Box 225, Seguin, TX, 78155).

Bassham, L. (1989). *Mental management seminar, part 2. Mental tools and techniques* [Videotape]. (Available from Mental Management Systems, P.O. Box 225, Seguin, TX, 78155).

Bassham, L. (1989). *Mental management seminar part 3. Mental tools and techniques* [Videotape]. (Available from Mental Management Systems, P.O. Box 225, Seguin, TX, 78155.

Blanchard, K. (1994). *The golf university swing school videos: Mastering the mental game of golf* [Videotape]. (Available from The Golf University, 17550 Bernardo Oaks Drive, San Diego, CA 92128, 1-800-426-0966, $24.95).

Botterill, C., & Orlick, T. (1988). *Visualization: What you see is what you get* [Videotape]. (Available from Coaching Association of Canada, 1600 James Naismith Drive, Gloucester, ON K1B 5N4 Canada, 613-748-5624, $19.95 Canadian). Video Review: Murphy, S.M. (1991). Visualization: What you see is what you get [Review of the video program *Visualization: What you see is what you get*]. *The Sport Psychologist, 5*, 94–95.

Braden, V. (1994). *Mental tennis: Hidden secrets to why you win and lose!* [Videotape]. (Available from Vic Braden Tennis College, 23335 Avenida La Caza, Coto de Caza, CA 92769; 1-800-42COURT, $39.95).

Cairns, K. (1989). *Our inner selves, (Program 2)* [Videotape]. (Available from Human Kinetics Publishers, P.O. Box 5076, Champaign, IL 61825-5076; 1-800-747-4457, $15.95).

Cohn, P., & Waite, G. (1996). *Make your most confident stroke: A guide to a one putt mindset* [Videotape]. (Available from Peak Performance Sports, 7380 Sand Lake Rd., Suite 500, Orlando, FL 32819; 1-888-742-7225, $22.95).

Cox, B. (1982). *Sports psychology for youth coaches* [Videotape]. (Available from Distinctive Home Videos, 391 El Portal Road, San Mateo, CA 94402; 415-344-7756, $59.95).

Cox, B. (1982). *Tom Tutko's coaching clinic* [Videotape]. (Available from Distinctive Home Videos, 391 El Portal Road, San Mateo, CA 94402; 415-344-7756, $39.95).

Curtis, J. (1988). *The mindset for winning* [Videotape]. (Available from Cambridge Career Products, Cambridge Physical Education & Health, P.O. Box 2153, Department PE15, Charleston, WV 25328-2153; 1-800-468-4227, $39.95).

Duda, J., & Retton, M. L. (1994). *Mental readiness* [Videotape]. (Available from USA Gymnastics, 1036 N. Capital Ave., Suite E. 235, Indianapolis, IN, 46204; 1-800-4USAGYM, $4.95).

Ellis, R. (1990). *Mental mechanics and hitting simplification* [Videotape]. (Available from Championship Books and Video Productions, 2730 Graham St., Ames, IA 50010; 1-800-873-2730, $29.95).

Goshen, B. (1987). *The mental game* (Videotape]. (Available from Professional Image, 9422 E. 55th Place, Tulsa, OK, 74145-8154, 918-622-8899, $39.95). Video Review: Sime, W.E. (1992). The mental game [Review of the video program *The mental game*]. *The Sport Psychologist, 6*, 204–205.

Gould, D. (1987). *Sport psychology* [Videotape]. Champaign, IL: Human Kinetics Publishers. (Available from Human Kinetics Publishers, P.O. Box 5076, Champaign, IL 61825-5076; 1-800-747-4457, $70.00).

Hamshire, R., Iveson, I., & Catell, R. (1994). *Winning with sports psychology* [Videotape]. Available from I.C.C. Entertainment P/L, The Marina 13/1 Bradley Ave., Kirribill, NSW, 2061, Australia, 6129955-2297; US $29.95). Video Review: Sargent, G. (1995). Winning with sports psychology [Review of the video program *Winning With Sports Psychology*]. *The Sport Psychologist, 4*, 433–434.

Hogan, C. (1988). *Nice shot* [Videotape]. (Available from Cambridge Career Products, Cambridge Physical Education & Health, P.O. Box 2153, Department PE15, Charleston, WV 25328-2153; 1-800-468-4227, $29.95). Video Review: Armstrong, H.E. (1990) *Nice Shot* [Review of the video program *Nice Shot*]. *The Sport Psychologist, 4,* 433–434.

Jacobs, A., Hill, C., & Allen, L. (1987). *Sports psychology: The winning edge in sports.* (Available from Cambridge Career Products, Cambridge Physical Education & Health P.O. Box 2153, Department PE15, Charleston, WV 25328-2153; 1-800-468-4227, $89.95). Video Review: Weinberg, R. (1990). Sports psychology: The winning edge in sports [Review of the video program *Sports psychology: The winning edge in sports*]. *The Sport Psychologist, 4,* 192–194.

LaTreill, D., & Theilen, A. (1994). *Mental golf* [Videotape]. (Availability, Vestron Video, 15400 Sherman Way, P.O. Box 10124, Van Nuys, CA 91410-0124; $19.95).

Loehr, J. (1989). *Mental toughness training for tennis: "The 16 Second Cure"* [Videotape]. (Available from LGE/Sport Science, 9757 Lake Nona, Orlando, FL 32827-7017; 1-800-543-7764, $30.00).

Loehr, J. (1989). *Tips to mental toughness* [Videotape]. (Available from LGE/Sport Science, 9757 Lake Nona, Orlando, FL 32827-7017; 1-800-543-7764, $40.00).

Martin, C., & Winter, G. (1990). *What is sport psychology?* [Videotape]. (Available from South Australian Sports Institute, P.O. Box 219, Brooklyn Park, SA 5032).

Martin, G. (1989). *Sport psychology for figure skaters.* [Videotape]. (Available from Canadian Figure Skating Association, 200 Main St., Winnipeg, Manitoba R3C 4MZ; 204-985-4064, $28.00 Canadian). Video Review: Jackson, S. (1991). Sport psyching for figure skaters. [Review of the video program *Sport psyching for figure skaters*]. *The Sport Psychologist, 5,* 194–195.

Mudra, D. (1986). *The creative edge in sports psychology.* [Videotape]. (Availabe from Championship Books and Video Productions, 2730 Graham St., Ames, IA 50010; 1-800-873-2730, $29.95).

Murphy, S., & McCann, S. (1994). *Sports mental training.* [Videotape]. (Available from USOC, Judine Anseimo, Sports Science & Technology Division, USOC, One Olympic Plaza, Colorado Springs, CO 80909; $4.99).

National Collegiate Athletic Association. (1988). *Athletes at risk.* [Videotape]. (Available from Karol Media, 350 N. Pennsylvania Ave., Wilkesbarre, PA 18773, 1-800-526-4773, $17.95).

National Collegiate Athletic Association. (1988). *Drugs and the collegiate athlete.* [Videotape]. (Available from Karol Media, 350 N. Pennsylvania Ave., Wilkesbarre, PA 18773, 1-800-526-4773, $17.95).

National Collegiate Athletic Association. (1989). *Afraid to eat: Eating disorders and student-athletes.* [Videotape]. (Available from Karol Media, 350 N. Pennsylvania Ave., Wilkesbarre, PA 18773, 1-800-526-4773, $17.95).

National Collegiate Athletic Association. (1989). *Eating disorders: What can you do?* [Videotape]. (Available from Karol Media, 350 N. Pennsylvania Ave., Wilkesbarre, PA 18773, 1-800-526-4773, $14.95).

Nideffer, R., & Coffey, R. (1989). *Psychological preparation of the elite athlete.* [Videotape]. (Availabe from Australian Coaching Council, P.O. Box 176, Belconnen, ACT 2616).

Orlick, T. (1995). *Coaching the spirit of sport: Building self-esteem.* [Videotape]. Ontario, Canada: Canadian Sport Association. (Available from The Spirit of Sport Foundation, 1600 J. Naismith Drive, Gloucester, Ontario, K1B 5N4; 1-800-672-7775, $17.95).

Porter, K., & Foster, J. (1985). *Mental training for peak athletic performance.* Eugene, OR: Westcom Productions, Inc. (Available from Cambridge Career Products, Cambridge Physical Education & Health, P.O. Box 2153, Department PE15, Charleston, WV 25328-2153, 1-800-468-4227, $59.95). Video Review: Gould, D. (1987). Mental training for peak athletic performance [Review of the video program *Mental training for peak athletic performance*]. *The Sport Psychologist, 1,* 364–365.

Ravizza, K. (1989). *Stress management for baseball: 3–2 count bases loaded, "no sweat."* [Videotape]. (Available from Australian Baseball Federation, P.O. Box 58, Malvern, Victoria, Australia, 3144).

Scolinos, J. (1983). *Mental approach to baseball.* [Videotape]. (Available from Australian Baseball Federation, P.O. Box 58, Malvern, Victoria, Australia, 3144).

Stewart, A., & Heading, R. (1990). *Psychology and motivation in Australian football.* [Videotape]. (Available from National Football Council, 120 Jolimont Road, Jolimont, Victoria, Australia).

Stockton, B.A. (1985). *Coaching psychology.* [Videotape]. (Available from Championship Books and Video Productions, 2730 Graham St., Ames, IA 50010; 1-800-873-2730, $39.95).

Sutphen, R. (1989). *Golf: Mindprogramming to increase your skill.* [Videotape]. (Available from Valley of the Sun Publishing, P.O. Box 683, Ashland, OR 97520-0023; 1-800-225-4717, $19.95).

Voderman, C. (1988). *Mind over matter.* [Videotape]. (Available from National Coaching Foundation, 4 College Close, Beckett Park, Leeds, England LS6 3QHUK).

Whitaker, J. (1991). *Brainwaves golf.* [Videotape]. (Available from Televisual Communications, 300 S. Duncan Ave., Suite 112, Clearwater, FL 34615; 813-442-6480, $19.95).

Geographical Listing of Graduate Programs

There are five countries represented in this directory. The total number of programs represented is 109, as follows:

Australia:	7	programs
Canada:	12	programs
Great Britain:	5	programs
South Africa:	1	program
United States:	84	programs (in 37 states)
Total:	109	programs

Australia

University of Canberra
Deakin University, Rusden Campus
University of Queensland
University of Southern Queensland
Victoria University of Technology
University of Western Australia
University of Wollongong

Canada

University of Alberta
Lakehead University
University of Manitoba
McGill University
Université de Montréal
University of Ottawa
Université du Québec à Trois-Rivières
Queen's University
Université de Sherbrooke
University of Waterloo
University of Western Ontario
York University

Great Britain

Chichester Institute of Higher Education
DeMontfort University Bedford
University of Exeter
Manchester Metropolitan University
Staffordshire University

South Africa

University of Stellenbosch

United States

Alabama
Auburn University

Arizona
Arizona State University
University of Arizona

California
California State University, Fullerton
California State University, Long Beach
California State University, Sacramento
University of California, Berkeley
University of California, Los Angeles
The University for Humanistic Studies
Humboldt State University
John F. Kennedy University
San Diego State University
San Francisco State University
San Jose State University
University of Southern California

Colorado
University of Colorado
University of Northern Colorado

Connecticut
Southern Connecticut State University

Florida
Florida State University
University of Florida

Georgia
University of Georgia
Georgia Southern University

Idaho
Boise State University
University of Idaho

Illinois
Illinois State University
University of Illinois
Northern Illinois University
Southern Illinois University, Carbondale
Southern Illinois University, Edwardsville
Western Illinois University

Indiana
Ball State University
Indiana University
Purdue University

Iowa
Iowa State University
University of Iowa

Kansas
Kansas State University
University of Kansas

Kentucky
Spalding University

Louisiana
Southeastern Louisiana University

Maryland
University of Maryland, College Park

Massachusetts
Boston University
Springfield College (Graduate Studies)
Springfield College (Psychology
    Department)

Michigan
Michigan State University
Wayne State University

Minnesota
Mankato State University
University of Minnesota

Missouri
University of Missouri, Columbia
University of Missouri, Kansas City

Montana
University of Montana

New Hampshire
University of New Hampshire

New Mexico
University of New Mexico

New York
Brooklyn College of the City University of
    New York
Ithaca College

North Carolina
University of North Carolina, Chapel Hill
University of North Carolina, Greensboro

North Dakota
University of North Dakota

Ohio
Bowling Green State University
Cleveland State University
Miami University
Xavier University

Oregon
Oregon State University

Pennsylvania
The Pennsylvania State University
Temple University

South Carolina
Furman University

Tennessee
University of Memphis (Human Movement
    Sciences and Education)
University of Memphis (Psychology)
University of Tennessee, Knoxville

Texas
University of Houston
University of North Texas
University of Texas, Austin
Texas Christian University (Kinesiology and
    Physical Education)
Texas Christian University (Psychology)
Texas Tech University

Utah
Utah State University
University of Utah

Virginia
University of Virginia
Virginia Commonwealth University
Virginia Polytechnic Institute and
    State University

Washington
University of Washington
Western Washington University

West Virginia
West Virginia University

Wisconsin
University of Wisconsin, Milwaukee

Wyoming
University of Wyoming

Contact Persons

University of Alberta	Anne Jordan
	John Hogg
Arizona State University	Daniel M. Landers
University of Arizona	Jean M. Williams
	Peggy Collins
Auburn University	T. G. Reeve
Ball State University	S. Jae Park
Boise State University	Linda M. Petlichkoff
Boston University	Leonard Zaichkowsky
Bowling Green State University	Vikki Krane
	Janet Parks
Brooklyn College of City University of New York	Vivian Acosta
California State University, Fullerton	Carol A. Weinmann
California State University, Long Beach	Michael Lacourse
California State University, Sacramento	Karen L. Scarborough
University of California, Berkeley	Brenda Jo Light Bredemeier
University of California, Los Angeles	Graduate Program Director
University of Canberra	John B. Gross
Chichester Institute of Higher Education	Jan Graydon
Cleveland State University	Susan Ziegler
University of Colorado	Penny McCullagh
Deakin University, Rusden Campus	Rob Sands
	Sue South
DeMontfort University Bedford	Howard K. Hall
University of Exeter	Stuart Biddle
Florida State University	David Pargman
University of Florida	Robert N. Singer
Furman University	Frank M. Powell
University of Georgia	Rod K. Dishman
	Patrick J. O'Connor
Georgia Southern University	Jim McMillan
	Kevin L. Burke
University of Houston	Dale G. Pease
University for Humanistic Studies	Cristina Bortoni Versari
Humboldt State University	Chris Hopper
University of Idaho	Damon Burton
Illinois State University	Sally A. White
	Bill Vogler
University of Illinois	Glyn Roberts
	Jim Misner
Indiana University	John S. Raglin
Iowa State University	Sharon Mathes
University of Iowa	Dawn E. Stephens

283

Ithaca College	Craig Fisher
Kansas State University	David Dzewaltowski
University of Kansas	David Templin
John F. Kennedy University	Gail Solt
Lakehead University	Jane Crossman
Manchester Metropolitan University	Dave Collins
University of Manitoba	Garry Martin
	Dennis Hrycaiko
Mankato State University	Wayne C. Harris
University of Maryland, College Park	Donald H. Steel
	Brad D. Hatfield
McGill University	Graham Neil
University of Memphis (Hum. Mvmt. Sciences & Educ.)	Mary Fry
University of Memphis (Psychology)	Andrew Meyers
Miami University	Robert Weinberg
Michigan State University	John Haubenstricker
University of Minnesota	March L. Krotee
	Diane Wiese-Bjornstal
University of Missouri, Columbia	Richard H. Cox
University of Missouri, Kansas City	Cynthia Pemberton
University of Montana	Lewis A. Curry
Université de Montréal	Wayne R. Halliwell
University of New Hampshire	Heather Barber
University of New Mexico	Joy Griffin
University of North Carolina, Chapel Hill	John M. Silva
University of North Carolina, Greensboro	Diane L. Gill
	Daniel Gould
	David L. Rudolph
University of North Dakota	Robert Eklund
University of North Texas	Peggy Richardson
	Scott Martin
University of Northern Colorado	Robert Brustad
Northern Illinois University	Keith Lambrecht
Oregon State University	Vicki Ebbeck
University of Ottawa	John Salmela
The Pennsylvania State University	Shannon L. Mihalko
	Sam Slobunov
	David Yukelson
Purdue University	Joan L. Duda
Université du Québec à Trois-Rivières	Pierre Lacoste
Queen's University	John Albinson
University of Queensland	Sue Jackson
	Stephanie Hanrahan
	Trish Gorely
San Diego State University	Dennis J. Selder

San Francisco State University
San Jose State University
Université de Sherbrooke
Southeastern Louisiana University
University of Southern California
Southern Connecticut State University
Southern Illinois University, Carbondale
Southern Illinois University, Edwardsville

University of Southern Queensland

Spalding University
Springfield College (Graduate Studies)
Springfield College (Psychology)
Staffordshire University
University of Stellenbosch
Temple University

University of Tennessee, Knoxville
University of Texas, Austin
Texas Christian University (Kinesiology and P.E.)
Texas Christian University (Psychology)
Texas Tech University
Utah State University
University of Utah
Victoria University of Technology

University of Virginia
Virginia Commonwealth University
Virginia Polytechnic Institute and State University
University of Washington
University of Waterloo
Wayne State University
University of Western Australia

Western Illinois University
University of Western Ontario
West Virginia University
Western Washington University
University of Wisconsin, Milwaukee
University of Wollongong
University of Wyoming
Xavier University
York University

Andrea B. Schmid
David M. Furst
Paul Deshaies
Edmund O. Acevedo
John Callaghan
David S. Kemler
Elaine Blinde
Curt L. Lox
Darren C. Treasure
Gershon Tenenbaum
Steven Christensen
Thomas Titus
Betty L. Mann
Al Petitpas
Bruce Hale
Justus R. Potgieter
Carole A. Oglesby
Michael L. Sachs
Craig A. Wrisberg
John B. Bartholomew
Gloria B. Solomon
Michael Richardson
Carl Hayashi
Richard Gordin
Evelyn Hall
Vance Tammen
Mark Andersen
Maureen Weiss
Steven J. Danish
Richard Stratton
Office
L. R. Brawley
Jeff Martin
J. Robert Grove
Sandy Gordon
Laura Finch
Craig R. Hall
Andrew Ostrow
Ralph A. Vernacchia
Barbara B. Meyer
Postgraduate Coordinator
Bonnie Berger
W. Michael Nelson III
Barry Fowler

Telephone Number Listing of Contact Persons

The following listing provides telephone numbers for the contact persons listed in this directory (in some cases, only one person, generally the "primary" sport psychology contact person, is listed per program). The listing is provided by area code first, and then telephone number within area code. Occasionally students wish to find institutions in particular geographical areas and, within those areas, in particular area codes. The following listing will help locate institutions by area code more efficiently. Telephone numbers are provided first for the United States, then for Australia, Canada, Great Britain, and South Africa.

United States

203-392-6040	Southern Connecticut St. Univ.	David S. Kemler
206-543-8687	University of Washington	Office
208-385-1231	Boise State University	Linda Petlichkoff
208-885-2186	University of Idaho	Damon Burton
213-740-2479	Univ. of Southern California	John Callaghan
215-204-1948	Temple University	Carole A. Oglesby
215-204-8718	Temple University	Michael L. Sachs
216-687-4876	Cleveland State University	Susan Ziegler
217-333-6563	University of Illinois	Glyn Roberts
301-405-2489	Univ. of Maryland, College Park	Brad Hatfield
301-405-2490	Univ. of Maryland, College Park	Donald H. Steel
303-492-8021	University of Colorado	Penny McCullagh
303-351-1737	Univ. of Northern Colorado	Robert Brustad
304-293-3295	West Virginia University	Andrew Ostrow
307-766-2494	University of Wyoming	Bonnie Berger
309-298-2350	Western Illinois University	Laura Finch
309-438-2809	Illinois State University	Sally A. White
310-825-2617	UCLA	Graduate Program Director
313-577-1381	Wayne State University	Jeff Martin
317-285-1458	Ball State University	S. Jae Park

319-335-9348	University of Iowa	Dawn E. Stephens
334-844-1463	Auburn University	T. G. Reeve
352-392-0584	University of Florida	Robert N. Singer
360-650-3514	Western Washington University	Ralph Vernacchia
406-243-5242	University of Montana	Lewis A. Curry
408-924-3039	San Jose State University	David M. Furst
413-748-3125	Springfield Coll. (Grad. School)	Betty L. Mann
413-748-3325	Springfield Coll. (Psych.)	Al Petitpas
414-229-6080	Univ. of Wisconsin, Milwaukee	Barbara B. Meyer
415-338-1786	San Francisco State University	Andrea B. Schmid
419-372-7233	Bowling Green State University	Vikki Krane
419-372-6906	Bowling Green State University	Janet Parks
423-974-1283	Univ. of Tennessee, Knoxville	Craig A. Wrisberg
435-797-1506	Utah State University	Richard Gordin
502-585-9911	Spalding University	Thomas Titus
504-549-3870	Southeastern Louisiana Univ.	Edmund O. Acevedo
505-277-3360	University of New Mexico	Joy Griffin
507-389-1818	Mankato State University	Wayne C. Harris
510-254-0110	John F. Kennedy University	Gail Solt
510-530-1225	U. of California, Berkeley	Brenda Bredemeier
512-471-4407	University of Texas, Austin	John B. Bartholomew
513-529-2700	Miami University	Robert Weinberg
513-745-3533	Xavier University	W. Michael Nelson III
515-294-8766	Iowa State University	Sharon Mathes
517-355-4741	Michigan State University	J. Haubenstricker

520-621-6984	University of Arizona	Jean M. Williams
520-621-7456	University of Arizona	Peggy Collins
540-231-5617	Virginia Polytech Inst. & SU	Richard Stratton
541-737-6800	Oregon State University	Vicki Ebbeck
562-985-4558	Cal. State Univ., Long Beach	Michael Lacourse
573-882-7602	Univ. of Missouri, Columbia	Richard H. Cox
602-621-6989	University of Arizona	Jean M. Williams
602-965-7664	Arizona State University	Daniel M. Landers
603-862-2058	University of New Hampshire	Heather Barber
607-274-3112	Ithaca College	Craig Fisher
612-625-0538	University of Minnesota	March L. Krotee
612-625-6580	University of Minnesota	Diane Wiese-Bjornstal
617-353-3378	Boston University	L. Zaichkowsky
618-453-3119	Southern Illinois U., Carbondale	Elaine Blinde
618-692-5961	Southern Illinois U., Edwardsville	Curt L. Lox
618-692-2306	Southern Illinois U., Edwardsville	Darren C. Treasure
619-259-9733	Univ. for Humanistic Studies	C. B. Versari
619-594-1920	San Diego State University	Dennis J. Selder
701-777-3230	University of North Dakota	Robert Eklund
706-542-4382	University of Georgia	Patrick O'Connor
706-542-9840	University of Georgia	Rod K. Dishman
707-826-4536	Humboldt State University	Chris Hopper
713-743-9838	University of Houston	Dale G. Pease
714-278-3316	Cal. State Univ., Fullerton	Carol A. Weinmann
718-951-5879	Brooklyn College of CUNY	Vivian Acosta
765-494-3172	Purdue University	Joan L. Duda
801-581-7646	University of Utah	Evelyn Hall

803-294-3418	Furman University	Frank M. Powell
804-924-7860	University of Virginia	Maureen Weiss
804-828-4384	Virginia Commonwealth Univ.	Steven J. Danish
806-742-3371	Texas Tech University	Carl Hayashi
812-335-0682	Indiana University	John S. Raglin
814-865-1326	Pennsylvania State University	Shannon L. Mihalko
814-865-3146	Pennsylvania State University	Sam Slobounov
814-865-0407	Pennsylvania State University	David Yukelson
815-753-1407	Northern Illinois University	Keith Lambrecht
816-235-2751	Univ. of Missouri, Kansas City	Cynthia Pemberton
817-565-3427	University of North Texas	Scott Martin
817-565-3427	University of North Texas	Peggy Richardson
817-921-7665	Texas Christian U. (Kinesiology)	Gloria B. Solomon
817-921-7410	Texas Christian U. (Psych)	Michael Richardson
901-678-4986	Univ. of Memphis (Human Mvmt.)	Mary Fry
901-678-2146	Univ. of Memphis (Psych.)	Andrew Meyers
904-644-6058	Florida State University	David Pargman
910-334-3037	U. North Carolina, Greensboro	Daniel Gould
910-334-5573	U. North Carolina, Greensboro	Diane L. Gill
910-334-3694	U. North Carolina, Greensboro	David L. Rudolph
912-681-5267	Georgia Southern University	Kevin L. Burke
912-681-0495	Georgia Southern University	Jim McMillan
913-532-0708	Kansas State University	D. Dzewaltowski
913-864-0778	University of Kansas	David Templin
916-278-7309	Cal. State Univ., Sacramento	Karen Scarborough
919-962-5176	U. North Carolina, Chapel Hill	John M. Silva

Australia

(03) 9244 7244	Deakin Univ., Rusden Campus	Rob Sands
(06) 2012009	University of Canberra	John B. Gross

61-3-9248-1132	Victoria Univ. of Technology	Mark Andersen
61-3-9248-1131	Victoria Univ. of Technology	Vance Tammen
61-73-365-6985	University of Queensland	Trish Gorely
61-73-365-6453	University of Queensland	Stephanie Hanrahan
61-73-365-6845	University of Queensland	Sue Jackson
61-8-9380-2361	Univ. of Western Australia	Sandy Gordon
61-8-9380-2361	Univ. of Western Australia	J. Robert Grove
61-42-213732	University of Wollongong	Mark Anshel
76-311703	Univ. of Southern Queensland	Gershon Tenenbaum

Canada

204-474-8589	University of Manitoba	Garry Martin
204-474-8764	University of Manitoba	Dennis Hrycaiko
403-492-3198	University of Alberta	Anne Jordan
403-492-5910	University of Alberta	John Hogg
416-736-5728	York University	Barry Fowler
514-398-4188	McGill University	Graham Neil
514-343-7008	Université de Montréal	Wayne Halliwell
519-679-2111	University of Western Ontario	Craig R. Hall
519-885-1211	University of Waterloo	L. R. Brawley
613-562-5800	University of Ottawa	John Salmela
613-545-2666	Queen's University	John Albinson
807-343-8642	Lakehead University	Jane Crossman
819-376-5128	U. du Québec à Trois-Rivières	Pierre Lacoste
819-821-8000	Université de Sherbrooke	Paul Deshaies

Great Britain

01234-793316	DeMontfort Univ., Bedford	Howard K. Hall
01243-816320	Chichester Inst. of Higher Ed.	Jan Graydon
44-161-247-5429	Manchester Metropolitan Univ.	Dave Collins
44-1782-412515	Staffordshire University	Bruce Hale
44-0-1392-264751	University of Exeter	Stuart Biddle

South Africa

27-21-8084915	University of Stellenbosch	Justus Potgieter

Electronic Mail Addresses for Contact Persons

The following listing provides electronic mail (e-mail) addresses for the contact persons listed in this directory. The listing is provided alphabetically by program first, and then alphabetically by individual. Please note that e-mail addresses change frequently, and some of the addresses in this directory are most likely outdated by the time you read this. For those addresses which don't work, or for those individuals who don't have addresses listed, doing some surfing on the Internet, particularly accessing Gopher or the Web, may allow you to locate a college/university address directory and find the correct address or locate an address when one is not listed.

Alphabetically by Program

University of Alberta
    John Hogg   jhogg@PER.ALBERTA.CA
    Anne Jordan   Ajordan@PER.ALBERTA.CA

Auburn University
    T. G. Reeve   reevetg@mail.auburn.edu

Boise State University
    Linda Petlichkoff   lpetli@bsu.idbsu.edu

Boston University
    Leonard Zaichkowsky   sport@acs.bu.edu

Bowling Green State University
    Vikki Krane   VKRANE@BGNET.BGSU.EDU
    Janet Parks   JPARKS@BGNET.BGSU.EDU

California State University, Long Beach
    Michael Lacourse   mlacours@csulb.edu

California State University, Sacramento
    Karen Scarborough   scarboro@csus.edu

University of California, Berkeley
    Brenda Jo Light Bredemeier   BRENDA@UCLINK2.BERKELEY.EDU

University of Canberra
    John Gross   gross@science.canberra.edu.au

Chichester Institute of Higher Education
    Jan Graydon   100443.2067@compuserve.com

University of Colorado
Penny McCullagh   MCCULLAGH@COLORADO.EDU

Deakin University, Rusden Campus
Rob Sands   rsands@deakin.edu.au

DeMontfort University Bedford
Howard K. Hall   HKHall@DMU.AC.UK

University of Exeter
Stuart Biddle   S.J.H.BIDDLE@EXETER.AC.UK

Florida State University
David Pargman   Pargman@SY2000.cet.fsu.edu

University of Florida
Robert Singer   RSINGER@HHP.UFL.EDU

Furman University
Frank M. Powell   frank.powell@furman.edu

University of Georgia
Rod K. Dishman   rdishman@uga.cc.uga.edu
Patrick J. O'Connor   poconnor@uga.cc.uga.edu

Georgia Southern University
Kevin L. Burke   KevBurke@gsaix2.cc.GASOU.edu
Jim McMillan   McMillan@GVSMS2.CC.GASOU.EDU

University of Houston
Dale G. Pease   DPEASE@UH.EDU

University for Humanistic Studies
Cristina Bortoni Versari   Cversari@aol.com

University of Idaho
Damon Burton   dburton@uidaho.edu

Illinois State University
Sally A. White   SWhite@ilstu.edu

Indiana University
John S. Raglin   raglinj@indiana.edu

Iowa State University
Sharon Mathes   SMATHES@iastate.edu

292

University of Iowa
  Dawn Stephens   DAWN-E-STEPHENS@UIOWA.EDU

Ithaca College
  Craig Fisher   cfisher@ithaca.edu

Kansas State University
  David Dzewaltowski   DADX@KSU.KSU.EDU

Lakehead University
  Jane Crossman   Jane.Crossman@lakeheadu.ca

Manchester Metropolitan University
  Dave Collins   D.COLLINS@MMU.AC.UK

University of Maryland, College Park
  Donald H. Steel   BH5@UMAIL.UMD.EDU

McGill University
  Graham Neil   Neil@EDUCATION.MCGILL.CA

University of Memphis (Hum. Mvmt. Sci.)
  Mary Fry   fry.mary@coe.memphis.edu

University of Memphis (Psychology)
  Andrew Meyers   AMEYERS@MEMPHIS.EDU

Miami University
  Robert Weinberg   WEINBERG_R@MIAMIU.MUOHIO.EDU

University of Minnesota
  March L. Krotee   Krote001@tc.umn.edu
  Diane Wiese-Bjornstal   dwiese@ZX.CIS.UMN.EDU

University of Missouri, Columbia
  Richard H. Cox   rhcox@showme.missouri.edu

University of Missouri, Kansas City
  Cynthia Pemberton   CPEMBERTON@smtpgate.umkc.edu

University of Montana
  Lewis A. Curry   curry58@selway.umt.edu

University of New Hampshire
  Heather Barber   HB@CHRISTA.UNH.EDU

University of North Carolina, Chapel Hill
John Silva   Silva@UNC.edu

University of North Carolina, Greensboro
Diane Gill   diane_gill@uncg.edu
Dan Gould   GOULDD@iris.uncg.edu
David L. Rudolph   dlrudolph@homans.uncg.edu

University of North Dakota
Robert Eklund   REKLUND@BADLANDS.NODAK.EDU

University of North Texas
Scott Martin   SMARTIN@COEFS.COE.UNT.EDU
Peggy Richardson   RCHRDSN@COEFS.COE.UNT.EDU

University of Northern Colorado
Robert Brustad   bbrustad@hhs.UnivNorthCo.edu

Oregon State University
Vicki Ebbeck   EBBECKV@CCMAIL.ORST.EDU

University of Ottawa
John Salmela   JSALMELA@UOTTAWA.CA

The Pennsylvania State University
Sam Slobounov   sms18@PSU.EDU
David Yukelson   Y39@PSU.EDU

Purdue University
Joan Duda   LYNNE@VM.CC.PURDUE.EDU

Queens University
John Albinson   ALBINSON@QUCDN.QUEENSU.CA

University of Queensland
Trish Gorely   tgorely@hms.uq.edu.au
Stephanie Hanrahan   steph@hms.uq.edu.au
Sue Jackson   suejac@hms.uq.edu.au

San Diego State University
Dennis J. Selder   DSELDER@MAIL.SDSU.EDU

San Jose State University
David M. Furst   furstd@sjsuvm1.sjsu.edu

Université de Sherbrooke
    Paul Deshaies   PDESHAIES@FEPS.USHERB.CA

Southeastern Louisiana University
    Edmund O. Acevedo   eacevedo@selu.edu

University of Southern California
    John Callaghan   callagha@mizar.usc.edu

Southern Connecticut State University
    David S. Kemler   Kemler@scsu.ctstateu.edu

Southern Illinois University, Carbondale
    Elaine Blinde   Blinde@SIUCVMB.EDU

Southern Illinois University, Edwardsville
    Curt L. Lox   clox@siue.edu
    Darren C. Treasure   dtreasu@siue.edu

University of Southern Queensland
    Gershon Tenenbaum   tenenbau@usq.edu.au

Staffordshire University
    Bruce Hale   SCTBDH@CR41.STAFFS.AC.UK

University of Stellenbosch
    Justus R. Potgieter   JRP@MATIES.SUN.AC.ZA

Temple University
    Carole A. Oglesby   REDS@ASTRO.TEMPLE.EDU
    Michael L. Sachs   MSACHS@VM.TEMPLE.EDU

University of Tennessee, Knoxville
    Craig A. Wrisberg   wrisberg@utkux.utcc.utk.edu

University of Texas, Austin
    John B. Bartholomew   john.bart@mail.utexas.edu

Texas Christian University
    Gloria B. Solomon (Kinesiology)   G.SOLOMON@TCU.EDU

Texas Tech University
    Carl Hayashi   UNHAY@TTACS.TTU.EDU

Utah State University
    Richard Gordin   gordin@cc.usu.edu

University of Utah
    Evelyn Hall   EHall@deans.health.utah.edu

Victoria University of Technology
    Mark Andersen   marka@dingo.vut.edu.au
    Vance Tammen   vancet@dingo.vut.edu.au

University of Virginia
    Maureen Weiss   mrw5d@curry.edschool.virginia.edu

Virginia Commonwealth University
    Steven J. Danish   sdanish@saturn.vcu.edu

Virginia Polytechnic Institute & State University
    Richard Stratton   rstratto@VT.EDU

University of Washington
    Office   dormont@u.washington.edu

University of Waterloo
    L. R. Brawley   lrbrawle@healthy.uwaterloo.ca

Wayne State University
    Jeff Martin   jeff_martin@mts.cc.wayne.edu

University of Western Australia
    Sandy Gordon   sgordon@cyllene.uwa.edu.au
    J. Robert Grove   Bob.Grove@uwa.edu.au

Western Illinois University
    Laura Finch   LM-Finch@wiu.edu

University of Western Ontario
    Craig R. Hall   CHALL@JULIAN.UWO.CA

West Virginia University
    Andrew Ostrow   aostrow2@wvu.edu

Western Washington University
    Ralph A. Vernacchia   anthony@cc.wwu.edu

University of Wisconsin-Milwaukee
    Barbara B. Meyer   bbmeyer@csd.uwm.edu

University of Wollongong
    Mark Anshel   Mark_Anshel@UOW.EDU.AU

University of Wyoming
    Bonnie Berger   BBERGER@UWYO.EDU

Xavier University
    W. Michael Nelson III   xupsych@xavier.xu.edu

York University
    Barry Fowler   EAHS@YORKU.CA

Alphabetically by Contact Person

Edmund O. Acevedo   eacevedo@selu.edu
    Southeastern Louisiana University

John Albinson   ALBINSON@QUCDN.QUEENSU.CA
    Queens University

Mark Andersen   marka@dingo.vut.edu.au
    Victoria University of Technology

Mark Anshel   Mark_Anshel@UOW.EDU.AU
    University of Wollongong

Heather Barber   HB@CHRISTA.UNH.EDU
    University of New Hampshire

John B. Bartholomew   john.bart@mail.utexas.edu
    University of Texas, Austin

Bonnie Berger   BBERGER@UWYO.EDU
    University of Wyoming

Stuart Biddle   S.J.H.BIDDLE@EXETER.AC.UK
    University of Exeter

Elaine Blinde   Blinde@SIUCVMB.EDU
    Southern Illinois University, Carbondale

L. R. Brawley   lrbrawle@healthy.uwaterloo.ca
    University of Waterloo
Brenda Jo Light Bredemeier   BRENDA@UCLINK2.BERKELEY.EDU
    University of California, Berkeley

Robert Brustad   bbrustad@hhs.UnivNorthCo.edu
    University of Northern Colorado

Kevin L. Burke   KevBurke@gsaix2.cc.GASOU.edu
    Georgia Southern University

Damon Burton   dburton@uidaho.edu
    University of Idaho

John Callaghan   callagha@mizar.usc.edu
    University of Southern California

Dave Collins   D.COLLINS@MMU.AC.UK
    Manchester Metropolitan University

Richard H. Cox   rhcox@showme.missouri.edu
    University of Missouri, Columbia

Jane Crossman   Jane.Crossman@lakeheadu.ca
    Lakehead University

Lewis A. Curry   curry58@selway.umt.edu
    University of Montana

Steven J. Danish   sdanish@saturn.vcu.edu
    Virginia Commonwealth University

Paul Deshaies   PDESHAIES@FEPS.USHERB.CA
    Université de Sherbrooke

Rod K. Dishman   rdishman@uga.cc.uga.edu
    University of Georgia

Joan Duda   LYNNE@VM.CC.PURDUE.EDU
    Purdue University

David Dzewaltowski   DADX@KSU.KSU.EDU
    Kansas State University

Vicki Ebbeck   EBBECKV@CCMAIL.ORST.EDU
    Oregon State University

Robert Eklund   REKLUND@BADLANDS.NODAK.EDU
    University of North Dakota

Richard Fenker   re131ps@tcuamus.bitnet
    Texas Christian University

Laura Finch   LM-Finch@wiu.edu
    Western Illinois University

Craig Fisher   cfisher@ithaca.edu
    Ithaca College

Barry Fowler   EAHS@YORKU.CA
    York University

Mary Fry   fry.mary@coe.memphis.edu
    University of Memphis (Hum. Mvmt. Sciences)

David M. Furst   furstd@sjsuvm1.sjsu.edu
    San Jose State University

Diane Gill   diane_gill@uncg.edu
    University of North Carolina, Greensboro

Trish Gorely   tgorely@hms.uq.edu.au
    University of Queensland

Richard Gordin   gordin@cc.usu.edu
    Utah State University

Sandy Gordon   sgordon@cyllene.uwa.edu.au
    University of Western Australia

Dan Gould   GOULDD@iris.uncg.edu
    University of North Carolina, Greensboro

Jan Graydon   100443.2067@compuserve.com
    Chichester Institute of Higher Education

John Gross   gross@science.canberra.edu.au
    University of Canberra

J. Robert Grove   Bob.Grove@uwa.edu.au
    University of Western Australia

Bruce Hale   SCTBDH@CR41.STAFFS.AC.UK
    Staffordshire University

Craig R. Hall   CHALL@JULIAN.UWO.CA
    University of Western Ontario

Evelyn Hall   EHall@deans.health.utah.edu
    University of Utah

Howard K. Hall   HKHall@DMU.AC.UK
    DeMontfort University Bedford

Stephanie Hanrahan   steph@hms.uq.edu.au
    University of Queensland

Carl Hayashi   UNHAY@TTACS.TTU.EDU
    Texas Tech University

John Hogg   jhogg@PER.ALBERTA.CA
    University of Alberta

Sue Jackson   suejac@hms.uq.edu.au
    University of Queensland

Anne Jordan   Ajordan@PER.ALBERTA.CA
    University of Alberta

David S. Kemler   Kemler@scsu.ctstateu.edu
    Southern Connecticut State University

Vikki Krane   VKRANE@BGNET.BGSU.EDU
    Bowling Green State University

March L. Krotee   Krote001@tc.umn.edu
    University of Minnesota

Michael Lacourse   mlacours@csulb.edu
    California State University, Long Beach

Curt L. Lox   clox@siue.edu
    Southern Illinois University, Edwardsville

Jeff Martin   jeff_martin@mts.cc.wayne.edu
    Wayne State University

Scott Martin   SMARTIN@COEFS.COE.UNT.EDU
    University of North Texas

Sharon Mathes   SMATHES@iastate.edu
    Iowa State University

Penny McCullagh
University of Colorado

MCCULLAGH@COLORADO.EDU

Jim McMillan
Georgia Southern University

McMillan@GVSMS2.CC.GASOU.EDU

Barbara Meyer
University of Wisconsin, Milwaukee

bbmeyer@csd.uwm.edu

Andrew Meyers
University of Memphis (Psychology)

AMEYERS@MEMPHIS.EDU

Graham Neil
McGill University

Neil@EDUCATION.MCGILL.CA

W. Michael Nelson III
Xavier University

xupsych.@xavier.xu.edu

Patrick J. O'Connor
University of Georgia

poconnor@uga.cc.uga.edu

Carole A. Oglesby
Temple University

REDS@ASTRO.TEMPLE.EDU

Andrew Ostrow
West Virginia University

aostrow2@wvu.edu

David Pargman
Florida State University

Pargman@SY2000.cet.fsu.edu

Janet Parks
Bowling Green State University

JPARKS@BGNET.BGSU.EDU

Dale G. Pease
University of Houston

DPEASE@UH.EDU

Cynthia Pemberton
University of Missouri, Kansas City

CPEMBERTON@smtpgate.umkc.edu

Linda Petlichkoff
Boise State University

lpetli@bsu.idbsu.edu

Justus R. Potgieter
University of Stellenbosch

JRP@MATIES.SUN.AC.ZA

Frank M. Powell
    Furman University

frank.powell@furman.edu

John S. Raglin
    Indiana University

raglinj@indiana.edu

T. G. Reeve
    Auburn University

reevetg@mail.auburn.edu

Peggy Richardson
    University of North Texas

RCHRDSN@COEFS.COE.UNT.EDU

David L. Rudolph
    University of North Carolina, Greensboro

dlrudolph@homans.uncg.edu

Michael L. Sachs
    Temple University

MSACHS@VM.TEMPLE.EDU

John Salmela
    University of Ottawa

JSALMELA@UOTTAWA.CA

Rob Sands
    Deakin University, Rusden Campus

rsands@deakin.edu.au

Karen Scarborough
    California State University, Sacramento

scarboro@csus.edu

Dennis J. Selder
    San Diego State University

DSELDER@MAIL.SDSU.EDU

John Silva
    University of North Carolina, Chapel Hill

Silva@UNC.edu

Robert N. Singer
    University of Florida

RSINGER@HHP.UFL.EDU

Sam Slobounov
    The Pennsylvania State University

sms18@PSU.EDU

Gloria B. Solomon
    Texas Christian University (Kinesiology)

G.SOLOMON@TCU.EDU

Donald H. Steel
    University of Maryland, College Park

BH5@UMAIL.UMD.EDU

Dawn Stephens
    University of Iowa

DAWN-E-STEPHENS@UIOWA.EDU

Richard Stratton   rstratto@VT.EDU
    Virginia Polytechnic Institute & State University

Vance Tammen   vancet@dingo.vut.edu.au
    Victoria University of Technology

Gershon Tenenbaum   tenenbau@usq.edu.au
    University of Southern Queensland

Darren C. Treasure   dtreasu@siue.edu
    Southern Illinois University, Edwardsville

Ralph A. Vernacchia   anthony@cc.wwu.edu
    Western Washington University

Cristina Bortoni Versari   Cversari@aol.com
    The University for Humanistic Studies

Robert Weinberg   WEINBERG_R@MIAMIU.MUOHIO.EDU
    Miami University

Maureen Weiss   mrw5d@curry.edschool.virginia.edu
    University of Virginia

Diane Wiese-Bjornstal   dwiese@ZX.CIS.UMN.EDU
    University of Minnesota

Sally A. White   swhite@ilstu.edu
    Illinois State University

Craig A. Wrisberg   wrisberg@utkux.utcc.utk.edu
    University of Tennessee, Knoxville

David Yukelson   Y39@PSU.EDU
    The Pennsylvania State University

Leonard Zaichkowsky   sport@acs.bu.edu
    Boston University

Surfing the Net—Using the Internet for Success

Kevin L. Burke, Vince J. Granito, and Michael L. Sachs
Georgia Southern University, John F. Kennedy University,
and Temple University

Getting information about the field of sport psychology in general, or graduate programs specifically, is in many cases as easy as typing on a computer keyboard. Thanks to the convenience of the Internet, there is a wealth of sport psychology information at your fingertips. Many colleges and universities make available much of the same graduate program information that is placed in graduate catalogues through their World Wide Web sites (check the listing of available web sites as of December 1, 1997 for the graduate programs in this directory in Appendix P). You may be able to find graduate program applications, assistantship information and applications, graduate course offerings and requirements, and information (perhaps even pictures!) of the graduate faculty involved in the programs in which you are interested.

The Internet, specifically electronic mail (e-mail), can allow you to contact faculty at potential programs (see Appendix N for e-mail addresses of contact persons for the graduate programs in this directory). Other sources (AAASP Membership Directory) provide additional e-mail addresses for other colleagues in the field with whom you can have conversations about the hot sport psychology topics of the day and/or where to eat at the site of the next sport psychology conference. E-mail is certainly a viable (and in some ways preferable) option for communication, as opposed to letters, faxes, or telephone calls.

There are numerous sites on the Internet which address exercise- and sport-related issues. The most established site in sport psychology is SPORTPSY, originally established in 1987 at the University of Maryland at Baltimore and still coordinated by Michael Sachs at Temple University. SPORTPSY deals with a wide variety of areas in exercise and sport psychology, from discussions on issues such as certification and confidentiality, to conference information, job announcements, and requests for information on topics within sport psychology. Most individuals can join by sending the following command at their command line:

TELL LISTSERV AT VM.TEMPLE.EDU SUB SPORTPSY your name

or sending the following message to LISTSERV@VM.TEMPLE.EDU

SUB SPORTPSY your name

SPORTPSY is at VM.TEMPLE.EDU and if the above commands don't work, just write to Michael Sachs directly at V5289E@VM.TEMPLE.EDU and he can add you himself (given his "vast" powers as list coordinator).

The World Wide Web has grown exponentially, and a dizzying number of sites have been developed from a diverse population ranging from individual faculty members to international organizations. There are so-called search engines which are available to help users search for information on various topics (see your local Internet/World Wide Web guru for suggestions on the latest/best resources). The listing which follows was compiled by the three authors (with some helpful additions from Dr. Jack Lesyk, of the Ohio Center for Sport Psychology—check out his Web site under Sport Psychology Related Sites), and addresses are hopefully still correct. Information on the organization or source is provided where available. No attempt has been made to screen these sites for the quality of their information. Almost all the information should be of good quality and derived from reputable sources. However, especially for "personal" web sites, there is no screening of what one can post on a site. Therefore, the cardinal rule is always "User Beware" (as in "Buyer beware").

Enjoy your surfing (always physical activity involved!) through the Internet.

WEB SITES FOR SPORT AND EXERCISE PSYCHOLOGY

Associations and Organizations

North American Society for Psychology of Sport and Physical Activity
http://grove.ufl.edu/~naspspa/

American College of Sports Medicine
http://www.acsm.org/

Association for the Advancement of Applied Sport Psychology
http://spot.colorado.edu/~aaasp/

Division 47 (Exercise and Sport Psychology) of the American Psychological Association
http://www.psyc.unt.edu/apadiv47/

Fitness Information Technology
http://www.fitinfo.com/

Human Kinetics Publishers
http://www.humankinetics.com/

Michigan State University's Youth Sports Institute
http://www.educ.msu.edu/units/Dept/PEES/ysi/ysihome.html

American Sport Education Program
http://www.asep.com/

National Alliance for Youth Sports
http://www.nays.org/

Coaching Association of Canada
http://www.coach.ca/

American Alliance for Health, Physical Education, Recreation and Dance
http://www.aahperd.org/

National Association for Girls and Women in Sport
http://www.aahperd.org/nagws/nagws.html

National Association for Sport and Physical Education
http://www.aahperd.org/naspe/naspe.html

Women's Sports Foundation
http://www.lifetimetv.com/wosport/

Sport Psychology—Related Sites

Sport psychology information
http://spot.colorado.edu/~collinsj/

Sport psychology articles
   http://www.potentium.ca/

Ohio Center for Sport Psychology
   http://pwd.netcom.com./~jjlesyk/ocsp.html

Eileen Udry, Ph.D., University of Oregon, (home page)
   http://darkwing.uoregon.edu/~udryem/EMUd2.html

University of Washington's Husky Sport Psychology Services
   http://weber.u.washington.edu/~hsps/

Sport Psychology & Weight Lifting
   http://www.waf.com/weights/randal1.htm

Ithaca College Health Science and Human Performance Department
   http//www.ithaca.edu/Admissions/Schools/HSHP/Majors/Sport_studies.html

John Murray (articles on the mental side of tennis)
   http://tennisserver.com/

Noel Blundell
   http://www.golf.com.au/netcoach/library/blundell.html

Brent Russell (sport psychology workshops offered for coaches)
   http://www.rohan.sdsu.edu/dept/coachsci/intro.html

Cristina Versari self-help and psychology magazine)
   http://www.cybertowers.com/selfhelp/

Mind Tools column on Sport Psychology
   http://www.mindtools.com/

Sport Psychology Questions and Answers
   http://www.sportdoc.com/

Sport Psychology in Spain
   http://www.ucm.es/OTROS/Psyap/hispania/cruz.htm

Psychology in Spain
   http://www.cop.es/

Performance Enhancement
   http://bubba.ucc.okstate.edu/wellness/athlete.htm

Golf Psych; The Lergry Golf Psychology System
   http://www.golfpsych.com/
Golf Web—Patrick Cohn—Peak Performance Sports

Sport psychology and golf
   http://golfweb.com/instruction/cohn/

The Mental Edge Article
   http://www.ultranet.com/~dupcak/mntledge.html

RESOURCE LIST

Explanation of sport science journals (including sport psychology)
   http://teach.virginia.edu/curry/resources/library/handouts/explainsj.html

The Prevention Researcher (resource list in both psychology and sport psychology)
http://www.integres.org/prevres/v2n2abst.htm

Just SPORTS for Women (issues related to women and sport)
http://justwomen.com/

Mental Health Net (Web resource for health and sport psychology)
http://www.cmhc.com/guide/pro07.htm

Psychology of Sport and Exercise link
http://www.livjm.ac.uk/sports_science/psycholo.html

Sport Psychology—internet information
http://www.gettysburg.edu/response/ref/sportspsy.html

Sport Psychology—research sources
http://server.bmod.athabascau.ca/html/aupr/sport.htm

SPECIFIC SPORT INFORMATION SITES

ESPN's Sport Zone
http://www.sportzone.com/

USA Today Sports Section
http://www.usatoday.com/sports/sfront.htm

CNN Sports
http://www.cnn.com/SPORTS/index.html

Sports Illustrated On-Line
http://pathfinder.com/si/

Major League Baseball
http://www.majorleaguebaseball.com/

National Basketball Association
http://www.nba.com/

American Basketball League (women's pro league)
http://ableague.com/

National Hockey League
http://www.nhl.com/

USA Hockey
http://www.usahockey.com/

United States Golf Association
http://www.usga.org/

GOLF
http://www.igolf.com/

Golf Web
http://www.golfweb.com/

American Youth Sport Soccer Organization
http://www.soccer.org/

U.S. Youth Soccer Association
http://www.usysa.org/

Amateur Softball Association
http://www.softball.org/

United States Swimming
http://www.usswim.org/

United States Tennis Association
http://www.usta.com/

USA Wrestling
http://www.usawrestling.org/

The Grandstand
http://www.gstand.com/

Stadiums and Arenas
http://www.wwcd.com/stadiums.html

Sydney 2000 Olympic Games
http://www.sydney.olympic.org/

Winter Paralympics 2002
http://www.vsnet.ch/Sion2002/para_e.html

Sport Information Resource Center (SIRC)
http://sirc.ca/

Title IX Information
http://www.arcade.uiowa.edu/proj/ge/

Sport information
http://www.sportquest.com/

Parents, Kids, and Sports
http://www.uvol.com/family/pbseries.html

Web Sites for Programs

The following listing provides web site addresses for the programs listed in this directory. The listing is provided alphabetically by program. Only those programs which submitted Web site addresses by July 1997, are included in this list. Because Web addresses frequently change and because some programs have no Web site listed, you are encouraged to surf the Web to locate the current address of a program.

Arizona State University
  http://www.asu.edu/clas/espe/

Boston University
  http://www.education.bu.edu/sport psychology/

Bowling Green State University
  http://www.bgsu.edu/departments/hper/gp.html

California State University, Fullerton
  http://www.fullerton.edu/hdcs/322kines.html

California State University, Long Beach
  http://www.csulb.edu/~kpe/

California State University, Sacramento
  http://www.hhs.csus.edu/

University of Canberra
  http://science.canberra.edu.au/sportstud/

University of Colorado
  http://www.colorado.edu/kines/

DeMontfort University Bedford
  http://www.dmu.ac.uk/dept/schools/pesl/spob/research_psych.html

University of Exeter
  http://www.exeter.ac.uk/education/

Furman University
  http://www.furman.edu/

University of Georgia
  http://www.coe.uga.edu/exs/

Georgia Southern University
  http://www.gasou.edu/

University of Houston
  http://www.coe.uh.edu/

Indiana University
  http://www.indiana.edu/~kines/

Iowa State University
  http://www.iastate.edu/

University of Iowa
http://www.uiowa.edu/~shlps/grad.htm

Ithaca College
http://www.ithaca.edu/grad/grad1/

University of Kansas
http://www.soe.ukans.edu/courses/hper892/

John F. Kennedy University
http://www.jfku.edu/

Lakehead University
http://www.lakeheadu.ca/

University of Memphis (Psychology)
http://www.memphis.edu/psych.htm

Michigan State University
http://www.educ.msu.edu/units/dept/pees/

University of Minnesota
http://www.coled.umn.edu/Kls/

University of Missouri, Columbia
http://tiger.coe.missouri.edu/~ecp/

University of Missouri, Kansas City
http://www.CCTR.UMKC.EDU/DEPT/PHYSED/

University of North Carolina, Chapel Hill
http://www.unc.edu/depts/exercise/SP_cover.html

University of North Carolina, Greensboro
http://www.uncg.edu/

University of North Texas
http://www.coe.unt.edu/

University of Northern Colorado
http://www.hhs.univnorthco.edu/

Northern Illinois University
http://www.Niu.edu/acad/phed/

Oregon State University
http://www.orst.edu/dept/hhp/

University of Ottawa
http://www.uottawa.ca/academic/health/sportstudies-etudes/

University of Queensland
http://www.uq.edu.au/hms/

San Jose State University
http://www.sjsu.edu/depts/casa/dept/hup.html

University of Southern California
http://www.usc.edu/dept/LAS/exsci/

Southern Connecticut State University
    http://scsu.ctstateu.edu/

Spalding University
    http://www.spalding.edu/

Springfield College (Graduate Studies)
    http://www.springfieldcollege.edu/

Springfield College (Psychology)
    http://www.spfldcol.edu/

Staffordshire University
    http://www.staffs.ac.uk/sands/scis/sport/

Temple University
    http://www.temple.edu/HPERD/phys.html

University of Tennessee, Knoxville
    http://www.coe.utk.edu/units/cultural.html

Texas Tech University
    http://www.ttu.edu/~hper/

Victoria University of Technology
    http://www.vut.edu.au/

Virginia Tech University
    http://www.chre.vt.edu/coe/COE_admin/programs/hpe/hpe_p.html

University of Washington
    http://www.weber.u.washington.edu/~psychol/

University of Waterloo
    http://www.ahs.uwaterloo.ca/kin/kinhome.html

University of Western Australia
    http://www.general.uwa.edu.au/~hmweb/

Western Illinois University
    http://www.wiu.edu/users/mipe/

University of Western Ontario
    http://www.uwo.ca/kinesiology/

West Virginia University
    http://www.wvu.edu/~physed/sportbeh/htm

University of Wisconsin, Milwaukee
    http://www.uwm.edu/SAHP/gp/hk/ghkmenu.htm

University of Wyoming
    http://www.uwyo.edu/

Xavier University
    http://www.xu.edu/

York University
    http://www.york.ca/academics/bfowier

Location of Graduate Programs:
Physical Education and Psychology, Master's and Doctoral Level

Physical Education Programs *

Master's Programs (92 programs)

University of Alberta
Arizona State University
Auburn University
Ball State University
Boise State University
Bowling Green State University
Brooklyn College, City University of
    New York
California State University, Fullerton
California State University, Long Beach
California State University, Sacramento
University of California, Berkeley
University of Canberra
Chichester Institute of Higher Education
Cleveland State University
University of Colorado
Deakin University, Rusden Campus
DeMontfort University Bedford
University of Exeter
University of Florida
Furman University
University of Georgia
Georgia Southern University
University of Houston
Humboldt State University
University of Idaho
Illinois State University
University of Illinois
Indiana University
Iowa State University
University of Iowa
Ithaca College
Kansas State University
University of Kansas

Lakehead University
Manchester Metropolitan University
University of Manitoba
University of Maryland, College Park
McGill University
University of Memphis
Miami University
Michigan State University
University of Minnesota
University of Missouri, Kansas City
University of Montana
Université de Montréal
University of New Hampshire
University of New Mexico
University of North Carolina, Chapel Hill
University of North Carolina, Greensboro
University of North Dakota
University of North Texas
University of Northern Colorado
Northern Illinois University
Oregon State University
University of Ottawa
The Pennsylvania State University
Purdue University
Université du Québec à Trois-Rivières
Queen's University
University of Queensland
San Diego State University
San Francisco State University
San Jose State University
Universite de Sherbrooke
Southeastern Louisiana University
University of Southern California
Southern Connecticut State University
Southern Illinois University, Carbondale
Southern Illinois University, Edwardsville
Springfield College (Health, Physical Educa-
    tion, and Recreation)

*Primarily found in Departments of Physical Education, but also found under many other
names, including Kinesiology, Exercise and Sport Sciences, etc.

Staffordshire University
University of Stellenbosch
Temple University
University of Tennessee, Knoxville
University of Texas, Austin
Texas Christian University
Texas Tech University
Utah State University
University of Utah
Victoria University of Technology
University of Virginia
Virginia Polytechnic Institute and State University
University of Waterloo
Wayne State University
University of Western Australia
Western Illinois University
University of Western Ontario
West Virginia University
Western Washington University
University of Wisconsin, Milwaukee
University of Wyoming
York University

Doctoral Programs (43 programs)

University of Alberta
Arizona State University
University of California, Berkeley
Chichester Institute of Higher Education
University of Colorado
Deakin University, Rusden Campus
DeMontfort University Bedford
University of Exeter
University of Florida
University of Georgia
University of Houston
University of Idaho
University of Illinois
University of Iowa
University of Kansas
Manchester Metropolitan University
University of Maryland, College Park
Michigan State University
University of Minnesota

University of Missouri, Kansas City
Université de Montréal
University of New Mexico
University of North Carolina, Greensboro
University of Northern Colorado
Oregon State University
University of Ottawa
The Pennsylvania State University
Purdue University
University of Queensland
University of Southern California
Springfield College (Health, Physical Education, and Recreation)
Staffordshire University
University of Stellenbosch
Temple University
University of Tennessee, Knoxville
Texas Tech University
University of Utah
Victoria University of Technology
University of Virginia
University of Waterloo
University of Western Australia
University of Western Ontario
West Virginia University

Psychology Programs

Master's Programs (13 programs)

Boston University**
Florida State University***
The University for Humanistic Studies
John F. Kennedy University
University of Manitoba
Mankato State University
University of Memphis
University of Missouri, Columbia
University of Queensland
University of Southern Queensland
Spalding University
Springfield College (Psychology)
University of Wollongong

Doctoral Programs (19 programs)

University of Arizona
Boston University**
University of California, Los Angeles
Florida State University***
The University for Humanistic Studies
John F. Kennedy University
University of Manitoba
University of Memphis
University of Missouri, Columbia
University of Montana****
University of North Texas
University of Queensland
University of Southern Queensland
Spalding University
Texas Christian University
Virginia Commonwealth University
University of Washington
University of Wollongong
Xavier University

**Department of Developmental Studies and Counseling
***Department of Educational Research, Program in Educational Psychology
***Department of Counselor Education

Quick Chart of Program Information:
Degrees Offered, Program Emphasis Rating, and Internship Possibility

Institution	Master's	Doctoral	Rating*	Internship
Univ. of Alberta	MA/MS	PhD	—	N
Arizona State Univ.	MS	PhD	5	Y
University of Arizona		PhD	5	Y
Auburn UniversityMS/MEd		—	Y	
Ball State University	MA/MS		4	Y
Boise State University	MS		—	Y
Boston University	MEd	EdD	4	Y
Bowling Green State Univ.	MEd		4	N
Brooklyn College — CUNY	MS		3	N
Cal. State U., Fullerton	MS		3	Y
Cal. State U., Long Beach	MS		=	Y
Cal. State U., Sacramento	MS		4	Y
Univ. of Cal., Berkeley	MS	PhD	—	Y
Univ. of Cal., Los Angeles		PhD	—	Y
University of Canberra	GradDip		2	Y
Chichester Inst. Higher Ed.	MPhil/MS	PhD	—	Y
Cleveland State Univ.	MEd		—	N
Univ. of Colorado	MS	PhD	6	Y
Deakin Univ., Rusden Campus	MAS	PhD	—	N
DeMontfort Univ. Bedford	MPhil/MS	PhD	7	N
University of Exeter	MS/MPhil	PhD	4	Y
Florida State Univ.	MS	PhD	4	Y
Univ. of Florida	MS	PhD	6=	Y
Furman University	MA		4=	Y
Univ. of Georgia	MA	PhD	7	N
Georgia Southern Univ.	MS		2	Y
Univ. of Houston	MEd/MS	EdD	6=	N
U. of Humanistic Studies	MA	PhD	2	Y
Humboldt State Univ.	MA		—	Y
Univ. of Idaho	MS	PhD	4	Y
Illinois State Univ.	MS		7	Y
Univ. of Illinois	MS	PhD	—	Y
Indiana University	MS		7	N
Iowa State University	MS		4	Y
University of Iowa	MA	PhD	7	N
Ithaca College	MS		2=	N
Kansas State University	MS		—	Y
University of Kansas	MS	EdD/PhD	—	Y(PhD)
John F. Kennedy Univ.	MA	PsyD	2=	Y
Lakehead University	MA/MS		4	Y

Institution	Masters	Doctoral	Rating*	Internship
Manchester Metropolitan U.	MS/MPhil	PhD	—	N
University of Manitoba	MA/MS	PhD	4	Y
Mankato State Univ.	MA		—	Y
Univ. of MD, College Park	MA	PhD	6	N
McGill University	MA		—	N
University of Memphis (Psych)	MA/MS	PhD	6	N
University of Memphis (HMS)	MS		—	Y
Miami University	MS		4	Y
Michigan State Univ.	MS	PhD	4	Y
University of Minnesota	MA/MEd	PhD	4	Y
U. of Missouri, Columbia	MA	PhD	4	Y
U. of Missouri, Kansas City	MA	PhD	5	Y
University of Montana	MS	EdD	3=	Y
Université de Montréal	MSc	PhD	—	N
Univ. of New Hampshire	MS		4	Y
Univ. of New Mexico	MS	EdD/PhD	—	Y
U. of NC, Chapel Hill	MA		4	Y
U. of NC, Greensboro	MS	PhD	4=	Y
Univ. of North Dakota	MS		—	Y
Univ. of North Texas	MS	PhD	=	Y
Univ. of Northern Colorado	MA	EdD	6=	Y
Northern Illinois Univ.	MSEd		4	Y
Oregon State University	MS	PhD	6	N
University of Ottawa	MA/MS	PhD	2=	Y
Pennsylvania State Univ.	MS	PhD	6	Y
Purdue University	MS	PhD	—	Y
U. Québec, Trois-Rivières	MS		—	Y
Queen's University	MA		—	Y
University of Queensland	MA/MS	PhD	4=	Y
San Diego State Univ.	MA		4	Y
San Francisco State Univ.	MA/CC		—	Y
San Jose State University	MA		6=	Y
Université de Sherbrooke	MS		5	N
Southeastern Louisiana Univ.	MA		—	Y
Univ. of Southern California	MA	PhD	6	N
S. Connecticut St. Univ.	MS		4=	Y
Southern Illinois Univ., Carbondale	MS		—	Y
Southern Illinois Univ., Edwardsville	MS		—	Y
Univ. of Southern Queensland	MPsy/MPhl	PhD	—	Y
Spalding University	MA	PsyD	4=	Y
Springfield College (Grad. Studies)	MS	DPE	4	Y

Institution	Master's	Doctoral	Rating	Internship
Springfield College (Psy.)	MEd/MS	CAS	4=	Y
Staffordshire University	MPhil/MS	PhD	6=	Y
University of Stellenbosch	MHMvt	PhD	6	N
Temple University	MEd	PhD	5	Y
Univ. of Tennessee, Knoxville	MS	PhD	4	Y
Univ. of Texas, Austin	MA/MEd		—	Y
Texas Christian Univ. (Psych.)		PhD	—	Y
Texas Christian Univ. (Kines.)	MS		—	Y
Texas Tech University	MS/MEd	EdD	6	Y
Utah State University	MS		3	Y
University of Utah	MS	PhD	—	Y
Victoria U. of Technology	MAP/MAS	PhD	=	Y
University of Virginia	MEd	EdD/PhD	—	Y
Virginia Commonwealth U.		PhD	5	Y
Virginia Poly Inst. & SU	MS		5	Y
University of Washington		PhD	5	Y
University of Waterloo	MS	PhD	—	Y(PhD)
Wayne State University	MEd		7	Y
Univ. of Western Australia	MS	PhD	4	Y
Western Illinois Univ.	MS		—	Y
Univ. of Western Ontario	MA	PhD	6	Y
West Virginia University	MS	EdD	5	Y
Western Washington Univ.	MS		4	Y
U. of Wisconsin, Milwaukee	MS		5=	Y
University of Wollongong	MS/MPsy	PhD	4	Y
University of Wyoming	MS		5	Y
Xavier University		PsyD	—	N
York University	MScMA		7	Y

Keys

Master's Degrees

CC—Coaching Certificate
GradDip—Graduate Diploma in Applied Psychology
MA—Master of Arts
MAP—Master of Applied Psychology
MAS—Master of Applied Science
MEd—Master of Education
MHK—Master of Human Kinetics
MHMvt—Master of Human Movement

MPE—Master of Physical Education
MPhil—Master of Philosophy
MPsy—Master of Psychology
MSEd—Master of Science in Education
MS—Master of Science

Doctoral degrees

DPE—Doctorate in Physical Education
EdD—Doctor of Education
PhD—Doctor of Philosophy
PsyD—Doctor of Psychology
CAS—Certificate of Advanced Study (not a doctoral degree but represents advanced study beyond the master's)

Program Emphasis Rating

Programs were asked to rate on a seven-point Likert Scale the number that best reflected the emphasis/orientation of their program. The scale looked like the following:

Program Rating:

1	2	3	4	5	6	7
Applied Orientation			Equal Emphasis			Research Orientation

An equals sign (=) indicates that the program offers opportunities to pursue an applied orientation OR a research orientation (as opposed to an equal emphasis on both)

Internship Possibility

Y—yes (possible or required)
N—no